THE UNTILLED FIELD

THE
UNTILLED FIELD

BY

GEORGE MOORE

with an Introduction by
Richard Allen Cave

This edition first published in 2000 by Colin Smythe Limited
Gerrards Cross, Buckinghamshire SL9 8XA

ISBN 0-86140-199-9

Produced in Great Britain
Printed and bound by
Guernsey Press Co.Ltd, Vale, Guernsey, C.I. GY1 3BW

CONTENTS

INTRODUCTION BY RICHARD ALLEN CAVE   vii

PREFACE   xxix

THE EXILE   1

HOME SICKNESS   21

SOME PARISHIONERS   33

PATCHWORK   45

THE WEDDING FEAST   57

THE WINDOW   67

A LETTER TO ROME   85

A PLAY-HOUSE IN THE WASTE   97

JULIA CAHILL'S CURSE   107

THE WEDDING GOWN   113

THE CLERK'S QUEST   121

ALMS-GIVING   125

SO ON HE FARES   129

THE WILD GOOSE   139

FUGITIVES   179

Appendices

IN THE CLAY   199

THE WAY BACK   212

INTRODUCTION

George Moore liked to be daring, to astonish. Throughout his long career he regularly attempted virtuoso acts on the high wire of aesthetic brilliance; sometimes he lost his footing and fell headlong into vulgarity or bad taste; more frequently he sustained performances remarkable for their deftness, assurance and dexterity, when in terms of taste and tone he seemingly could not put a foot wrong. In his sixties (Moore was born in Mayo in 1852) he conceived the idea of writing a novel about the adult life of Christ; all the familiar episodes leading up to the Crucifixion were to be there, but Christ was not to die on the cross; the Messiah, retrieved from Golgotha by Joseph of Arimathea, would be found to be in a coma and would be steadily restored to health and sanity by Joseph's patient care. There would be a miraculous resurrection but not of the kind venerated traditionally, rather it would be an awakening by an overly cerebral mind to the joy of living in the body and the senses; it would be a catharsis in the depths of consciousness effecting a total transformation of Christ's modes of perception. Much of the resulting novel, *The Brook Kerith* (1916), is taken up with evoking this slow process of change and the writing is simple, imaginatively compelling, exact. The whole enterprise could have been a disaster: sensational, exploitative, crude. Instead Moore rose to the challenge of his subject with integrity and produced that rarest of kinds of fiction: a novel about the spiritual life and the relationship between personality and faith.

If Moore could write convincingly at this time in his career about the idea of a resurrection, it was because on several occasions his own life had undergone such a complete transformation. *The Untilled Field* is the record of one such awakening, perhaps the most momentous of them all. The collection of stories can be viewed retrospectively not only as a personal landmark, but also as a point of major cultural change: with them modern Irish fiction came into being.

Moore had taken to writing novels in the 1880s in order to make a decent living, as the income accruing from rents on his family

estate near Lough Carra was fast dwindling in consequence of the
activities of the Land League. Like many an Irish author at the time
he deliberately chose to turn for his models to figures of
contemporary note *outside* the English tradition; this may in his
case (at least initially) have been less a nationalist cultural gesture
than a matter of necessity: much of his adult life throughout the
1870s had been spent in Paris where he numbered among his friends
many of the Impressionist painters, poets like LaForgue and writers
of the Medan circle that grouped themselves around the novelist,
Zola. Paris, he used to boast in later life, had been his university;
though London became his next home for some twenty years, it was
to France that he repeatedly turned for inspiration.

He was attracted first by the social realism of Balzac, Flaubert
and Zola and, after a passable start with *A Modern Lover*, he
produced two fine novels in the style: *A Mummer's Wife* and *Esther
Waters*. Keen to keep up with avant-garde taste however extreme, he
tried next to imitate (as his near-contemporary, Wilde, was currently
doing) the heavy, self-consciously poetic prose of Huysmans and
his typical cast of characters (burned-out intellectuals, repentant
sensualists and effete, world-weary aesthetes). They were an
unlovely bunch and, lacking Wilde's wit and epigrammatic skill,
Moore could not get any life into his writing. He was himself too
vigorous, earthy and enthusiastic an individual to carry off with
conviction the tone of exhausted boredom and spiritual desperation
that characterises Huysmans' work: in Moore it all seems a bit of a
pose, less manner than mannerism. By the time he completed *Sister
Teresa* (published in 1901), Moore felt trapped in a style that was
increasingly uncongenial and affected.

It was not an entirely wasted period in his career: he had been
trying, he realised, to find ways of depicting what he termed the
'underlife of the soul' in fiction, the movements of consciousness in
educated sensibilities. He was in quest of a new kind of realism in
fact, a psychological as distinct from a social realism, to evoke the
nature of impulse and intuition and the ways they define perception
and identity. Imitating Huysmans took him labouring up what
proved a *cul de sac*, but that did not mean that Moore's ambition
was futile: he needed to find a different path.

Moore was exceptionally adept at seizing opportunities when
they offered and turning them to his advantage; and in his time of
crisis one such opportunity now offered itself. Involvement in the
early seasons of the dramatic movement that by 1904 would bring
about the founding of the Abbey Theatre took Moore back to

Ireland, which he had not visited since the time (true disciple of Zola as he then was) that he was researching the Dublin Season and the receptions for debutantes at the Castle in preparation for his novel, *A Drama In Muslin* (1886). Moore's cousin, Edward Martyn, and the poet W.B.Yeats, who with Lady Gregory had started the Irish Literary Theatre Society, had little experience of professional actors, rehearsal techniques or stage management and they turned to Moore, who had a wide circle of theatrical friends, to help them out.

Mounting an Irish drama for Irish audiences was startlingly innovative at a time when theatre in Ireland meant English touring companies or imitative revivals of London successes. Innovation demands enthusiasm and enthusiasm was infectious where Moore was concerned. Dublin intellectual circles seemed alive with new schemes, ideas of revival and renaissance, a preoccupation with language and freshness of expression; art and scholarship were becoming politicised and fervently anti-English. This was exactly what Moore's enervated inspiration needed. An intellectual revolution was in the making. Back in London once the first season of plays was over, Moore began campaigning for the new Ireland, championing the cause of the Gaelic League and the theatrical movement. As his involvement deepened, he found it necessary to spend longer time in Ireland; the fervent jingoism of England in the throes of the Boer War became unbearably offensive and constricting to his imagination. In the spring of 1901 Moore moved his home to Upper Ely Place in Dublin and set about becoming a Nationalist.

Work in drama helped tighten up what was already quite a strength in Moore's better fiction his command and use of dialogue; plays demand the utmost economy of expression: points have to be made tellingly, with precision, subtlety of implication and they have to be made rapidly. Every detail should be rich in nuance yet advance the action appreciably, whether that action be social or psychological. It was good training for a writer who had been pursuing a style remarkable for its expansive indulgence in purple prose; dramatic composition concentrated Moore's mind wonderfully, allowing his inspiration no space to be arbitrary, wilful, pedestrian or intrusively exhibitionist. Theatre alone, however, was not responsible for his acquiring a necessary creative discipline.

During the late Nineties, Moore had become an intimate friend of a young, Slade-trained artist, Clara Christian, who in his autobiography, *Hail and Farewell*, he was subsequently to call 'Stella' (echoing Swift's name for his personal muse).[1] Clara was trained by

Tonks and Wilson Steer in the Impressionist manner, learning to delight in the play of natural light over a subject and to record its transient effects with effortless dexterity and wit. Little is known of her beyond what has been recorded by Moore in his autobiography; but she was clearly a woman with a great strength of character, who daringly chose to follow Moore to Dublin (she lived privately at a house in Tallaght), where she pursued her art and her relationship with the novelist. That that relationship was valued profoundly by Moore is evident in the fact that he never in his writing betrayed her actual identity and he never subjected her to satire and caricature as was generally the fate of his acquaintance. The episodes concerning her in *Hail and Farewell* are handled with a distinctive lyricism, expressive of affection, respect and gratitude. This was proper since what those episodes show is how much she influenced the process of awakening and transformation in Moore, simply by the force of her personality: assured, witty, relaxed, joyous.

They were both great walkers as well as talkers and spent a deal of time in each other's company exploring the countryside around Dublin and south towards Wicklow. Clara made their walks subtle lessons in artistic decorum, as she laughed and teased Moore out of his affectations. She found it preposterous that he could not look at anything and see it simply for what it was in itself; everything for him had to look like something else. In commenting on what drew his attention he had to impose himself on the subject to show what a benefit he was conferring in deigning to make it a topic of his conversation. His approach was freely evocative but self-consciously judgemental; and, in judging, he laid himself open to judgement. Repeatedly so with Clara, who quietly ridiculed his pomposity and egotism. In return for his patience with her teasing, she appears to have taught him how to view landscape with a painter's interest in form and contour, texture, mass and colour, the patterning of light and shadow that accentuates density and structure, the balancing of relations between foreground and background.[2] Sensing the distinctions between her way of seeing and his own, he learned the extent to which perception and discrimination are highly personal and therefore immediately indicative of a particular personality. Clara taught Moore a new language through which to define the 'underlife of the soul'.

Moore had used landscape figuratively in his fiction prior to this and to especially good effect in *A Mummer's Wife, A Drama in Muslin* and *Esther Waters*; but the technique is applied there in a generalised way and almost invariably to define the hardship and misery of each heroine's lot in life as distinct from the vitality, abundance and energy for renewal apparent in the natural world. Moore's use was in the tradition of the pathetic fallacy and as such a kind of poetic licence. Now he had discovered in himself the degree to which perception is subject to change and that taught him an exact way of determining the quality of a consciousness at a precise moment in time within the flux of feeling and awareness that shapes identity. To find a means of expressing this in prose would allow him to depict character with both solidity and flexibility without the need for intrusive commentary. Because the method would rely on evocation rather than statement, it would actively engage the reader's imagination in interpreting and advancing the action. More importantly the method would allow him considerable freedom to write about both educated and untutored sensibilities without the risk of appearing to patronise his subject. Through 'Stella', Moore had found not only a new discipline over himself but also a new means of securing an apt decorum for evoking character in fiction.

This was to become a pressing need once he determined on his next subject which focused largely on the peasantry of the West of Ireland, for which his late, Huysmansesque style would have proved absurdly inappropriate. Indeed Moore had shown how disastrously inappropriate such a style could be for such a subject over a decade earlier, when in the first phase of his enthusiasm for Huysmans he had turned some of his research material gleaned for *A Drama in Muslin* into a series of sketches about Ireland for a French newspaper. These he subsequently translated into English and published in book-form as *Parnell and his Island* (1887). The tone throughout preserves the lofty superiority of the cosmopolitan artist returning from cultured Europe to visit with barely concealed scorn and distaste the countryside of his youth; the work is decidedly nasty and Moore had to work hard in some Nationalist circles in Dublin after his return to Ireland to redeem his reputation. *The Untilled Field* was for many Irish readers to justify his repatriation. Circumstances were steadily making the writing of that work a possibility, but it was a departure in his career, a renewal, a re-making of the self, that few could have predicted in 1901.

To his chagrin Moore found himself rather rapidly *of* the activity that constituted the cultural renaissance but not exactly *in* it. 1901 had witnessed the last of the three seasons of plays mounted by the Irish Literary Theatre Society; Martyn had left the venture somewhat disgruntled by the criticism Yeats and Moore had launched against his efforts to write a satirical drama about the relations between England and Ireland called *A Tale of a Town*; Yeats and Moore's efforts at collaborating on a dramatisation of the story of Diarmuid and Grania had been fraught with difficulties as their respective styles and methods of composition were quite different; the play had been completed and staged by Frank Benson's company but relations between the two dramatists were so sour that an attempt to embark on a second project was doomed to failure almost from the start; they had devised a scenario together which Yeats with Lady Gregory's help proceeded to flesh out with dialogue as *Where There Is Nothing* without fully consulting Moore over this plan and Moore in rage threatened litigation; Moore promptly abandoned the scheme for a national theatre to Yeats (who next joined with the Fays, Synge and Lady Gregory to form the group that eventually with Annie Horniman's financial support were to open the Abbey).

Moore's hopes of being a leading light with the Gaelic League were in a short while dashed too. This was the group that was most suspicious of the seriousness of purpose of the man who had written *Parnell and his Island*. It was difficult for Moore to cut an impressive figure in public on the language issue when he himself did not know Gaelic, as his critics were quick to point out. The fact that he had arranged for his young nephews to be taught Irish over at Moore Hall in Mayo was scarcely proof of his personal zeal and commitment. A scheme he devised with Edward Martyn for a troupe of touring players to travel to remote areas of Ireland playing dramas in Gaelic gave him some excitement for a while; but the idea was suppressed by some clerical members of the executive committee of the Gaelic League who thought it improper, not to say downright scandalous, for actresses to be members of such a company. Then Moore proposed to the executive that they consider publishing translations of internationally recognised masterpieces of fiction for the benefit of those Gaelic scholars who had achieved proficiency in the language. The problem was to find the right works (which meant works acceptable to the Catholic hierarchy); Moore's suggestion of *Tales from the Arabian Nights* provoked only shock and outrage. Moore's frustration knew no bounds: his brain was teeming with proposals but every one was turned down for what seemed to him the most specious of reasons; his creativity had found new verve but had no outlet for its abundant energies. It was at this point that a Jesuit acquaintance, Father Tom Finlay, suggested that Moore should himself write a work of fiction to be translated into Irish which he would arrange to have published in

The New Ireland Review. If the work was successful, Father Tom would encourage its publication in book form and recommend its adoption as a school text by the Intermediate Board of Education. Suddenly Moore was embarked on a venture for which he had exclusive responsibility. The problem now was what kind of fiction to write.

Chance again gave Moore his solution. He spoke of his plans while in conversation with the librarian, 'John Eglinton' (W.K.Magee), who, musing on the idea, asked whether Moore had in mind a collection of stories the like of Turgenev's *A Sportsman's Sketches*. It was a canny suggestion. Moore had been fascinated by Turgenev's work for many years and had viewed the Russian as a kind of honorary Frenchman whose works were wholly in accord with the prevailing canons of French realism. Though Moore had written essays about Turgenev's novels and stories, he had never till now considered him as a possible influence and model. (There is a hint of Turgenev about Moore's handling of landscape in the later chapters of *A Drama in Muslin*, but the lure of Huysmans became irresistible and the aesthetic connection with Turgenev was not at that time developed.) Eglinton's remark was just the spur to creativity that Moore needed at that stage of his career.

In *A Sportsman's Sketches* Turgenev had had to address the issue of an appropriate tone and decorum for writing about the serfs from the standpoint of a landowner while avoiding any charge of being patronisingly superior. He developed a technique of subtextual implication that allowed his readers to *imagine* the characters being depicted free of the need for easy and possibly class-conscious judgement. Readers have to bring a close attention to detail, an emotional sensitivity and a delicacy of moral scruple to the act of reading to a degree that makes the contribution of their imaginative resources a necessary part of the creative act by which the full meaning of each tale is discovered.

On the surface the tales may appear simple, direct, even perhaps austere, since Turgenev resolutely eschews rhetorical or emotional emphasis and colour; the richness lies beyond mere statement and precise definition. *A Sportsman's Sketches* demonstrate Turgenev's art at its finest, where the discovery of a fictional character is part of a process of self-discovery by the reader too. Psychological analysis in these stories would be heavy-handed and would tend to keep the characters at a distance when what Turgenev seeks is to foster the reader's total engagement and understanding. (Henry James explained the matter perfectly: 'As we read, we are always looking and listening; and we seem, indeed, at moments, for want of a running thread of explanation, to see rather more than we understand.'⁴) Turgenev's Russian readers would after all be predominantly of the landowning classes; he sought to make them look again at characters and situations they quite likely took for granted and see the unique individuals that lie behind people they might well otherwise dismiss as mere types; and he succeeded in this because his art always invites a profound respect for his subjects rather than pity.

Several of Moore's friends were surprised by the apparent lack of stylistic 'finish' in the stories he wrote under the influence of *A Sportsman's Sketches*; it is true that they are not overtly artful or showy. Moore recommended that they should undertake a careful re-reading of *The Untilled Field*, admitting it was a 'dry book' that was not designed 'to claim the affections at once'.⁵ *Dry* might seem a perverse epithet to use of a book designed to achieve a greater inwardness and warmth than was apparent in Moore's more recent fiction, but it does intimate a conscious choice on his part not to wear his heart, his culture or his intellect too openly upon his sleeve. Seen from the standpoint of Turgenev's artistry, *dry* would seem an exact and felicitous description. *The Untilled Field* sets out to render the quality of peasant and urban working-class life, to evoke what it is in Ireland to be poor and near-destitute in terms of material well-being; sentimentality and pathos have no place in such fiction: they would demean the subject. 'Dryness' in such a context is the proper decorum. To judge by the evolution of the tales, it was not a quality that Moore expected to master at all easily.

Only three of the stories found their way as originally planned into Father Tom Finlay's *New Ireland Review*, where they appeared at irregular intervals throughout 1902 in both English and Irish versions (the translations were by Padraic O'Sullivan): 'The Wedding Gown', 'The Clerk's Quest' and 'Alms-Giving'. Interestingly they were all revised versions of short stories Moore had published in English magazines over the previous fourteen years or so, but which he had not collected into a volume. The earliest written of these, 'The Wedding Gown', had appeared in the Christmas number of the *Lady's Pictorial* in 1887; it was also the first of the stories that make up *The Untilled Field* to be published in Ireland and in Irish. In its revised form its control of tone is superb for a subject that could easily have descended into mawkishness or bathos. It treats of family affection, different kinds of generosity and sympathy, the indulgence by the elderly of the enthusiasms and exuberance of the young, and an adolescent girl's discovery of the force of her intuitions and her sudden awareness in a moment of apparent elation of the nature and meaning of mortality. The tale evokes in its final version delicate and subtle movements of consciousness as a young girl gains access to adulthood through confronting and conquering her fear of death; and it is all done indirectly through the rhythmic modulations of the prose. At first the situation is defined objectively as the characters are introduced; but at the climax of the narrative the style changes to capture Molly's breathless haste as she races home through the darkness from the ball at the Big House, and then changes again to render the studied calm that comes over her when she faces what she has most feared to find that her great-aunt is dead. In revising his text Moore has pared away all emotive language and authorial commentary. One is not informed how to respond; instead the style works to draw one into a complete empathy with the central character.

'The Clerk's Quest' and 'Alms-Giving' also pose problems over tone: the one is a story about a man's sudden awakening to the power of his instincts after leading a life of studied routine and the tragic consequences for him when his previously repressed emotions become the prey of an uncontrollable infatuation; the other is an exploration of the motives and feelings that influence our instinct to be charitable. 'The Clerk's Quest' could easily have become an exercise in sustained ridicule, especially given the role of practised womaniser that Moore himself liked to play on occasions; the earliest version published in the *St. James Gazette* in September, 1890 (and even that included in *The New Ireland Review*) did not entirely skirt the temptation, as can be gauged from the fact that the clerk was originally called not 'Dempsey' but 'Dumpty'. The urge to scoff and disparage was disciplined out of existence through the process of revision as Moore rose to the challenge of evoking a mind overwhelmed by sentimentality without himself resorting to sentimentality in doing so. The final version pitches the tone beautifully, allowing a gentle hint of comedy to keep a sense of proportion throughout the telling without any loss of respect for the subject and his private anguish.

Several of the stories invite the reader like this to look beyond a character's apparent absurdity and discover it to be the corollary of an unusual strength of personality. There is Biddy M'Hale in 'The Window' who is viewed as 'cracked' by the parish priest on account of her mania to pay for the installation of a stained glass window in her local church, but who is shown in time to be a visionary and mystic. Moore sustains a delicate irony throughout the tale that makes for a tragi-comic undertow to the narrative: Biddy's essential goodness, so free from any taint of practised piety, excites in Father Maguire only cupidity, anger and envy. He sees but he cannot believe; she believes and what she sees is transfigured.

Then there is Father MacTurnan in 'A Letter To Rome' writing to the Pope to suggest the Irish Catholic clergy be freed of their oath of celibacy so that they may marry and repopulate an Ireland laid waste by famine and emigration. The story would verge on farce were it not for the very real misery and degradation of MacTurnan's parishioners that compel him in sheer desperation to search for a possible cure. Ridiculous as his solution may be, it is the product of a mind anxious to express compassion for a people whom he knows at heart are placed by social circumstance beyond the reach of anyone's pity. Again the carefully judged tone of this story is exemplary.

Just how successful these stories are can be sensed by comparing them with 'Alms-Giving', which, though improved by revision (it was first published as 'Charity' in *The Sketch* in September, 1893), mars the powerful effect of its artistry by its conclusion. The tale, a first-person narrative, tells of the deepening relationship between the 'author' and a blind beggar; the blind man's simple tales of the consolations he has found in life to offset his disability excite the narrator's imagination and through that empathy his own perceptions are cleansed of their self-conscious and self-satisfied impulses, made pristine and attentive and invested with the quality of wonder. In many ways 'Alms-Giving' openly enacts the very strategy that in the remaining tales of the collection works on the reader by the power of suggestion. As in several of Turgenev's stories the significant changes in the narrator's sensibility are conveyed through passages of natural description, which show how his perceptions are being affected by the situation. The implied injunction to the reader is still to *imagine*. But then in the final sentences Moore's discipline falters and with it his trust of the reader's sensitivity to the implications of the way his style has been modulating through the narrative, as he suddenly starts to define and explain the emotional state in which his narrator-figure will be left at the conclusion. The steady movement towards an experience of pure wonder in nature is instantly reduced to a pedestrian, near-banal statement ('We're here,' I said, 'for the purpose of learning what life is, and the blind beggar has taught me a great deal, something that I could not have learnt out of a book, a deeper truth than any book contains. . .'), which risks making the whole story seem emotionally contrived, a great deal of ado about relatively little.

Moore was an inveterate reviser of his works (generally for their improvement), but oddly he never saw fit to revise the close of this tale. The early editions of *The Untilled Field* show Moore constantly changing the order of the stories till he settled on the sequence that best pleased him; always 'Alms-Giving' is placed late in the collection. Was the story and its placing a deliberate strategy to teach the reader how to respond to his new technique, how to move beyond imaginative engagement into awareness? Is the story to be seen as an injunction to us to look back over our experience of *The Untilled Field* and ponder its significance, the better to understand our creative relation to its artistry? If so, it was to misprize the power of his new-found inspiration, sensitivity and scruple and their relation to the question of proper modes of address to the reader. The matter is however a local failure (there are analogous moments in *A Sportsman's Sketches*) and of a kind to make us relish the virtuosity with which the tales that proceed 'Alms-Giving' in the collection are accomplished. The style of *The Untilled Field* was a radical departure from Moore's previous work and one can appreciate his anxiety lest he be misunderstood.

Several stories were appearing in English and American magazines during 1902 when 'The Wedding Gown', 'The Clerk's Quest' and 'Alms-Giving' were being published in Father Finlay's journal. 'Home-Sickness' and 'The Exile' appeared respectively in August and September in *Harper's Weekly* and in September and October in *Pall Mall Magazine*, while 'Julia Cahill's Curse' had been published as 'The Golden Apples' in *The English Illustrated Magazine* as early as April. Six of the tales ('The Exile', 'Home-Sickness', 'The Window', 'A Playhouse in the Waste', 'The Wedding Gown' and a part of the story that was to be called 'The Wild Goose', here entitled 'Patriotism') were published in Gaelic translations by Padraic O'Sullivan as *An T-Ur-Gort* in Dublin early in 1903 just prior to Fisher Unwin's publication in London of *The Untilled Field* in April of that year. The English edition included thirteen tales in all; 'The Window' had been extended by the inclusion of three further stories centred on Father Maguire to make a short novella of rural life entitled 'Some Parishioners' (in later editions the sections were separated to form four distinct tales, with the two titles already mentioned being supplemented by two more, 'Patchwork' and 'The Wedding Feast'); 'The Wild Goose' had been considerably lengthened; and there were four stories that had hitherto gone unpublished ('A Letter to Rome', 'So On He Fares', 'In The Clay' and 'The Way Back').

The two stories last listed (which are included as an Appendix to this edition) originally framed the collection so that *The Untilled Field* was viewed by the reader between the account of the philistine zeal that drove the sculptor, Rodney, out of Ireland for good and the tale of Lucy Delaney, his former model, whose efforts to make a bid for a similar freedom were ended when duty compelled her to return to Dublin and a loveless marriage. Compared with the carefully realised texture of implication that is the mark of the other stories, these seem shallow, rushed, overly preoccupied with plot at the expense of psychological interest, and in a style quite different from the rest of the group, lacking everything that gives them distinction. Moore seems to have become dissatisfied immediately with this arrangement: he omitted 'In The Clay' and 'The Way Back' from the Tauchnitz edition published in May of 1903 and they were omitted from subsequent English editions until that of April 1931 when 'Fugitives' first appeared based on the subject matter of those earlier tales. This is a tighter version of the material, but it still falls short of the quality of the rest of the collection.

The other story that continued to give Moore trouble was 'The Wild Goose'. As it first appeared as 'Tir-grad' ('Patriotism') in *An T-Ur-Gort*, it was a short account of the breakdown of a marriage caused by intellectual, political and religious differences between a husband and wife. By the time of the first edition of *The Untilled Field* it had been expanded to include a portrayal of the courtship and early idyllic phase of the relationship which threw into sharp contrasting relief the growing division between the couple. This in turn accentuated the instrumental role of the wife's confessor in bringing about the breakdown through encouraging her continually to attempt to restrict her husband's free thinking and politically subversive views, a situation aggravated by his financial dependence on her. The problem now was that the story was so long and expansive that it occupied a rather obtrusive place in the collection; this was for a number of reasons. Firstly the setting was suburban and the characters educated and articulate which for reasons of verisimilitude demanded a method of presentation different from most of the tales. Then the subject-matter of marital breakdown in consequence of subtle forms of emotional blackmail was one that Moore had treated before and to particularly good effect in *Vain*

Fortune (1891); not surprisingly the handling here lacks a certain freshness of invention. But most important of all is the sense that the story is written less to render the quality of a particular way of life than to illustrate an idea, and one Moore clearly thought of some urgency of appeal.

Not even when 'The Wild Goose' was completely re-written and shortened for Heinemann's third revised English edition of 1926 (the text reprinted here) were these difficulties resolved. The reason why this tale seems as out of place in the collection as 'In The Clay', 'The Way Back' and their revised version, 'Fugitives', is that they are not fundamentally about 'the underlife of the soul' but about ideologies, political and cultural, and the social dangers attendant on adopting unorthodox intellectual positions in modern Ireland. As such they are vehicles for Moore's own contemporary attitudes and exasperation and sustain a bias in the presentation of the characters not apparent elsewhere in *The Untilled Field*. Where the majority of the stories are achieved through a disciplined act of depersonalisation in imitation of Turgenev's sincere humility before his subject, these three strain to provoke readers' concern and to influence response. They are not necessarily flawed in their artistry; it is because their chosen method is propagandist that they seem out of keeping in the context in which they appear. Why their method and subject are so different from the rest is worth exploring, since the reasons for it relate closely to the intricate continuum of experience in which Moore conceived the whole group of tales; and to understand this is to develop a greatly enhanced appreciation of Moore's astonishing personal achievement in composing the rest of the stories that make up *The Untilled Field*.

Throughout his life Moore was fond of claiming that he lived by a dictum frequently uttered by the painter, Manet: that one should be ashamed of nothing but to be ashamed. This was the source of Moore's daring as artist and man; but that daring had an adverse side on occasion that manifested itself as a thoughtless, foolhardy impulsiveness, which in retrospect could bring Moore deep regret. In his autobiography, *Hail and Farewell!* (1911-1914), which assesses his life during the decade Moore spent in Ireland after 1901, the novelist makes it clear that circumstances made him quickly repent of his sudden move back to his native land and that the writing of *The Untilled Field* was welcomed by him as a means of assuaging the guilt and fury he felt at his apparent rashness. The tales were his justification for being in Ireland, for having faith in the possibility of a cultural renaissance. In retrospect he could

readily see the importance of this period to him as an artist: it was
the occasion of a personal renaissance of some magnitude. But at
the time as a *lived* experience these months must have been
anything but settled and reassuring.

Any renaissance, personal or national, is a time not only of
reawakening but also of taking stock of the past; and Moore's past
for many of his Irish contemporaries was that of an absentee
Catholic landlord turned renegade agnostic novelist. It was not an
easy reputation to live with, especially in Nationalist circles; but to
Moore himself that past and present explained his freedom to
question everything and be what he thought all true revolutionaries
should be: subversive. He found himself working for the cause of
the renaissance with individuals who clearly thought the credentials
of the true revolutionary should be absolutely 'safe' and above
suspicion or reproach. Moore came to believe this resulted from the
presence of a weighty number of Catholic clergy on most of the
committees handling the affairs of the various movements for
cultural change, men who hindered genuine efforts to advance by
their repressive bigotry and narrow minds. He found the situation
increasingly irksome, and that inevitably inclined one of his
temperament to become combative.

Some months after the publication of *The Untilled Field* Moore
was to write to *The Irish Times* publicly declaring himself to be a
Protestant. It was a flamboyant gesture, the stark manner of which
he came to regret (though he never regretted what the gesture
actually avowed). *The Lake*, which tells of a priest's awakening as a
consequence of his painful loss of faith in his calling, *Hail and
Farewell!* and *The Brook Kerith* were more studied considerations
in fiction and autobiography of how his identity had been shaped by
his continually changing beliefs: they were scrupulous expressions
of the movements of consciousness that brought him to know why
one should be ashamed of nothing but to be ashamed. They were all
written after the occasion of his letter to *The Times* (24th September,
1903); and are in some ways to be seen as an explanation and
apology for its hasty composition. The stories in *The Untilled Field*
were all conceived during the months of growing rage that
precipitated his declaration (Moore claimed that it was a review
disparaging the tales as coming from the pen of a man who was
born a Catholic which actually prompted his letter). What is
remarkable in the circumstances is that the tales are not uniformly
shrill in tone, satirical and challenging in a pugnacious manner. That
two of the fifteen ('The Wild Goose' and 'Fugitives' as they are

called in the present edition) are moving in this direction only emphasizes how consummately controlled and dispassionate is the artistry of the remaining thirteen.

Hail and Farewell! recounts how out of concern for what he believed were the proper interests of a cultural renaissance Moore was driven to adopt an increasingly anti-clerical stance. His autobiography is a taking stock of the events in his life that led him inexorably to embrace independence of mind and the challenge of evolving a personal conscience. Finding little of such freedom in the lives of the artists, intellectuals and writers he worked with in Dublin, he ends by offering the autobiography as a Gospel for the New Ireland, an account of how to cultivate a genuine renaissance in the self, which he sees as the only way a larger movement for social and aesthetic revolution will begin to be a possibility in the country. Through three substantial volumes Moore traces the shaping of his sensibility and shows how efforts during his years in Dublin to curtail or censor its expression steadily taught him to recognise its true worth.[6] He takes time in other words to substantiate his anti-clerical argument.

The short-story format does not afford the necessary space to initiate and develop subtle arguments; they have to be expressed somewhat tersely as the opinions of the characters; and this risks making challenging ideas sound like so much opinionating, unless the writer can find ways of investing a considerable degree of intellectual distinction and authority in his characters. This Moore signally fails to do in the cases of Ned Carmady, the sculptor Rodney and the novelist Harding in 'The Wild Goose' and 'Fugitives'; he is more preoccupied with what they are saying than with such necessary questions of address to the reader as why and how they are voicing such issues and attitudes. He presents their ideas about the intellectual parochialism of Ireland as self-evident and as such beyond the need for debate. This is a serious failure in artistic scruple.

Ned, a journalist and social reformer, and the two artists have ways of life close to Moore's own, yet he never contrives to have us imaginatively inhabit their lives in the way that we are brought to live within the more constricted experience of Father MacTurnan or Biddy M'Hale. Moore identifies intellectually with Carmady, Rodney and Harding to a degree that prevents him imaginatively engaging with them. It is as if he thought his wholesale enthusiasm for their opinions would be enough to characterise them. Moore succumbs in fact to the danger of propagandist art: these two tales offer statements of intent rather than strategies that subtly draw the reader into a process of discovery. One is left distanced from the stories and can contribute little as reader to the shaping of their respective meanings.

Consider by contrast the deft way in which different kinds of affection are defined and distinguished in the opening tale, 'The Exile'. There is the close emotional bond between the two Phelan brothers; the watchful care of them shown by their father, which is coloured by his deep love of his inheritance, the farm, and his concern for its future; there is James Phelan's infatuation for their neighbour Catherine; her respect for the sincerity of his feelings that is matched by her scruple to preserve her integrity, since at heart she loves his brother, Peter; and there is Peter's anxiety not to stand in the way of his brother's hopes. The situation is what Thomas Hardy might have described as one of life's 'little ironies'. Moore could have worked hard to build up the pathos and irony but his concern is more with the characters' quiet dignity and patience as they realise and accept the painfulness of their dilemma and seek to resolve it honourably.

One is impressed as one reads less by the situation than by the way pain and self-awareness release a need to act generously in each of the characters; but this is less a conscious decision than a ready impulse borne of long experience of each other's company; a sense of decorum that is innate rather than tutored governs their actions. And yet none of this is directly described; it is all intimated through the precise way in which the narrative evolves and through the brief exchanges of conversation by which the unexpected transitions in the story are effected. Moore intrudes no commentary regarding tone, motive, expected response into the dialogue; these are left for a reader to infer from one's growing sense of the identities of the characters. Fundamental decency is far from easy to evoke in fiction; it can seem colourless, insipid, banal or, worse, appear an object for gentle (and consequently patronising) mockery; Moore's treatment of it here is exemplary.

What particularly impresses one on reading 'The Exile' is how Moore contrives through pace and tone to keep the focus firmly on the inner lives of his characters. The effect of this is augmented by his technique of subtly blurring the distinction between authorial commentary and what appears to be a kind of précis of his characters' own intimate musing and reverie. The opening paragraph of the tale is typical of his method. The story begins with a simple statement of fact: 'Pat Phelan's pigs were ready for Castlebar market'. This is immediately qualified ('but so were his bullocks') in a manner which introduces a conversational thrust and rhythm. The clause that then completes the sentence opens with a verb ('and he was of a mind to. . .') which firmly internalises the whole experience as the play of Pat Phelan's mind. The next sentence ('But James was set on staying at home to help Catherine with the churning, and his son Peter was a bad hand at a bargain') gives the context for the old man's anxiety, explaining why each clause in all we have read so far is prefaced by the word 'but', thus qualifying and limiting the statement that immediately preceded it. Through a simple dilemma and an old man's indecision we have subtly been introduced to the emotional patterns within the relationships that make up the household out of which the story will be built. Next a comment that further stresses Peter's feeble bargaining powers intrudes with what seems at first to be dialogue till the verb ('he said to himself') establishes it as unspoken reverie. The ensuing dependent clause describes the physical disposition of the old man and his sons beside the kitchen fireplace which, as he smokes his pipe, has stimulated the particular drift of Pat Phelan's thoughts. The question 'Now, what's to be done?' that ends his silent contemplation seems to compel a change in the situation: 'and as if Peter had guessed what was passing in his father's mind, he knocked the ashes out of his pipe and bade his father and brother, 'Good-night''. The father's troubled musing has built up a tension between the three men; Peter knows his father well enough to sense that Pat's silence is in some measure a judgement against him and realises that the old man would find it easier to unburden himself to his other son, James, if they were left alone. The sensitivity of the three men towards each other is carefully evoked and their fundamental kindliness established; furthermore it is intimated that the family have so great and intimate an awareness of each other that their more serious communing is on levels other than direct speech. Four sentences alone have been all that Moore required to establish his basic story-line, to instruct his readers to look behind the surface of what his prose offers and relish the subtextual implications, and to show that the subject of his tale is to be the 'underlife' of his characters, the quality of their inner experience and its power to shape their individual identities. The paragraph is characteristic of Moore's style at its best in *The Untilled Field*: succinct, allusive, undemonstrative, dry. Here lies richness within an apparent austerity of expression; it is a triumph of creative tact.

The Untilled Field marked a breakthrough in Moore's career: he had discovered a technique that he was to explore avidly through the remaining thirty years of his life. With *The Lake* (1905) he created the first stream-of-consciousness novel in English; with *Hail and Farewell!* (1911-14) he transformed traditional autobiographical writing making it a study of the evolution and continual re-shaping of his sensibility as it is played upon by pressures to conform to certain inherited patterns of awareness and as it struggles to discover its own unique modes of perception and understanding; and with *The Brook Kerith* (1916) Moore began a series of historical novels in which the past is not viewed with antiquarian interest but revitalised with a rare immediacy. A particular felicity of Moore's new-found stylistic method for many Irish readers was that it bore no obvious relation to contemporary English models. Moreover his preoccupation in the stories that make up *The Untilled Field* with revealing to the alert, sensitive reader the inner wealth of individuals who might on first acquaintance appear to lead grey, quiet lives was wholly in accord with the aims of the cultural renaissance at large, which sought in every branch of the arts to redeem the presentation of Irish characters from British modes of perception which tended to reduce them to type-figures at best and at worst to caricatures. Moore brought dignity and emotional complexity to the study of Irish rural life even as Joyce subsequently was to bring them to the study of the Dublin poor. But where Joyce's Dubliners are without exception trapped by social circumstance, emotionally paralysed and stunted of their potential for growth (they are in every sense a *subject* people), most of Moore's characters can in some inspired way grow free of their imprisoning tendencies or find spiritual consolation like Biddy M'Hale for an existence that seems outwardly one of unrelieved drudgery.

The only characters of *The Untilled Field* who remain trapped and desperate are the Catholic priests. But their portraits (at least in the earlier stories) are not maliciously conceived or satirical. The youth and inexperience of the zealous Father Maguire are stressed; he is unthinking and uncharitable, too obsessed with the letter of his faith to be illumined in his activities by its spirit. But Moore is careful to withhold an overtly judgemental tone from his presentation: instead he offsets Maguire against a more compassionate and warmly witty cleric, his uncle Father Stafford, or against the unworldly, unselfconsciously pious Biddy. Father MacTurnan is a genuinely tragic creation in his doomed efforts to bring a little dignity and relief into the lives of his sorely tried parishioners. His efforts are tragic precisely because they are absurd in the circumstances, yet the writing carefully displaces any tendency the reader may have to mock.

Brilliantly the second tale concerning him, 'The Playhouse in the Waste', opens with a set of Dublin wags pouring ridicule on the man when rumours reach them of his letter to Rome, the subject of the previous tale. It is profoundly shocking to the sensitive reader after the deeply felt insight with which the tale has been conducted, but it precisely illustrates Moore's theme implicit throughout the stories about the degree to which perception is a judgement on the perceiver. The perspective has changed radically from the charitable to the malicious, but this, we discover, is part of a larger strategy within the pair of tales. One of the group of tattling intellectuals admits that he has travelled in connection with his work to the vicinity of MacTurnan's parish; he has stayed with the priest and discovered another story about him concerning an attempt to build a playhouse. What starts as a grand yarn for an audience inclined to scoff steadily changes its tone as the priest once again becomes the centre of attention. This is a short story with a dramatised narrator who in the course of telling how he became engrossed imaginatively by the plight of MacTurnan's parishioners and by the selflessness of the priest totally captures his audience imaginatively too. Accuracy and fairness of character-portrayal become the prime motive for the story-telling and in quest of that objective the narrator is seen increasingly to depersonalise himself. The telling of the tale enacts a process whereby a particular sensibility gains access to a complete imaginative sympathy; and, gaining it, finds a way of instilling that same heightened quality of response in his listeners. The story embodies Moore's method throughout *The Untilled Field* and explains the source throughout all but the last two tales of his artistic control, tact and unfailing judgement when it comes to questions of decorum and an appropriate level of address to the reader.

One has only to compare stories like 'The Exile', 'The Wedding Gown', 'The Window', 'A Letter to Rome' and 'A Playhouse in the Waste' with the shorter fiction of an older generation of Irish novelists such as the works W.B.Yeats selected for his *Representative Irish Tales* (1891) to perceive the extent of Moore's break with the past. The way of life Moore is describing in *The Untilled Field* is not appreciably different from that being evoked in the stories of Carleton, Griffin, Kickham or Rosa Mulholland; it is a way of life that has largely vanished. Yet where one has to make a conscious adjustment to what seem dated conventions of tone, presentation and diction in their works, a reader responds to Moore's method as distinctively immediate and modern. When one turns to more recent, Irish writers of short stories, James Joyce, Elizabeth Bowen, William Trevor or Bernard MacLaverty, for example, one finds that the subject matter has strayed into paths vastly different from Moore's, but their technique is still recognisably close to his: a pursuit of understatement and a concomitant refusal to indulge in rhetorical display or self-consciously fine writing that might intervene between the reader and the subject. They too cultivate a style of considerable flexibility that allows them (often within a single sentence by a clever manipulation of the tenses or moods of the verbs) to move dextrously between inner and outer worlds of experience to define the fluctuating qualities of a particular consciousness or sensibility.

This might at first sight seem not only a dry technique, but a rather cold one. Flaubert recognised that this might be a possible misconception about Turgenev's method in his short stories: 'But one thing about you has never had sufficient praise, your heart; your unfailing feeling, I mean, your indescribable deep and hidden sensibility.'[7] The crucial epithet here is 'hidden'. It is the prime secret of the technique and the source of its subtle virtuosity, because by hiding his own developed sensibility the author excites the reader's powers of discrimination and thereby encourages the reader's participation in creating meaning in the given story. This is Moore's strength in *The Untilled Field*. It was his gift to the tradition of modern Irish fiction.

RICHARD ALLEN CAVE

1. For a more detailed account of Clara Christian's life and of her relationship with Moore, see my article: 'George Moore's "Stella"' in *The Review of English Studies*, New Series, Vol. XXVIII, Number 110; May, 1977; pp. 181-8.
2. Moore had gone to Paris on attaining his majority with the intention of training to be a painter but, as he recounts in *Confessions of a Young Man*, he discovered he was signally lacking in talent and had the courage to abandon his aspirations and take up a career as a writer. Throughout his life he numbered many artists among his friends: Manet, Degas, Sickert, Wilson Steer, Tonks, J-E. Blanche. He repeatedly found them, like Clara Christian, a source of inspiration.
3. For a more detailed account of the influence of Turgenev's stories on Moore's volume, see my article: 'Turgenev and Moore: *A Sportsman's Sketches* and *The Untilled Field*' in *The Way Back: Essays on George*

Moore's The Untilled Field *and* The Lake', edited by Robert Welch (Dublin: Wolfhound Press, 1982) pp. 45-63.

4. Henry James: 'Ivan Turgenieff' in *French Poets and Novelists* (London, 1878), p.285.

5. Quoted in J.M.Hone, *The Life of George Moore* (London, 1936), p.246.

6. For a full account of the themes and structure of Moore's autobiography, see the introduction to my annotated edition of *Hail and Farewell* (Gerrards Cross: Colin Smythe, 1976, revised 1985).

7. Gustave Flaubert, *Letters*, selected with an introduction by Richard Rumbold and translated by J.M.Cohen, (London, 1950); p.240.

PREFACE

IT must have been somewhere at the end of the nineties, not unlikely in ninety-nine, that dear Edward said to me in the Temple: 'I should like to write my plays in Irish.' And it was not long afterwards, in the beginning of 1900, that Yeats persuaded him to come to Ireland to found a literary theatre. In search of a third person, they called on me in Victoria Street, and it is related in Ave how we packed our bags and went away to do something.

We all did something, but none did what he set out to do. Yeats founded a realistic theatre, Edward emptied two churches he and Palestrina between them and I wrote *The Untilled Field*, a book written in the beginning out of no desire of self-expression, but in the hope of furnishing the young Irish of the future with models.

Yeats said that I had learned the art of presentation in Paris, and in 1900 we believed that the Irish language could be revived.

'You see, it is necessary,' I observed to Edward, 'that Ireland's future writers should have models, and the stories will be published in a Jesuit magazine.' 'If the Jesuits assume all responsibility,' he muttered, and fell to pondering over his pipe, but he raised no further objection and invested with full authority I wrote 'The Wedding Gown', 'Almsgiving', 'The Clerk's Quest', and 'So On He Fares', in English rather than in Anglo-Irish, for of what help would that pretty idiom, in which we catch the last accents of the original language, be to Tiagh Donoghue, my translator? As soon as his translations were finished, my manuscripts were to be burnt; but these first stories begot a desire to paint the portrait of my country, and this could only be done in a Catholic atmosphere, and as I had just come out of *Evelyn Innes* and *Sister Teresa*, 'The Exile' rose up in my mind quickly, and before putting the finishing hand to it I began 'Home Sickness'. The village of Duncannon in the story set me thinking of the villages round Dublin, and I wrote 'Some Parishioners', 'Patchwork', 'The Wedding Feast', and 'The Window'. The somewhat harsh rule of Father Maguire set me thinking of a gentler type of priest, and the pathetic figure of Father MacTurnan tempted me. I wrote 'A Letter to Rome' and 'A

Playhouse in the Waste'; and as fast as these stories were written
they were translated into Irish and published in a very pretty book
of which nobody took any notice, and that the Gaelic League could
not be persuaded to put in its window; and one evening a
disheartened man was driven to the bitter extremity of collecting his
manuscripts for a London publisher. The cheque they brought back
on account of royalties did not soothe me; in 1903 England was
hateful on account of the Boer War, and the sale of one hundred
copies of the book that I could not read would have pleased me
more than ten thousand of the book that I could. In a word, I was
hipped with my book, and willingly forgot it in the excitement of
The Lake, a thing an author should never do, for to forget a book or
to speak contemptuously of it brings bad luck. And so Synge was
raised up against me in Ireland, and for the last ten years we have
been thinking and talking of him as the one man who saw Irish life
truly and wrote it candidly.

*It was just as if on purpose to make an omadaun of me that Yeats
brought him over from Paris in the year 1903, though he had no
English on him at the time. only the like that's heard in the National
Schools, and if you don't believe me, will you be throwing your eye
over the things he wrote in them days for the weekly papers, and
faith you'll see the editors were right to fire them out. Wasn't he
dreaming, too, he could be writing like a French fellow of the name
of Loti, that knew the trick with a couple of twists of the pen of
turning every country in the wide world into a sweet-shop? But 'tis
little of the taste of sugar-candy he got into his articles, and his
book about the Aran Islands has more of the tang of old leather, like
as if he'd be chewing the big brogues he did be always wearing on
his feet. And, morebetoken, his language in the same book is as bald
as the coat of a mangy dog, and trapsed along over a page of print
like the clatter of a horse that was gone in the legs. It's many a heart
scald this same must have given to my bold Yeats, for it's the grand
judge entirely he is of the shape and the colour and the sound of
words. So one day he up and said to Synge. 'Give up your
schoolmaster words that have no guts left in them, and leave off
thinking of Loti and his barley-sugar, and go down into the County
Wicklow and listen to what the people do be saying to 'other when
they're at their ease without any notion of an ear cocked to carry off
what they say. I hear tell that they speak a language that isn't worn
out yet, and that has some of the youth of the world in it. I'd like to
write in it myself, but I'd be afeard of muddying the clear English
well that I'm used to dabbling in. Besides, if you pick it up anyway*

decent you might yet prove to the world that it wasn't a mare's nest I found when I discovered you,' he said. And if Synge didn't pack up his few duds and tramp off that very minute, and if he hadn't the luck of the old boy himself in finding a lodging in a house in the hills of Wicklow that was like as if it was made on purpose for him a room over the kitchen with an old broken boarded floor to it, the way he could see and hear all that was going on below, and nobody a penny the wiser but himself. Lying flat on his belly, with an ear or an eye to the slits, he took in all that was said and done, and put it down in a bookeen with the stump of a pencil and made a play out of it.

There is the pretty idiom of the Irish peasants as they chatter it the roads, about their firesides, in the marketplaces, reported truthfully without exaggeration or refinements. But Synge put polish upon it and enlivened it with bright colours, and drew out of it the poetry of the country with which it is saturated as with dew. We listened delighted to *The Shadow of the Glen*, admitting to ourselves as we sat in our seats and to our friends as we left the hall that we preferred the cooing of Synge's dialogue to grey thoughts. We told him so in the street, and he went away to the Aran Islands for the summer-time, hoping to return in the autumn with another play, written in the same idiom, of course, but enriched by direct translation from the Irish. Why good English can be discovered by translating word for word from the Irish is one of the many great mysteries that beset our lives; but it is so. And when the news was passed round that Synge had brought back a play from Aran, we assembled in the Molesworth Hall, and it seemed to us that he had raised a tombstone over the intellectual drama. Dear Edward was the only dissident; he averred, and stood stiffly to it, that he hated peasant language. Yeats cried: 'Sophocles!' and then revising his judgment, said: 'No, Eschylus.' John Eglinton, Æ, and myself looked upon these two plays as two remarkable exercises in language. We were interested; we approved the plays, and on tiptoe Dublin waited for Synge's new play, which came two years after, *The Well of the Saints*, another remarkable exercise in language, hardly more; for the play is but an adaptation of Clemenceau's *Voile du Bonheur*, with an Irish couple substituted for the Chinese couple and country idiom for Clemenceau's Parisian speech. But Synge's indebtedness did not trouble us; why should it? we asked. Is not a plagiarist one who spoils the original text, and an original writer one who improves upon his predecessor? And satisfied with this definition, we waited, and whenever a circle of men and women

drew round a fire, the subject of the *Playboy* was discussed. Yeats
had communicated it so that we might be prepared to accept a
parricide as a hero, and a Mayo village as nothing loth to do the
same. At first sight the subject seemed wildly improbable, having
no roots in human nature, but it was defended on the ground that
brigands have always been popular heroes. And when the play was
produced, our little group discovered extenuating circumstances for
Christy Mahon. Into an extremely ingenious paradoxical story,
Synge had brought real men and women, and amazed we asked
each other how it was that Synge, who had never before shown any
sense of form, should suddenly become possessed of an exquisite
construction. We fell to wondering how the miracle had come about,
and we continued wondering, and myself was still head-scratching
in Vale, asking how Synge had sprung at once out of pure board-
school English into a beautiful style, finding it in an idiom that had
hitherto been used only as a means of comic relief. Tricks of speech
a parrot can learn, but it is impossible to learn through a crack how
character acts and reacts upon character. Never before did anyone
hear that the intelligence may be lifted through eavesdropping on to
a higher plane. Yeats told us that Synge read only Racine and
Clement Marot; but we turned up our noses at these herrings, and
the history of *The Playboy* was wrapped in unsearchable mystery
until I began to read *The Untilled Field* for this new edition, and
found myself thinking that if perchance any of my writings should
survive me for a few years, as likely as not it would be these stories.
And as this little vanity dispersed, I became more and more
interested, for it seemed to me that I had come upon the source of
Synge's inspiration. *The Untilled Field* was a landmark in Anglo-
Irish literature, a new departure, and Synge could not have passed it
by without looking into it. It was not Racine nor Clement Marot. I
would not, however, seem invidious to Synge's fame; my hope is
not to pluck a leaf from the wreath that Yeats has placed upon his
brow. I would merely explain his talent, and if that be impossible, I
would explain how he came by it; to do this with becoming modesty
is surely commendable. And if my critics think that I am
exaggerating the importance of *The Untilled Field* in Synge's
literary life, they will have to seek for another explanation, and for
all I know they may prefer to fall back on Yeats's terrible great
conjurations in the Nassau Hotel: Yeats standing over an entranced
Synge, his pearl pale, or is it his ivory hand sweeping the strings of
a harp of applewood, rousing a masterpiece out of the abyss.

In Professor Tonks's studio on Saturday nights the doctrine

always implicit in the conversation, sometimes explicit, is that art is correction, and Michael Angelo's drawings are often produced as testimony that he sought with unwearying eagerness a new line more perfect than the last.

'If,' I said as I returned home down the long King's Road that leads into longer Ebury Street, 'Michael Angelo held that art is correction, he would not shrink from the avowal that correction of form is virtue, and virtue being available to the smallest as to the greatest, the new edition of *The Untilled Field* will allow me to seek an outline that eluded me in the first version of 'The Wild Goose', and should I find the needed outline, the story will become, perhaps, dearer to me than the twelve that precede it and that need no correction.'

January 1926.

PUBLISHER'S NOTE (1931) Edition)

The first English edition of *The Untilled Field* (1903) contained two stories: 'In The Clay' and 'The Way Back' which were removed from the second (1914) and subsequent editions. In the present edition the author has included a new tale, 'Fugitives', based upon the subject matter of the other two, and here printed for the first time.

April 1931.

THE EXILE

PAT PHELAN'S pigs were ready for Castlebar market, but so were his bullocks, and he was of a mind to send his son James with the bullocks to Westpost fair where they would fetch a higher price. But James was set on staying at home to help Catherine with the churning, and his son Peter was a bad hand at a bargain. 'The divil a worse in the county of Mayo,' he said to himself as he smoked his pipe in front of his two sons, and they sitting on the other side of the fireplace facing him. 'Now, what's to be done?' he asked himself; and as if Peter had guessed what was passing in his father's mind, he knocked the ashes out of his pipe and bade his father and brother, 'Good-night.'

As soon as the door was closed behind him, Pat said: 'Now, James, what do you be thinking? Are we safe to send Pether with the bullocks to the fair?'

'Do ye mane he won't be getting the full price for them?'

'Well, I'm not sure, you see; for myself would be getting as much as thirteen pound ten a head for them, I'm thinking.'

'You should, indeed!'

'I was thinking, James, that they might be bating him down, for his thoughts do be often away a bad habit while buying or selling.... But wouldn't you like to be going with him, James?'

A cloud came into James's face, and he said: 'It's time we were getting into our beds.'

'I wouldn't be saying you were wrong, James. Wisdom often comes to us in our beds, and unless a dream is put upon me I think I must be letting the bullocks go with Pether; it'll be easier selling them than the pigs. But now you won't wake him. At three you'll just push him out of bed with your foot, and there will be some breakfast for him on the table.'

It was while eating the fried eggs that Pat gave Peter his orders. He would meet him about midday at the crossroads. And he was there waiting for his son sure enough about eleven o'clock, his pigs having gone from him sooner than he had expected, the buyers being at him the moment they had cast their eyes over the pigs. 'Just

1

the kind of pig we do be wanting for the Liverpool market.' He had caught the words out of the mouth of one jobber whispering in the ear of his mate. Michael was right; they were fine pigs. And, sitting on the stile waiting, he had begun to turn it over in his mind that if he had gotten five shillings more than he had expected for the pigs, it was reasonable to suppose that Peter might be getting fourteen pounds a head for the bullocks, they being better value than the pigs. Well, if he did, it would be a great day for them all, and if he got no more than thirteen pounds ten shillings it would be a great day all the same. And so did he go on dreaming till, looking up the road suddenly, whom should he see coming down the road but Peter and the bullocks in front of him.

'Well, now, can a man believe his own eyes?' he said. 'For all I can see they're me own bullocks, three of the finest I ever sent to a fair, and they coming back from the fair unsold.'

It was a long story that Peter had to tell him about the two men that had offered him eleven pounds ten shillings, and who, when he wouldn't sell them at that, had stood laughing at the bullocks, doing their level best to keep off other buyers. Peter was given to sulking when anybody found fault with him, and so Pat let him go on talking without saying a word, the bullocks trotting in front of them till they were about five miles from home.

'And fifteen miles is hard on fat animals,' Pat kept saying to himself, 'and this day I am six pounds out of pocket six pounds out of pocket, if I take into account the price of their keep.'

And while Pat was thinking, Peter kept on talking and telling his story again and again till they came to Michael Quinn's public-house, and it was there he asked his father—

'Well, father, how did the pigs do with you at the fair?'

Pat Phelan was too heartsick to answer him, and he had to say his words again and again.

'Now, father, did you get three pounds apiece for the pigs? Will ye be telling me?'

'I did, and three pounds five.'

'Wasn't that a fine price one that we might have a drink out of?'

It seemed to Peter that the men inside were laughing at him, or at the lemonade he was drinking, and, seeing among them one who had been interfering with him all day, he told him he would put him out of the house, and he would have done it if Mrs. Quinn had not spoken up saying that no one put a man out of her house without her leave.

'Go out before me. Do you hear me talking to you, Pether? If you can't best them at the fair, it will be little good it will be doing you to put them out of the public-house afterwards.'

And on that Peter swore he would never go to a fair again, and they walked on until they came to the priest's house.

'It was bad for me when I listened to you and James. If I hadn't I might have been in Maynooth now.'

'How can you be saying that? Didn't yourself come home talking of the polis?'

'Wasn't that after?'

'What do I be hearing you saying that I left Maynooth for the police?' And Peter talked on, telling of the authors he had read with Father Tom Caesar, Virgil, even Quintilian. The priest had said Quintilian was too hard for him, and Pat Phelan was in doubt whether the difficulty of Quintilian was a sufficient reason for preferring the police to the priesthood.

'Any way, it isn't a girl that's troubling him,' he said to himself. And he looked at Peter, and wondered how it was that Peter did not want to be married, for he was a great big fellow, over six feet high, one that many a girl would take a fancy to. Pat Phelan had long had his eye on a girl for Peter, and Peter's failure to sell the bullocks brought to mind all the advantages of this marriage, and he began to talk to his son, who listened, and seemed to take an interest in all that was said, expressing now and then a doubt if the girl would marry him; the possibility that she might not turning his thoughts, so it seemed to his father, once again towards the priesthood.

'Well, Pether, is it the cassock or the belt you're after?'

The bullocks stopped to graze, and Peter's doubts threw Pat Phelan fairly out of his humour.

'If it's a priest you want to be, go in there, and Father Tom will tell you what you must do, and I'll drive the bullocks home myself.'

And on that Pat laid his hand on the priest's green gate, and Peter walked through.

II

There were trees about the priest's house, and there were two rooms, on the right and left of the front door. The parlour was on the left, and when Peter came in the priest was sitting reading in his mahogany armchair. Peter wondered if it were this very mahogany chair that had put the idea of being a priest into his head. Just now, while walking with his father, he had been thinking that they had not even a wooden armchair in their house, though it was the best house in the village only some stools and some plain wooden chairs.

The priest could see that Peter had come to him for a purpose. But Peter did not speak; he sat raising his pale, perplexed eyes, looking at the priest from time to time, thinking that if he told Father Tom of his failure at the fair, Father Tom might think he only wished to become a priest because he had no taste for farming.

'You said, Father Tom, if I worked hard I should be able to read Quintilian in six months.'

The priest's face always lighted up at the name of a classical author, and Peter said he was sorry he had been taken away from his studies. But he had been thinking the matter over, and his mind was quite made up, and he was sure he would sooner be a priest than anything else.

'My boy, I knew you would never put on the policeman's belt. The bishop will hold an examination for the places that are vacant in Maynooth.' Peter promised to work hard, and he walked home, thinking that everything was at last decided, when suddenly, without warning, when he was thinking of something else, his heart misgave him. It was as if he heard a voice saying: 'My boy, I don't think you will ever put on the cassock. You will never walk with the biretta on your head.' The priest had said that he did not believe he would ever buckle on the policeman's belt. He was surprised to hear the priest say this, though he had often heard himself thinking the same thing. What surprised and frightened him now was that he heard himself saying he would never put on the cassock and the biretta. It is frightening to hear yourself saying you are not going to do the thing you have just made up your mind you will do.

He had often thought he would like to put the money he would get out of the farm into a shop, but when it came to the point of deciding he had not been able to make up his mind. He had always had a great difficulty in knowing what was the right thing to do. His uncle William had never thought of anything but the priesthood. James never thought of anything but the farm. A certain friend of his had never thought of anything but going to America. It was strange to know from the beginning.... It was like an animal. He heard somebody call him. 'Now, who can it be?' he asked himself. And who was it but Catherine, come to tell him for sure that she was going to marry James? She was another that always knew her own mind. He had heard tell that James wasn't the one she wanted, but Peter did not believe that, and he looked at Catherine and admired her face, and thought what a credit she would be to the family, for no one wore such beautifully knitted stockings as

Catherine, and no one's boots were so prettily laced.

But not knowing exactly what to say, he asked her if she had come from their house, and he went on talking, telling her she'd find nobody in the parish like James; that James was the best judge of cattle in the parish; and he said a great deal more in James's favour, till he saw that Catherine did not care to talk about James at all.

'I dare say all you say is right, Pether; but you see he's your brother.'

And then, fearing she had said something hurtful, she told him that she liked James as much as a girl could like a man who wasn't going to be her husband.

'And are you sure, Catherine, that James is not going to be your husband?'

'Yes,' she said, 'quite sure.'

'Now, isn't it wonderful like to be sure like that, for meself is never sure; and I don't know that I'd like to be if I could.' And Peter went away wondering why he hadn't told her he was going to Maynooth; for no one would have been able to advise him as well as Catherine, she had such good sense.

III

There was a quarter of a mile between the two houses, and while Peter was talking to Catherine, Pat Phelan was listening to his son James, who was telling his father that Catherine had said she would not marry him.

Pat was over sixty, but, all the same, old age seemed a long way from him; as a fine old oak, gnarled, without a withered bough and full of sap, he seemed to everybody; his long, thin, and shapely nose and his keen eyes drew attention to him. James was like him, but without the picturesqueness and without the streak of silliness that one liked in Peter. James sat holding his hands to the blaze, and when Peter opened the half-door, awaking the dozen hens that roosted on the beam, he glanced from one to the other, for he suspected his father to be telling James how he had failed to sell the bullocks. But the tone of his father's voice when he asked him what had detained him on the road put a doubt in his mind; and he remembered that Catherine had said she would not marry James.

'I met Catherine on the road, and I could do no less than walk as far as her door with her.'

'You could do no less than that, Pether,' said James.

'And what do you mean by that, James?'

'Only this, that it is always the crooked way, Pether; for if it had been you that had asked her she would have had you and jumping.'

'She'd have had me!'

'And now, don't you think you had better run after her, Pether, and ask her if she'll have you?'

'It's hurtful, James, you should think such a thing of me. I to try to get a girl from you!'

'I didn't mean that, Pether; but if she won't have me, you had better try if you can get her.'

And suddenly Peter felt a resolve come into his heart, and his manner grew exultant.

'I've seen Father Tom, and he said I can pass the examination. I'm going to be a priest.'

And when they were lying down side by side Peter said, 'James, it will be all right.' As there was a great heart-sickness on his brother, he put out his hand. 'As sure as I lie here she will be lying next you before this day twelvemonths. Yes, James, in this very bed, lying here where I am lying now.'

'I don't believe it, Pether.'

'I do, then.'

And not to stand in the way of his brother's marriage he took some money from his father and went to live at Father Tom's. And it was late one night when he went to bid them good-bye at home, having passed the bishop's examination all right.

'What makes you so late, Pether?'

'Well, James, I didn't want to meet Catherine on the road.'

'You're a good boy, Pether,' said the father, 'and God will reward you for the love you bear your brother. I don't think there are two better men in all this world. God is good, and he giving me two such sons.'

Then the three sat round the fire, and Pat Phelan began to talk family history.

'Well, Pether, you see, there has always been a priest in the family, and it would be a pity if there's not one in this generation. In '48 your grand-uncles joined the rebels, and they had to leave the country. You have an uncle a priest, and you are just like your uncle William.'

And then James talked, but he did not seem to know very well what he was saying, and his father told him to stop that Peter was going where God had called him.

'And you'll tell her,' Peter said, getting up, 'that I've gone.'

'I haven't the heart for telling her such a thing. She'll be finding it out soon enough.'

Outside the house for he was sleeping at Father Tom's that night Peter thought there was little luck in James's eyes; inside the house Pat Phelan and James thought that Peter was settled for life.

'He'll be a fine man standing on an altar,' James said, 'and perhaps he'll be a bishop some day.'

'And you'll see her when you're done reaping, and you won't forget what Pether told you,' said Pat Phelan.

And, after reaping, James put on his coat and walked up the hillside, where he thought he would find Catherine.

'I hear Pether has left you,' she said, as he opened the gate to let the cows through.

'He came last night to bid us good-bye.'

And they followed the cows under the tall hedges.

'I shall be reaping tomorrow,' he said. 'I will see you at the same time.'

And henceforth he was always at hand to help her to drive her cows home; and every night, as he sat with his father by the fire, Pat Phelan expected James to tell him about Catherine. One evening he came back overcome, looking so wretched that his father could see that Catherine had told him she would not marry him.

'She won't have me,' he said.

'A man can always get a girl if he tries long enough,' his father answered, hoping to encourage him.

'That would be true enough for another. Catherine knows she'll never get Pether. Another man might get her, but I'm always reminding her of Pether.'

She had told him the truth; he was sure of that when she said that if she didn't marry Peter she would marry no one, and James felt like dying.

At last he said, 'How is that?'

'I don't know. I don't know, James. But you mustn't talk to me about marriage again.'

He had had to promise her not to speak of marriage again: he kept his word, and at the end of the year she asked him if he had any news of Peter.

'The last news we had of him was about a month ago, and he said he hoped to be admitted into the minor orders.'

A few days afterwards he heard that Catherine had decided to go into a convent.

He seemed no longer fit for work on the farm, and was seen about the road smoking, and sometimes he went down to the ball-alley, and sat watching the games in the evening. It was thought that he would take to drink, but he took to fishing instead, and was out all day in his little boat on the lake, however hard the wind might blow. The fisherman said he had seen him in the part of the lake where the wind blew the hardest, and that he could hardly pull against the waves.

'His mind is away. I don't think he'll do any good in this country,' his father said.

And the old man was very sad, for when James was gone he would have no one, and he did not feel he would be able to work the farm for many years longer. He and James used to sit smoking on either side of the fireplace, saying nothing, Pat Phelan knowing that James was thinking of America, until one evening, as they were sitting like this, the door was opened suddenly.

'Pether!' said James. And he jumped up from the fire to welcome his brother.

'It is good for sore eyes to see the sight of you again,' said Pat Phelan. 'Well, tell us the news. Had we known you were coming we'd have sent the cart to fetch you.'

As Peter did not answer, they began to think that something must have happened. Perhaps Peter was not going to become a priest after all, and would stay at home with his father to learn to work the farm.

'You see, I didn't know myself until yesterday. It was only yesterday that—'

'So you are not going to be a priest? We are glad to hear that, Pether.'

'How is that?'

He had thought over what he should say, and without waiting to hear why they were glad, he told them the professor, who overlooked his essays, had refused to recognize their merits he had condemned the best things in them; and Peter said it was extraordinary that such a man should be appointed to such a place. And then he told them that the Church afforded little chances for the talents of young men unless they had a great deal of influence.

And they sat listening to him, hearing how the college might be reformed. He had a gentle, winning way of talking, and his father and brother forgot their own misfortunes thinking how they might help him.

'Well, Pether, you have come back none too soon.'

'And how is that? What have you been doing since I went away?

You all wanted to hear about Maynooth.'

'Of course we did, my boy. Tell him, James.'

'Oh! it is nothing particular,' said James. 'It is only this, Pether I'm going to America.'

'And who'll work the farm?'

'Well, Pether, we were thinking that you might work it yourself.'

'I work the farm! Going to America, James! But what about Catherine?'

'That's what I'm coming to, Pether. She has gone into a convent. And that's what's happened since you went away. I can't stop here, Pether I'll never do a hand's turn in Ireland and father will be getting too old to go to the fairs before long. That's what we were thinking when you came in.'

There was a faint tremble in his voice, and Peter saw how heartsick his brother was.

'I will do my best, James.'

'I knew you would.'

'Yes, I will,' said Peter; and he sat down by the fire. And his father said:

'You are not smoking, Pether.'

'No,' he said; 'I've given up smoking.'

'Will you drink something?' said James. 'We have got a drain of whisky in the house.'

'No, I have had to give up spirits. It doesn't agree with me. And I don't take tea in the morning. Have you any cocoa in the house?'

It was not the kind of cocoa he liked, but he said he would be able to manage.

IV

And when the old man came through the doorway in the morning buttoning his braces, he saw Peter stirring his cocoa. There was something absurd as well as something attractive in Peter, and his father had to laugh when he said he couldn't eat American bacon.

'My stomach wouldn't retain it. I require very little, but that little must be the best.'

And when James took him into the farmyard, he noticed that Peter crossed the yard like one who had never been in a farmyard before; he looked less like a farmer than ever, and when he looked at the cows, James wondered if he could be taught to see the difference between an Alderney and a Durham.

'There's Kate,' he said; 'she's a good cow, as good a cow as we have, and we can't get any price for her because of that hump on her back.'

They went to the styes; there were three pigs there and a great sow with twelve little bonhams, and the little ones were white with silky hair, and Peter asked how old they were, and when they would be fit for killing.

'Last year we had oats in the Holly field; next year you'll sow potatoes there.' And he explained the rotation of crops. 'And now,' he said, 'we'll go down to Crow's Oak. You have never done any ploughing, Pether; I'll show you.'

It was extraordinary how little Peter knew. He could not put the harness on the horse, and he reminded James that he had gone into the post-office when he left school. James gave in to him that the old red horse was hard to drive, but James could drive him better than Peter could lead him; and Peter marvelled at the skill with which James raised his hand from the shaft of the plough and struck the horse with the rein whilst he kept the plough steady with the other hand.

'Now, Pether, you must try again.'

At the end of the headland where the plough turned, Peter always wanted to stop and talk about something; but James said they would have to get on with the work, and Peter walked after the plough, straining after it for three hours, and then he said: 'James, let me drive the horse. I can do no more.'

'You won't feel it so much when you are accustomed to it,' said James.

Anything seemed to him better than a day's ploughing: even getting up at three in the morning to go to a fair.

He went to bed early, as he used to, and they talked of him over the fire, as they used to. But however much they talked, they never seemed to find what they were seeking his vocation until one evening an idea suddenly rose out of their talk.

'A good wife is the only thing for Pether,' said Pat.

And they went on thinking.

'A husband would be better for her,' said Pat Phelan, 'than a convent.'

'I can't say I agree with you there. Think of all the good them nuns be doing.'

'She isn't a nun yet,' said Pat Phelan.

And the men smoked on awhile, and they ruminated as they smoked.

'It would be better, James, that Pether got her than that she stayed in a convent.'

'I wouldn't say that,' said James.

'You see,' said his father, 'she didn't go into the convent because she had a calling, but because she was crossed in love.'

And after another long while James said, 'It is a bitter dose, I'm thinking, father, but you must go and tell her that Pether has left Maynooth.'

'And what would the Reverend Mother be saying to me if I went to her with such a story as that? Isn't your heart broke enough already, James, without wanting me to be breaking it still more? Sure, James, you could never see her married to Pether?'

'If she married Pether I'd be free to go to America, and that would be the only thing for me to do.'

'That would be poor comfort for you, James.'

'Well, it is the best I shall get, to see Pether settled, and to know that there will be someone to look after you, father.'

'You were always a good son, James.'

They talked on, and as they talked it became clearer to them that someone must go tomorrow to the convent and tell Catherine that Peter had left Maynooth.

'But wouldn't it be a pity,' said Pat Phelan, 'to tell her this if Pether is not going to marry her at all?'

'I will have him out of his bed,' said James, 'and he'll tell us before this fire if he will or won't.'

'It's a serious thing you are doing, James, to get a girl out of a convent, I'm thinking.'

'It will be on my advice that you will be doing this, father; and now I'll go and get Pether out of his bed.'

And Peter was brought in, asking what they wanted of him at this hour of the night; and when they told him what they had been talking about and the plans they had been making, he said he would be catching his death of cold, and they threw some sods of turf on the fire.

''Tis against myself that I am asking a girl to leave the convent, even for you, Pether,' said James. 'But what else can we do?'

'Pether will tell us if it is a sin that we'd be doing.'

'Surely we should tell Catherine all the truth before she takes her vows?'

'Pether, I'd take it as a great kindness. I shall never do a hand's turn in this country. I want to get to America. It will be the saving of me.'

'And now, Pether,' said his father, 'tell us for sure if you'll have the girl?'

'Faith I will, though I never thought of marriage, if it be pleasing James.' Seeing how heartsick his brother was, he said, 'I can't say I like her as you like her; but if she likes me I'll promise to do right by her. James, you're going away; we may never see you again. It's a great pity. And now you'll let me go back to bed.'

'Pether, I knew you would not say no to me; I can't bear this any longer.'

'And now,' said Peter, 'let me go back to bed. I am catching my death of cold.'

And he ran back to his room, and left his brother and father talking by the fire.

V

Pat thought the grey mare would take him in faster than the old red horse; and the old man sat, his legs swinging over the shaft, wondering what he should say to the Reverend Mother, and how she would listen to his story; and when he came to the priest's house a great wish came upon him to ask the priest's advice. The priest was walking up his little lawn reading his breviary, and a great fear came on Pat Phelan, and he thought he must ask the priest what he would do.

The priest heard the story over the little wall, and he was sorry for the old man.

It took him a long time to tell the story, and when he was finished the priest said:

'But where are you going, Pat?'

'That's what I stopped to tell you, your reverence. I was thinking I might be going to the convent to tell Catherine that Pether has come back.'

'Well, it wasn't yourself that thought of doing such a thing as that, Pat Phelan.'

But at every word the priest said Pat Phelan's face grew more stubborn, and at last he said:

'Well, your reverence, that isn't the advice I expected from you,' and he struck the mare with the ends of the reins and let her trot up the hill. Nor did the mare stop trotting till she had reached the top of the hill, and Pat Phelan had never known her do such a thing before. From the top of the hill there was a view of the bog, and Pat thought of the many fine loads of turf he had had out of that bog, and the many young fellows he had seen there cutting turf. 'But everyone is leaving the country,' the old man said to himself, and his chin dropped into his shirt-collar, and he held the reins loosely, letting the mare trot or walk as she liked. And he let many pass him without bidding them the time of day, for he was too much overcome by his own grief to notice anyone.

The mare trotted gleefully; soft clouds curled over the low horizon far away, and the sky was blue overhead; and the poor country was very beautiful in the still autumn weather, only it was empty. He passed two or three fine houses that the gentry had left to caretakers long ago. The fences were gone, cattle strayed through the woods, the drains were choked with weeds, the stagnant water was spreading out into the fields, and Pat Phelan noticed these things, for he remembered what this country was forty years ago. The devil a bit of lonesomeness there was in it then.

He asked a girl if they would be thatching the house that autumn; but she answered that the thatch would last out the old people, and she was going to join her sister in America.

'She's right they're all there now. Why should anyone stop here?' the old man said.

The mare tripped, and he took this to be a sign that he should turn back. But he did not go back. Very soon the town began, in broken pavements and dirty cottages; going up the hill there were some slated roofs, but there was no building of any importance except the church.

At the end of the main street, where the trees began again, the convent stood in the middle of a large garden, and Pat Phelan remembered he had heard that the nuns were doing well with their dairy and their laundry.

He knocked, and a lay-sister peeped through the grating, and then she opened the door a little way, and at first he thought he would have to go back without seeing either Catherine or the Reverend Mother. For he had got no farther than 'Sister Catherine,' when the lay-sister cut him short with the news that Sister Catherine was in retreat, and could see no one. The Reverend Mother was busy.

'But,' said Pat, 'you're not going to let Catherine take vows without hearing me.'

'If 'tis about Sister Catherine's vows—'

'Yes, 'tis about them I've come, and I must see the Reverend Mother.'

The lay-sister said Sister Catherine was going to be clothed at the end of the week.

'Well, that's just the reason I've come here.'

On that the lay-sister led him into the parlour, and went in search of the Reverend Mother.

The floor was so thickly bees-waxed that the rug slipped under his feet, and, afraid lest he might fall down, he stood quite still, awed by the pious pictures on the walls, and by the large books upon the table, and by the poor-box, and by the pious inscriptions. He began to think how much easier was this pious life than the life of the world the rearing of children, the failure of crops, and the loneliness. Here life slips away without one perceiving it, and it seemed a pity to bring her back to trouble. He stood holding his hat in his old hands, and the time seemed very long. At last the door opened, and a tall woman with sharp, inquisitive eyes came in.

'You've come to speak to me about Sister Catherine?'

'Yes, my lady.'

'And what have you got to tell me about her?'

'Well, my son thought and I thought last night we were all thinking we had better tell you last night was the night that my son came back.'

At the word Maynooth a change of expression came into her face, but when he told that Peter no longer wished to be a priest her manner began to grow hostile again, and she got up from her chair and said:

'But really, Mr. Phelan, I have got a great deal of business to attend to.'

'But, my lady, you see Catherine wanted to marry my son Pether, and 'tis because he went to Maynooth that she came here. I don't think she'd want to be a nun if she knew that he didn't want to be a priest.'

'I can't agree with you, Mr. Phelan, in that. I have seen a great deal of Sister Catherine she has been with us now for nearly a year and if she ever entertained the wishes you speak of, I feel sure she has forgotten them. Her mind is now set on higher things.'

'You may be right, my lady. It isn't for the likes of me to argue a point with you; but I have come a long way to see Catherine herself—'

'That is impossible. Catherine is in retreat.'

'So the lay-sister told me; but I thought—'

'Sister Catherine is going to be clothed next Saturday, and I can assure you, Mr. Phelan, that the wishes you tell me of are forgotten. I know her very well. I can answer for Sister Catherine.'

The rug slipped under the peasant's feet and his eyes wandered round the room; and the Reverend Mother told him how busy she was, she really couldn't talk to him any more that day.

'You see, it all rests with Sister Catherine herself.'

'That's just it,' said the old man; 'that's just it, my lady. My son Pether, who has come from Maynooth, told us last night that Catherine should know everything that has happened, so that she mayn't be sorry afterwards. Only for this I wouldn't come at all. I wouldn't be troubling you.'

'I am sorry, Mr. Phelan, that your son Peter has left Maynooth. It is sad indeed when one finds that one hasn't a vocation. But that happens sometimes. I don't think it will be Catherine's case. And now, Mr. Phelan, I must ask you to excuse me,' and the Reverend Mother persuaded the unwilling peasant into the passage, and he followed the lay-sister down the passage to the gate and got into his cart again.

'No wonder at all,' he said to himself; 'it wouldn't be suiting them to let Catherine out, and that after getting that fine farm. And I'm sure there isn't one of them in it could boil pig's food like Catherine herself.'

At the very same moment the same thoughts passed through the Reverend Mother's mind. She had not left the parlour yet, and stood thinking how she should manage if Catherine were to leave them. 'Why,' she asked, 'should he choose to leave Maynooth at such a time? It is indeed unfortunate. There is nothing,' she reflected, 'that gives a woman so much strength as to receive the veil. She always feels stronger after her clothing. She feels that the world is behind her.'

The Reverend Mother reflected that perhaps it would be better for Catherine's sake and for Peter's sake indeed, for everyone's sake if she were not to tell Catherine of Pat Phelan's visit until after the clothing. She might tell Catherine three months hence. The disadvantage of this would be that Catherine might hear that Peter had left Maynooth. In a country place news of this kind cannot be kept out of a convent. And if Catherine were going to leave, it were better that she should leave them now than leave them six months hence, after her clothing.

'There are many ways of looking at it,' the Reverend Mother reflected. 'If I don't tell her, she may never hear it. I might tell her later, when she has taught one of the nuns how to manage the farm.' She took two steps towards the door and stopped to think again, and she was thinking when a knock came to the door. She answered mechanically, 'Come in,' and Catherine wondered at the Reverend

Mother's astonishment.

'I wish to speak to you, dear mother,' she said timidly. But seeing the Reverend Mother's face change expression, she said, 'Perhaps another time will suit you better.'

The Reverend Mother stood looking at her, irresolute; and Catherine, who had never seen the Reverend Mother irresolute before, wondered what was passing in her mind.

'I know you are busy, dear mother, but what I've come to tell you won't take very long.'

'Well, then, tell it to me, my child.'

'It is only this, Reverend Mother. I had better be telling you now, and you are expecting the bishop, and my clothing fixed for the end of the week, and—'

'And,' said the Reverend Mother, 'you feel you aren't certain of your vocation.'

'That's it, dear mother. I didn't like to tell you before. I was thinking that the feeling would pass away; but it isn't everyone that has a vocation.'

The Reverend Mother asked Catherine to sit down by her; and Catherine told her she had come to the convent because she was crossed in love, and not as the others came, because they wished to give up their wills to God.

'Our will is the most precious thing in us, and that is why the best thing we can do is to give it up to you, for in giving it up to you, dear mother, we are giving it up to God. I know all these things, but—'

'You should have told me of this when you came here, Catherine, and then I shouldn't have advised you to come to live with us.'

'Mother, you must forgive me. My heart was broke, and I couldn't do else. And you told me yourself I made the dairy a success.'

'If you had stayed with us, Catherine, you would have made the dairy a success; but we have got no one to take your place. However, since it is the will of God, I suppose we must try to get on as well as we can without you. And now tell me, Catherine, when it was you changed your mind. It was only the other day you told me you wished to become a nun. You said you were most anxious for your clothing. How is it that you have changed your mind?'

Catherine's eyes brightened, and speaking like one illuminated by some inward light, she said:

'It was the second day of my retreat, mother. I was walking in the garden where the great cross stands amid the rocks. Sister Angela and Sister Mary were with me, and I was listening to what they were saying, when suddenly my thoughts were taken away and I remembered those at home. I remembered Mr. Phelan, and James, who wanted to marry me, but whom I would not marry; and it seemed to me that I saw him leaving his father it seemed to me that I saw him going away to America. I don't know how it was you won't believe me, dear mother but I saw the ship that is to take him away lying in the harbour. And then I thought of the old man sitting at home with no one to look after him, and it came over me suddenly that my duty was not here, but there. Of course you won't agree with me, but I can't resist it, it was a call.'

'But the Evil One, my dear child, calls us too; we must be careful not to mistake the devil's call for God's call.'

'I'm sure, mother.' Tears came to Catherine's eyes, she began to weep. 'I can't be arguing with you, mother, I only know—' She could not speak sobbing, and between her sobs she said, 'I only know that I must go home.'

She recovered herself very soon, and the Reverend Mother took her hand and said:

'Well, my dear child, I shan't stand in your way.'

Even the Reverend Mother could not help thinking that the man who got her would get a charming wife. Her face was rather long and white, and her eyes were full of tenderness. She had spoken out of so deep a conviction that the Reverend Mother had begun to believe that her mission was perhaps to look after this hapless young man; and when she told the Reverend Mother that yesterday she had felt a conviction that Peter was not going to be a priest, the Reverend Mother felt that she must tell her of Pat Phelan's visit.

'I did not tell you at once, my dear child, because I wished to know from yourself how you felt about this matter;' and the nun told Catherine that Peter had left Maynooth. A glow came into the postulant's eyes.

'How did he know that I cared for him?' the girl said, half to herself, half to the nun.

'I suppose his father or his brother must have told him,' the nun answered. And then Catherine, fearing to show too much interest in things that the nun deemed frivolous, said, 'I am sorry to leave before my work is done, ma'am. So it has all come true; it was extraordinary what I felt that morning in the garden,' she said, returning to her joy.

'The saints, of course, have had visions. We believe in the visions of the saints.'

'But after all, mother, there are many duties besides religious duties.'

'I suppose, Catherine, you feel it to be your duty to look after this young man?'

'Yes, I think that is it. I must go now, mother, and see Sister Angela, and write out for her all I know about the farm, and what she is to do, for if one is not very careful with a farm one loses a great deal of money. There is no such thing as making two ends meet. One either makes money or loses money.'

And then Catherine again seemed to be engulfed in some deep joy, out of which she roused herself with difficulty.

VI

When her postulant left the room, the Reverend Mother wrote to Pat Phelan, asking him to come next morning with his cart to fetch Catherine. And next morning, when the lay-sister told Catherine that he was waiting for her, the Reverend Mother said:

'We shall be able to manage, Catherine. You have told Sister Angela everything, and you'll not forget to come to see us, I hope.'

'Mr. Phelan,' said the lay-sister, 'told me to tell you that one of his sons is going to America today. Sister Catherine will have to go at once if she wishes to see him.'

'I must see James. I must see him before he leaves for America. Oh,' she said, turning to the Reverend Mother, 'do you remember that I told you I had seen the ship? Everything has come true. You can't believe any longer that it is not a call.'

Her box was in the cart, and as Pat turned the mare round he said: 'I hope we won't be after missing James at the station. 'Twas because of that I came for you so early. I thought you'd be liking to see him.'

'Why didn't you come earlier?' she cried. 'I shall never be happy again if I don't see James.'

The convent was already behind her, and her thoughts were now upon poor James, whose heart she had broken. She knew that Peter would never love her as well as James, but her vision in the garden consoled her, for she could no longer doubt that she was doing right in going to Peter, that her destiny was with him.

She knew the road well, she knew all the fields, every house and every gap in the walls. Sign after sign went by; at last they were within sight of the station. The signal was still up, and the train had not gone yet; at the end of the platform she saw James and Peter.

She let Pat Phelan drive the cart round; she could get to them quicker by running down the steps and crossing the line. The signal went down.

'Pether,' she said, 'we will have time to talk presently. I must speak to James now.'

And they walked up the platform, leaving Peter to talk to his father.

'Paddy Maguire is outside,' Pat said; 'I asked him to stand at the mare's head.'

'James,' said Catherine, 'it's bad news to hear you're going. Maybe we'll never see you again, and there is no time to be talking now, and me with so much to say.'

'I am going away, Catherine, but maybe I will be coming back some day. I was going to say maybe you would be coming over after me; but the land is good land, and you'll be able to make a living out of it.'

And then they spoke of Peter. James said he was too great a scholar for a farmer, and it was a pity he could not find out what he was fit for for surely he was fit for something great after all.

And Catherine said: 'I shall be able to make something out of Pether.'

His emotion almost overcame him, and Catherine looked aside so that she should not see his tears.

''Tis no time for talking of Pether,' she said. 'You are going away, James, but you will come back. You'll find better women than me in America, James. I don't know what to say to you. The train will be here in a minute. I am distracted. But one day you will be coming back, and we'll be proud of you when you do. I'll build up the house, and then we'll be happy. Oh! here's the train. Good-bye; you have been very good to me. Oh, James! when will I be seeing you again?'

Then the crowd swept them along, and James had to take his father's hand and his brother's hand. There were a great many people in the station hundreds were going away in the same ship as James. The wailing relatives ran alongside of the train, waving their hands until they could no longer keep up. James waved a red handkerchief till the train disappeared in a cutting, and a moment after Catherine and Peter remembered they were standing side by side. They were going to be married in a few days! They started a little, hearing a step beside them. It was old Phelan.

'I think,' he said, 'we'd better be after getting home.'

HOME SICKNESS

HE told the doctor he was due in the bar-room at eight o'clock in the morning; the bar-room was in a slum in the Bowery; and he had only been able to keep himself in health by getting up at five o'clock and going for long walks in the Central Park.

'A sea-voyage is what you want,' said the doctor. 'Why not go to Ireland for two or three months? You will come back a new man.'

'I'd like to see Ireland again.'

And he began to wonder how the people at home were getting on. The doctor was right. He thanked him, and three weeks after he landed in Cork.

As he sat in the railway-carriage he recalled his native village, built among the rocks of the large headland stretching out into the winding lake. He could see the houses and the streets, and the fields of the tenants, and the Georgian mansion and the owners of it; he and they had been boys together before he went to America. He remembered the villagers going every morning to the big house to work in the stables, in the garden, in the fields mowing, reaping, digging, and Michael Malia building a wall; it was all as clear as if it were yesterday, yet he had been thirteen years in America; and when the train stopped at the station the first thing he did was to look round for any changes that might have come into it. It was the same blue limestone station as it was thirteen years ago, with the same five long miles between it and Duncannon. He had once walked these miles gaily, in little over an hour, carrying a heavy bundle on a stick, but he did not feel strong enough for the walk today, though the evening tempted him to try it. A car was waiting at the station, and the boy, discerning from his accent and his dress that Bryden had come from America, plied him with questions, which Bryden answered rapidly, for he wanted to hear who were still living in the village, and if there was a house in which he could get a clean lodging. The best house in the village, he was told, was Mike Scully's, who had been away in a situation for many years, as a coachman in the King's County, but had come back and built a fine house with a concrete floor. The boy could recommend the loft,

21

he had slept in it himself, and Mike would be glad to take in a lodger, he had no doubt. Bryden remembered that Mike had been in a situation at the big house. He had intended to be a jockey, but had suddenly shot up into a fine tall man, and had become a coachman instead; and Bryden tried to recall his face, but could only remember a straight nose and a somewhat dusky complexion.

So Mike had come back from King's County, and had built himself a house, had married there were children for sure running about; while he, Bryden, had gone to America, but he had come back; perhaps he, too, would build a house in Duncannon, and — His reverie was suddenly interrupted by the carman.

'There's Mike Scully,' he said, pointing with his whip, and Bryden saw a tall, finely built, middle-aged man coming through the gates, who looked astonished when he was accosted, for he had forgotten Bryden even more completely than Bryden had forgotten him; and many aunts and uncles were mentioned before he began to understand.

'You've grown into a fine man, James,' he said, looking at Bryden's great width of chest. 'But you're thin in the cheeks, and you're very sallow in the cheeks too.'

'I haven't been very well lately —that is one of the reasons I've come back; but I want to see you all again.'

'And thousand welcome you are.'

Bryden paid the carman, and wished him 'Godspeed.' They divided the luggage, Mike carrying the bag and Bryden the bundle, and they walked round the lake, for the townland was at the back of the domain, and while walking he remembered the woods thick and well-forested, now they were wind-worn, the drains were choked, and the bridge leading across the lake inlet was falling away. Their way led between long fields where herds of cattle were grazing, the road was broken Bryden wondered how the villagers drove their carts over it, and Mike told him that the landlord could not keep it in repair, and he would not allow it to be kept in repair out of the rates, for then it would be a public road, and he did not think there should be a public road through his property.

At the end of many fields they came to the village, and it looked a desolate place, even on this fine evening, and Bryden remarked that the county did not seem to be as much lived in as it used to be. It was at once strange and familiar to see the chickens in the kitchen; and, wishing to re-knit himself to the old customs, he begged of Mrs. Scully not to drive them out, saying they reminded him of old times.

'And why wouldn't they?' Mike answered, 'he being one of ourselves bred and born in Duncannon, and his father before him.'

'Now, is it truth ye are telling me?' and she gave him her hand, after wiping it on her apron, saying he was heartily welcome, only she was afraid he wouldn't care to sleep in a loft.

'Why wouldn't I sleep in a loft, a dry loft! You're thinking a good deal of America over here,' said he, 'but I reckon it isn't all you think it. Here you work when you like and you sit down when you like; but when you've had a touch of blood-poisoning as I had, and when you have seen young people walking with a stick, you think that there is something to be said for old Ireland.'

'You'll take a sup of milk, won't you? You must be dry,' said Mrs. Scully.

And when he had drunk the milk Mike asked him if he would like to go inside or if he would like to go for a walk.

'Maybe resting you'd like to be.'

And they went into the cabin and started to talk about the wages a man could get in America, and the long hours of work.

And after Bryden had told Mike everything about America that he thought of interest, he asked Mike about Ireland. But Mike did not seem to be able to tell him much. They were all very poor poorer, perhaps, than when he left them.

'I don't think anyone except myself has a fivepound-note to his name.'

Bryden hoped he felt sufficiently sorry for Mike. But after all Mike's life and prospects mattered little to him. He had come back in search of health, and he felt better already, the milk had done him good, and the bacon and the cabbage in the pot sent forth a savoury odour, The Scullys were very kind, they pressed him to make a good meal; a few weeks of country air and food, they said, would give him back the health he had lost in the Bowery; and when Bryden said he was longing for a smoke, Mike said there was no better sign than that. During his long illness he had never wanted to smoke, and he was a confirmed smoker.

It was comfortable to sit by the mild peat fire watching the smoke of their pipes drifting up the chimney, and all Bryden wanted was to be left alone; he did not want to hear of anyone's misfortunes, but about nine o'clock a number of villagers came in, and Bryden remembered one or two of them he used to know them very well when he was a boy their talk was as depressing as their appearance, and he could feel no interest whatever in them. He was not moved when he heard that Higgins the stone mason was dead, he was not affected when he heard that Mary Kelly, who used to go to do the laundry at the Big House, had married; he was only interested when he heard she had gone to America. No, he had not met her there; America is a big place. Then one of the peasants asked him if he remembered Patsy Carabine, who used to do the gardening at the Big House. Yes, he remembered Patsy well. He had not been able to do any work on account of his arm; his house had fallen in; he had given up his holding and gone into the Poor-House. All this was very sad, and to avoid hearing any further unpleasantness, Bryden began to tell them about America. And they sat round listening to him, but all the talking was on his side, he wearied of it, and looking round the group he recognized a ragged hunchback with grey hair; twenty years ago he was a young hunchback, and, turning to him, Bryden asked him if he were doing well with his five acres.

'Ah, not much. This has been a poor season. The potatoes failed, they were watery there is no diet in them.'

These peasants were all agreed that they could make nothing out of their farms. Their regret was that they had not gone to America when they were young, and after striving to take an interest in the fact that O'Connor had lost a mare and a foal worth forty pounds, Bryden began to wish himself back in the slum.

And when they left the house he wondered if every evening would be like the present one. Mike piled fresh sods on the fire, and he hoped it would show enough light in the loft for Bryden to undress himself by.

The cackling of some geese in the street kept him awake, and he seemed to realize suddenly how lonely the country was, and he foresaw mile after mile of scanty fields stretching all round the lake with one little town in the far corner. A dog howled in the distance, and the fields and the boreens between him and the dog appeared as in a crystal. He could hear Michael breathing by his wife's side in the kitchen, and he could barely resist the impulse to run out of the house, and he might have yielded to it, but he wasn't sure that he mightn't awaken Mike as he came down the ladder. His terror increased, and he drew the blanket over his head. He fell asleep and awoke and fell asleep again, and lying on his back he dreamed of the men he had seen sitting round the fireside that evening, like spectres they seemed to him in his dream. He seemed to have been asleep only a few minutes when he heard Mike calling him. He had come halfway up the ladder, and was telling him that breakfast was ready. 'What kind of a breakfast will he give me ?' Bryden asked himself as he pulled on his clothes. There were tea and hot griddle cakes for breakfast, and there were fresh eggs; there was sunlight in the kitchen, and he liked to hear Mike tell of the work he was going to be at in the farm one of about fifteen acres, at least ten of it was grass; he grew an acre of potatoes, and some corn, and some turnips for his sheep. He had a nice bit of meadow, and he took down his scythe, and as he put the whetstone in his belt Bryden noticed a second scythe, and he asked Mike if he should go down with him and help him to finish the field.

'It's a long time since you've done any mowing, and its heavier work than you think for. You'd better go for a walk by the lake.' Seeing that Bryden looked a little disappointed, he added, 'If you like you can come up in the afternoon and help me to turn the grass over.' Bryden said he would, and the morning passed pleasantly by the lake shore a delicious breeze rustled in the trees, and the reeds were talking together, and the ducks were talking in the reeds; a cloud blotted out the sunlight, and the cloud passed and the sun shone, and the reed cast its shadow again in the still water; there was a lapping always about the shingle; the magic of returning health was sufficient distraction for the convalescent; he lay with his eyes fixed upon the castles, dreaming of the men that had manned the battlements; whenever a peasant driving a cart or an ass or an old woman with a bundle of sticks on her back went by, Bryden kept them in chat, and he soon knew the village by heart. One day the landlord from the Georgian mansion set on the pleasant green hill came along, his retriever at his heels, and stopped surprised at finding somebody whom he didn't know on his property. 'What, James Bryden!' he said. And the story was told again how ill-health had overtaken him at last, and he had come home to Duncannon to recover. The two walked as far as the pine-wood, talking of the county, what it had been, the ruin it was slipping into, and as they parted Bryden asked for the loan of a boat.

'Of course, of course!' the landlord answered, and Bryden rowed about the islands every morning ¡ and resting upon his oars looked at the old castles, remembering the prehistoric raiders that the landlord had told him about. He came across the stones to which the lake-dwellers had tied their boats, and these signs of ancient Ireland were pleasing to Bryden in his present mood.

As well as the great lake there was a smaller lake in the bog where the villagers cut their turf. This lake was famous for its pike, and the landlord allowed Bryden to fish there, and one evening when he was looking for a frog with which to bait his line he met Margaret Dirken driving home the cows for the milking. Margaret was the herdsman's daughter, and lived in a cottage near the Big House; but she came up to the village whenever there was a dance, and Bryden had found himself opposite to her in the reels. But until this evening he had had little opportunity of speaking to her, and he was glad to speak to someone, for the evening was lonely, and they stood talking together.

'You're getting your health again,' she said, 'and will be leaving us soon.'

'I'm in no hurry.'

'You're grand people over there; I hear a man is paid four dollars a day for his work.'

'And how much,' said James, 'has he to pay for his food and for his clothes?'

Her cheeks were bright and her teeth small, white and beautifully even; and a woman's soul looked at Bryden out of her soft Irish eyes. He was troubled and turned aside, and catching sight of a frog looking at him out of a tuft of grass, he said: 'I have been looking for a frog to put upon my pike line.'

The frog jumped right and left, and nearly escaped in some bushes, but he caught it and returned with it in his hand.

'It is just the kind of frog a pike will like,' he said.

'Look at its great white belly and its bright yellow back.'

And without more ado he pushed the wire to which the hook was fastened through the frog's fresh body, and dragging it through the mouth he passed the hooks through the hind-legs and tied the line to the end of the wire.

'I think,' said Margaret, 'I must be looking after my cows; it's time I got them home.'

'Won't you come down to the lake while I set my line?'

She thought for a moment and said:

'No, I'll see you from here.'

He went down to the reedy tarn, and at his approach several snipe got up, and they flew above his head uttering sharp cries. His fishing-rod was a long hazel-stick, and he threw the frog as far as he could in the lake. In doing this he roused some wild ducks; a mallard and two ducks got up, and they flew toward the larger lake in a line with an old castle; and they had not disappeared from view when Bryden came toward her, and he and she drove the cows home together that evening.

They had not met very often when she said: 'James, you had better not come here so often calling to me.'

'Don't you wish me to come?'

'Yes, I wish you to come well enough, but keeping company isn't the custom of the country, and I don't want to be talked about.'

'Are you afraid the priest would speak against us from the altar?'

'He has spoken against keeping company, but it is not so much what the priest says, for there is no harm in talking.'

'But if you're going to be married there is no harm in walking out together.'

'Well, not so much, but marriages are made differently in these parts; there isn't much courting here.'

And next day it was known in the village that James was going to marry Margaret Dirken.

His desire to excel the boys in dancing had caused a stir of gaiety in the parish, and for some time past there had been dancing in every house where there was a floor fit to dance upon; and if the cottager had no money to pay for a barrel of beer, James Bryden, who had money, sent him a barrel, so that Margaret might get her dance. She told him that they sometimes crossed over into another parish where the priest was not so averse to dancing, and James wondered. And next morning at Mass he wondered at their simple fervour. Some of them held their hands above their head as they prayed, and all this was very new and very old to James Bryden. But the obedience of these people to their priest surprised him. When he was a lad they had not been so obedient, or he had forgotten their obedience; and he listened in mixed anger and wonderment to the priest, who was scolding his parishioners, speaking to them by name, saying that he had heard there was dancing going on in their homes. Worse than that, he said he had seen boys and girls loitering about the road, and the talk that went on was of one kind love. He said that newspapers containing love stories were finding their way into the people's houses, stories about love, in which there was nothing elevating or ennobling. The people listened, accepting the priest's opinion without question. And their pathetic submission was the submission of a primitive people clinging to religious authority, and Bryden contrasted the weakness and incompetence of the people about him with the modern restlessness and cold energy of the people he left behind him.

One evening, as they were dancing, a knock came to the door, and the piper stopped playing, and the dancers whispered:

'Someone has told on us; it is the priest.'

And the awe-stricken villagers crowded round the cottage fire, afraid to open the door. But the priest said that if they didn't open the door he would put his shoulder to it and force it open. Bryden went towards the door, saying he would allow no one to threaten him, priest or no priest, but Margaret caught his arm and told him that if he said anything to the priest, the priest would speak against them from the altar, and they would be shunned by the neighbours.

'I've heard of your goings on,' he said, 'of your beer-drinking and dancing. I'll not have it in my parish. If you want that sort of thing you had better go to America.'

'If that is intended for me, sir, I'll go back tomorrow. Margaret can follow.'

'It isn't the dancing, it's the drinking I'm opposed to,' said the priest, turning to Bryden.

'Well, no one has drunk too much, sir,' said Bryden.

'But you'll sit here drinking all night,' and the priest's eyes went toward the corner where the women had gathered, and Bryden felt that the priest looked on the women as more dangerous than the porter. 'It's after midnight,' he said, taking out his watch.

By Bryden's watch it was only half-past eleven, and while they were arguing about the time Mrs. Scully offered Bryden's umbrella to the priest, for in his hurry to stop the dancing the priest had gone out without his; and, as if to show Bryden that he bore him no ill-will, the priest accepted the loan of the umbrella, for he was thinking of the big marriage fee that Bryden would pay him.

'I shall be badly off for the umbrella tomorrow,' Bryden said, as soon as the priest was out of the house. He was going with his father-in-law to a fair. His father-in-law was learning him how to buy and sell cattle. The country was mending, and a man might become rich in Ireland if he only had a little capital.

Margaret had an uncle on the other side of the lake who would give twenty pounds, and her father would give another twenty pounds.

Bryden had saved two hundred pounds. Never in the village of Duncannon had a young couple begun life with so much prospect of success, and some time after Christmas was spoken of as the best time for the marriage; James Bryden said that he would not be able to get his money out of America before the spring. The delay seemed to vex him, and he seemed anxious to be married, until one day he received a letter from America, from a man who had served in the bar with him. This friend wrote to ask Bryden if he were coming back. The letter was no more than a passing wish to see Bryden again. Yet Bryden stood looking at it, and everyone wondered what could be in the letter. It seemed momentous, and they hardly believed him when he said it was from a friend who wanted to know if his health were better. He tried to forget the letter, and he looked at the worn fields, divided by walls of loose stones, and a great longing came upon him.

The smell of the Bowery slum had come across the Atlantic, and had found him out in this western headland; and one night he awoke from a dream in which he was hurling some drunken customer through the open doors into the darkness. He had seen his friend in his white duck jacket throwing drink from glass into glass amid the din of voices and strange accents ¡ he had heard the clang of money as it was swept into the till, and his sense sickened for the bar-room. But how should he tell Margaret Dirken that he could not marry her? She had built her life upon this marriage. He could not tell her that he would not marry her ... yet he must go. He felt as if he were being hunted; the thought that he must tell Margaret that he could not marry her hunted him day after day as a weasel hunts a rabbit. Again and again he went to meet her with the intention of telling her that he did not love her, that their lives were not for one another, that it had all been a mistake, and that happily he had found out it was a mistake soon enough. But Margaret, as if she guessed what he was about to speak of, threw her arms about him and begged him to say he loved her, and that they would be married at once.

He agreed that he loved her, and that they would be married at once. But he had not left her many minutes before the feeling came upon him that he could not marry her that he must go away. The smell of the bar-room hunted him down. Was it for the sake of the money that he might make there that he wished to go back? No, it was not the money. What then? His eyes fell on the bleak country, on the little fields divided by bleak walls; he remembered the pathetic ignorance of the people, and it was these things that he could not endure. It was the priest who came to forbid the dancing. Yes, it was the priest. As he stood looking at the line of the hills the bar-room seemed by him. He heard the politicians, and the excitement of politics was in his blood again. He must go away from this place he must get back to the bar-room. Looking up, he saw the scanty orchard, and he hated the spare road that led to the village, and he hated the little hill at the top of which the village began, and he hated more than all other places the house where he was to live with Margaret Dirken if he married her. He could see it from where he stood by the edge of the lake, with twenty acres of pasture land about it, for the landlord had given up part of his demesne land to them. He caught sight of Margaret, and he called her to come through the stile.

'I have just had a letter from America.'

'About the money?'

'Yes, about the money. But I shall have to go over there.'

He stood looking at her, wondering what to say; and she guessed that he would tell her that he must go to America before they were married.

'Do you mean, James, you will have to go at once?'

'Yes,' he said, 'at once. But I shall come back in time to be married in August. It will only mean delaying our marriage a month.'

They walked on a little way talking, and every step he took James felt that he was a step nearer the Bowery slum. And when they came to the gate Bryden said:

'I must walk on or I shall miss the train.'

'But,' she said, 'you are not going now—you are not going today?'

'Yes, this morning. It is seven miles. I shall have to hurry not to miss the train.'

And then she asked him if he would ever come back.

'Yes,' he said, 'I am coming back.'

'If you are coming back, James, why don't you let me go with you?'

'You couldn't walk fast enough. We should miss the train.'

'One moment, James. Don't make me suffer; tell me the truth. You are not coming back. Your clothes where shall I send them?'

He hurried away, hoping he would come back. He tried to think that he liked the country he was leaving, that it would be better to have a farmhouse and live there with Margaret Dirken than to serve drinks behind a counter in the Bowery. He did not think he was telling her a lie when he said he was coming back. Her offer to forward his clothes touched his heart, and at the end of the road he stood and asked himself if he should go back to her. He would miss the train if he waited another minute, and he ran on. And he would have missed the train if he had not met a car. Once he was on the car he felt himself safe—the country was already behind him. The train and the boat at Cork were mere formulae; he was already in America.

And when the tall skyscraper stuck up beyond the harbour he felt the thrill of home that he had not found in his native village, and wondered how it was that the smell of the bar seemed more natural than the smell of fields, and the roar of crowds more welcome than the silence of the lake's edge. He entered into negotiations for the purchase of the bar-room. He took a wife, she bore him sons and daughters, the bar-room prospered, property came and went; he grew old, his wife died, he retired from business, and reached the age when a man begins to feel there are not many years in front of him, and that all he has had to do in life has been done. His children married, lonesomeness began to creep about him in the evening, and when he looked into the firelight, a vague, tender reverie floated up, and Margaret's soft eyes and name vivified the dusk. His wife and children passed out of mind, and it seemed to him that a memory was the only real thing he possessed, and the desire to see Margaret again grew intense. But she was an old woman, she had married, maybe she was dead. Well, he would like to be buried in the village where he was born.

There is an unchanging, silent life within every man that none knows but himself, and his unchanging, silent life was his memory of Margaret Dirken. The bar-room was forgotten and all that concerned it, and the things he saw most clearly were the green hillside, and the bog lake and the rushes about it, and the greater lake in the distance, and behind it the blue line of wandering hills.

SOME PARISHIONERS

THE way before Father Maguire was plain enough, yet his uncle's apathy and constitutional infirmity of purpose seemed at times to thwart him. Only two or three days ago, he had come running down from Kilmore with the news that a baby had been born out of wedlock, and what do you think? Father Stafford had shown no desire that his curate should denounce the girl from the altar.

'The greatest saints,' he said, 'have been kind, and have found excuses for the sins of others.'

And a few days later, when he told his uncle that the Salvationists had come to Kilmore, and that he had walked up the village street and slit their drum with a carving-knife, his uncle had not approved of his conduct, and what had especially annoyed Father Tom was that his uncle seemed to deplore the slitting of the drum in the same way as he deplored that the Kavanaghs had a barrel of porter in every Saturday, as one of those regrettable excesses to which human nature is liable. On being pressed, he agreed with his nephew that dancing and drinking were no preparation for the Sabbath, but he would not agree that evil could be suppressed by force. He even hinted that too strict a rule brought about a revolt against the rule, and when Father Tom expressed his disbelief at any revolt against the authority of the priest, Father Stafford said:

'They may just leave you, they may just go to America.'

'Then you think that it is our condemnation of sin that is driving the people to America.'

'My dear Tom, you told me the other day that you met a boy and girl walking along the roadside, and drove them home. You told me you were sure they were talking about things they shouldn't talk about; you have no right to assume these things. You're asking of the people an abstinence you don't practise yourself. Sometimes your friends are women.'

'Yes. But—'

Father Tom's anger prevented him from finding an adequate argument, and Father Stafford pushed the tobacco-bowl towards his nephew.

'You're not smoking, Tom.'

'Your point is that a certain amount of vice is inherent in human nature, and that if we raise the standard of virtuous living our people will escape from us to New York or London.'

'The sexes mix freely everywhere in Western Europe; only in Ireland and Turkey is there any attempt made to separate them.'

Later in the evening Father Tom insisted that the measure of responsibility was always the same.

'I should be sorry,' said his uncle, 'to say that those who inherit drunkenness bear the same burden of responsibility as those who come of parents who are quite sane—'

'You cannot deny, uncle John, that free will and predestination—'

'My dear Tom, I really must go to bed. It is after midnight.'

And as he walked home, Father Maguire thought of the great change he perceived in his uncle. He liked an hour's small-talk after dinner, his pipe, his glass of grog, his bed at eleven o'clock, and Father Maguire thought with sorrow of their great disputations, sometimes prolonged till after three o'clock. The passionate scholiast of Maynooth seemed to him unrecognizable in the esurient Vicar-General, only occasionally interested in theology, at certain hours and when he felt particularly well. The first seemed incompatible with the second, his mind not being sufficiently acute to see that after all no one can discuss theology for more than five and twenty years without wearying of the subject.

The moon was shining among the hills and the mystery of the landscape seemed to aggravate his sensibility, and he asked himself if the guardians of the people should not fling themselves into the forefront of the battle. If men came to preach heresy in his parish was he not justified in slitting their drum?

He had recourse to prayer, and he prayed for strength and for guidance. He had accepted the Church, and in the Church he saw only apathy, neglect, and bad administration on the part of his superiors.... He had read that great virtues are, like large sums of money, deposited in the bank, whereas humility is like the pence, always at hand, always current. Obedience to our superiors is the sure path. He could not persuade himself that it was right for him to allow the Kavanaghs to continue a dissolute life of drinking and dancing. They were the talk of the parish; and he would have spoken against them from the altar, but his uncle had advised him not to do so. Perhaps his uncle was right; he might be right regarding the Kavanaghs. In the main he disagreed with his uncle, but in this particular instance it might be well to wait and pray that matters might improve.

Father Tom believed Ned Kavanagh to be a good boy. Ned was going to marry Mary Byrne, and Father Tom had made up this marriage. The Byrnes did not care for the marriage they were prejudiced against Ned on account of his family. But he was not going to allow them to break off the marriage. He was sure of Ned, but in order to make quite sure he would get him to take the pledge. Next morning, when the priest had done his breakfast, the servant opened the door, and told him that Ned Kavanagh was outside, and wanted to see him.

It was a pleasure to look at this nice clean boy, with his winning smile, and the priest thought that Mary could not wish for a better husband. The priest had done his breakfast, and was about to open his newspaper, but he wanted to see Ned Kavanagh, and he told his servant to let him in. Ned's smile seemed a little fainter than usual, and his face was paler; the priest wondered, and presently Ned told the priest that he had come to confession, and, going down on his knees, he told the priest that he had been drunk last Saturday night, and that he had come to take the pledge. He would never do any good while he was at home, and one of the reasons he gave for wishing to marry Mary Byrne was his desire to leave home. The priest asked him if matters were mending, and if his sister showed any signs of wishing to be married.

'Sorra sign,' said Ned.

'That's bad news you're bringing me,' said the priest, and he walked up and down the room, and they talked over Kate's wilful character.

'From the beginning she didn't like living at home,' said the priest.

'I wouldn't be caring about living at home,' said Ned.

'But for a different reason,' said the priest. 'You want to leave home to get married, and have a wife and children, if God is pleased to give you children.'

He sat thinking of the stories he had heard. He had heard that Kate had come back from her last situation in a cab, wrapped up in blankets, saying she was ill. On inquiry it was found that she had only been three or four days in her situation; three weeks had to be accounted for. He had questioned her himself regarding this interval, but had not been able to get any clear and definite answer from her.

'She and mother do be always quarrelling about Pat Connex.'

'It appears,' said the priest, 'that your mother went out with a jug of porter under her apron, and offered a sup of it to Pat, who was talking with Peter M'Shane, and now he is up at your cabin every Saturday.'

'That's so,' said Ned.

'Mrs. Connex was here the other day, and I tell you that if Pat marries your sister he will find himself cut off with a shilling.'

'She's been agin us all the while,' said Ned. 'Her money has made her proud, but I wouldn't be blaming her. If I had the fine house she has, maybe I would be as proud as she.'

'Maybe you would,' said the priest. 'But what I'm thinking of is your sister Kate. She'll never get Pat Connex. Pat won't ever go against his mother.'

'Well, you see he comes up and plays the melodeon on Saturday night,' said Ned, 'and she can't stop him from doing that.'

'Then you think,' said the priest, 'that Pat will marry your sister?'

'I don't think she is thinking about him.'

'If she doesn't want to marry him, what's all this talk about?'

'She does like to be meeting Pat in the evenings and to be walking out with him, and him putting his arm round her waist and kiss her, saving your reverence's presence.'

'It is strange that you should be so unlike. You come here and ask me to speak to Mary Byrne's parents for you, and that I'll do, Ned, and it will be all right. You will make a good husband, and though you were drunk last night, you have taken the pledge today. And I will make a good marriage for Kate, too, if she'll listen to me.'

'And who may your reverence be thinking of?'

'I'm thinking of Peter M'Shane. He gets as much as six shillings a week and his keep on Murphy's farm, and his mother has got a bit of money, and they have a nice, clean cabin. Now listen to me. There is a poultry lecture at the schoolhouse tonight. Do you think you could bring your sister with you?'

'We did use to keep a great many hins at home, and Kate had the feeding of them, and now she's turned agin them, and she wants to live in town, and she even tells Pat Connex she would not marry a farmer, however much he was worth.'

'But if you tell her that Pat Connex will be at the lecture, will she come?'

'Yes, your reverence, if she believes me.'

'Then do as I bid you,' said the priest; 'you can tell her that Pat Connex will be there.'

II

After leaving the priest Ned crossed over the road to avoid the public-house, and went for a walk on the hills. It was about five when he turned towards the village. On his way there he met his father, and Ned told him that he had been to see the priest, and that he was going to take Mary to the lecture.

'They're quarrelling at home.'

Michael was very tired, and he thought it was pretty hard to come home after a long day's work to find his wife and daughter quarrelling.

'I am sorry your dinner isn't ready, father,' said Kate, 'but it won't be long now. I'll cut the bacon.'

'I met Ned on the road,' her father answered. 'It's sorry I am that he has gone to fetch Mary. He's going to take her to the lecture on poultry-keeping at the schoolhouse.'

'Ah, he has been to the priest, has he?' said Kate, and her mother asked her why she said that, and the wrangle began again.

Ned was the peacemaker; there was generally quiet in the cabin when he was there. And he dropped in as Michael was finishing his dinner, bringing with him Mary, a small, fair girl, who everybody said would keep his cabin tidy. His mother and sisters were broad-shouldered women with blue-black hair and red cheeks, and it was said that he had said he would like to bring a little fair hair in the family.

'We've just looked in for a minute,' said Mary. 'Ned said that perhaps you'd be coming with us.'

'All the boys in the village will be there tonight,' said Ned. 'You had better come with us.' And pretending he wanted to get a coal of fire to light his pipe, Ned whispered to Kate as he passed her, 'Pat Connex will be there.'

She looked at the striped sunshade she had brought back from the dressmaker's she had once been apprenticed to a dressmaker but Ned said that a storm was blowing and she had better leave the sunshade behind.

The rain beat in their faces and the wind came sweeping down the mountain and made them stagger. Sometimes the road went straight on, sometimes it turned suddenly and went uphill. After walking for a mile they came to the schoolhouse. A number of men were waiting outside, and one of the boys told them that the priest had said they were to keep a lookout for the lecturer, and Ned said that he had better stay with them, that his lantern would be useful to show her the way. The women had collected into one corner, and the priest was walking up and down a long, smoky room, his hands thrust into the pockets of his overcoat. Now he stopped in his walk to scold two children who were trying to light a peat fire in a tumble-down grate.

'Don't be tired, go on blowing,' he said. 'You are the laziest child I have seen this long while.'

Ned came in and blew out his lantern, but the lady he had mistaken for the lecturer was a lady who had come to live in the neighbourhood lately, and the priest said:

'You must be very much interested in poultry, ma'am, to come out on such a night as this.'

The lady stood shaking her waterproof.

'Now, then, Lizzie, run to your mother and get the lady a chair.'

And when the child came back with the chair, and the lady was seated by the fire, he said:

'I'm thinking there will be no lecturer here tonight, and that it would be kind of you if you were to give the lecture yourself. You have read some books about poultry, I am sure?'

'Well, a little but—'

'Oh, that doesn't matter,' said the priest. 'I'm sure the book you have read is full of instruction.'

He walked up the room towards a group of men and told them they must cease talking, and coming back to the young woman he said:

'We shall be much obliged if you will say a few words about poultry. Just say what you have in your mind about the different breeds.'

The young woman again protested, but the priest said:

'You will do it very nicely.' And he spoke like one who is not accustomed to being disobeyed. 'We will give the lecturer five minutes more.'

'Is there no farmer's wife who could speak?' the young lady asked in a fluttering voice. 'She'd know much more than I. I see Biddy M'Hale there. She has done very well with her poultry.'

'I dare say she has,' said the priest, 'but the people would pay no attention to her. She is one of themselves. It would be no amusement to them to hear her.'

The young lady asked if she might have five minutes to scribble a few notes. The priest said he would wait a few minutes, but it did not matter much what she said.

'But couldn't someone dance or sing?' said the young lady.

'Dancing and singing!' said the priest. 'No!'

And the young lady hurriedly scribbled a few notes about fowls for laying, fowls for fattening, regular feeding, warm houses, and something about a percentage of mineral matter. She had not half finished when the priest said:

'Now will you stand over there near the harmonium. Whom shall I announce?'

The young woman told him her name, and he led her to the harmonium and left her talking, addressing most of her instruction to Biddy M'Hale, a long, thin, pale-faced woman, with wistful eyes.

'This won't do,' said the priest, interrupting the lecturer—'I'm not speaking to you, miss, but to my people. I don't see one of you taking notes, not even you, Biddy M'Hale, though you have made a fortune out of your hins. Didn't I tell you from the pulpit that you were to bring pencil and paper and write down all you heard? If you had known years ago all this young lady is going to tell you, you would be rolling in your carriages today.'

Then the priest asked the lecturer to go on, and the lady explained that to get hens to lay about Christmas time, when eggs fetched the best price, you must bring on your pullets early.

'You must,' she said, 'set your eggs in January.'

'You hear that,' said the priest. 'Is there anyone who has got anything to say about that? Why is it that you don't set your eggs in January?'

No one answered, and the lecturer went on to tell of the advantages that would come to the poultry-keeper whose eggs were hatched in December.

As she said this, the priest's eyes fell upon Biddy M'Hale, and, seeing that she was smiling, he asked her if there was any reason why eggs could not be hatched in the beginning of January.

'Now, Biddy, you must know all about this, and I insist on your telling us. We are here to learn.'

Biddy did not answer.

'Then what were you smiling at?'

'I wasn't smiling, your reverence.'

'Yes; I saw you smiling. Is it because you think there isn't a brooding hin in January?'

It had not occurred to the lecturer that hens might not be brooding so early in the year, and she waited anxiously. At last Biddy said:

'Well, your reverence, it isn't because there are no hins brooding. You'll get brooding hins at every time in the year; but, you see, you couldn't be rearing chickens earlier than March. The end of February is the earliest ever I saw. But, sure, if you could be rearing them in January, all that the young lady said would be quite right. I have nothing to say agin it. I have no fault to find with anything she says, your reverence.'

'Only that it can't be done,' said the priest. 'Well, you ought to know, Biddy.'

The villagers were laughing.

'That will do,' said the priest. 'I don't mind your having a bit of amusement, but you're here to learn.'

And as he looked round the room, quieting the villagers into silence, his eyes fell on Kate. He looked for the others, and spied Pat Connex and Peter M'Shane near the door. 'They're here, too,' he thought. 'When the lecture is over I will see them and bring them all together. Kate Kavanagh won't go home until she promises to marry Peter. I have had enough of her goings on in my parish.'

But Kate had caught sight of Peter. She would get no walk home with Pat that night, and she suspected her brother of having done this for a purpose and got up to go.

'I don't want anyone to leave this room,' said the priest. 'Kate Kavanagh, why are you going? Sit down till the lecture is over.'

And as Kate had not strength to defy the priest, she sat down, and the lecturer continued for a little while longer. The priest could see that the lecturer had said nearly all she had to say, and he had begun to wonder how the evening's amusement was to be prolonged. It would not do to let the people go home until Michael Dunne had closed his public house, and the priest looked round the audience thinking which one he might call upon to say a few words on the subject of poultry-keeping.

From one of the back rows a voice was heard: 'What about the pump, your reverence?'

'Well, indeed, you may ask,' said the priest.

And immediately he began to speak of the wrong they had suffered by not having a pump in the village. The fact that Almighty God had endowed Kilmore with a hundred mountain streams did not release the authorities from the obligation of supplying the village with a pump. Had not the authorities put up one in the neighbouring village?

'You should come out,' he said, 'and fight for your rights. You should take off your coats like men, and if you do I'll see that you get your rights,' and he looked round for someone to speak.

There was a landlord among the audience, and as he was a Catholic the priest called upon him to speak. He said that he agreed with the priest in the main. They should have their pump, if they wanted a pump; if they didn't, he would suggest that they asked for something else. Farmer Byrne said he did not want a pump, and then everyone spoke his mind, and things got mixed. The Catholic landlord regretted that Father Maguire was against allowing a poultry-yard to the patients in the lunatic asylum. If, instead of supplying a pump, the Government would sell them eggs for hatching at a low price, something might be gained. If the Government would not do this, the Government might be induced to supply books on poultry free of charge. It took the Catholic landlord half an hour to express his ideas regarding the asylum, the pump, and the duties of the Government, and in this way the priest succeeded in delaying the departure of the audience till after closing time. 'However fast they walk,' he said to himself, 'they won't get to Michael Dunne's public-house in ten minutes, and he will be shut by then.' It devolved upon him to bring the evening's amusement to a close with a few remarks, and he said:

'Now, the last words I have to say to you I'll address to the women. Now listen to me. If you pay more attention to your poultry you'll never be short of half a sovereign to lend your husbands, your sons, or your brothers.'

These last words produced an approving shuffling of feet in one corner of the room, and seeing that nothing more was going to happen the villagers got up and they went out very slowly, the women curtseying and the men lifting their caps to the priest as they passed him.

He had signed to Ned and Mary that he wished to speak to them, and after he had spoken to Ned he called Kate and reminded her that he had not seen her at confession lately.

'Pat Connex and Peter M'Shane, now don't you be going. I will have a word with you presently.'

And while Kate tried to find an excuse to account for her absence from confession, the priest called to Ned and Mary, who were talking at a little distance. He told them he would be waiting for them in church tomorrow, and he said he had never made a marriage that gave him more pleasure. He alluded to the fact that they had come to him. He was responsible for this match, and he accepted the responsibility gladly. His uncle, the Vicar-General, had delegated all the work of the parish to him.

'Father Stafford,' he said abruptly, 'will be very glad to hear of your marriage, Kate Kavanagh.'

'My marriage,' said Kate....'I don't think I shall ever be married.'

'Now, why do you say that?' said the priest.

Kate did not know why she had said that she would never be married. However, she had to give some reason, and she said:

'I don't think, your reverence, anyone would have me.'

'You are not speaking your mind,' said the priest, a little sternly. 'It is said that you don't want to be married, that you like courting better.'

'I'd like to be married well enough.'

'Those who wish to make safe, reliable marriages consult their parents and they consult the priest. I have made your brother's marriage for him. Why don't you come to me and ask me to make up a marriage for you?'

'I think a girl should make her own marriage, your reverence.'

'And what way do you go about making up a marriage? Walking about the roads in the evening, and turning into public houses, and leaving your situations. It seems to me, Kate Kavanagh, you have been a long time making up this marriage.

'Now, Pat Connex, I've got a word with you. You're a good boy, and I know you don't mean any harm by it; but I have been hearing tales about you. You've been up to Dublin with Kate Kavanagh. Your mother came up to speak to me about this matter yesterday, and she said: " Not a penny of my money will he ever get if he marries her," meaning the girl before you. Your mother said: "I've got nothing to say against her, but I've got a right to choose my own daughter-in-law." Those are your mother's very words, Pat, so you had better listen to reason. Do you hear me, Kate ?'

'I hear your reverence.'

'And if you hear me, what have you got to say to that?'

'He's free to go after the girl he chooses, your reverence,' said Kate.

'There's been courting enough,' the priest said. 'If you aren't going to be married you must give up keeping company. I see Paddy Boyle outside the door. Go home with him. Do you hear what I'm saying, Pat? Go straight home, and no stopping about the roads. Just do as I bid you; go straight home to your mother.'

Pat did not move at the bidding of the priest. He stood watching Kate as if he were waiting for a sign from her, but Kate did not look at him.

'Do you hear what I'm saying to you?' said the priest.

'Yes, I hear,' said Pat.

'And aren't you going?' said the priest.

Everyone was afraid Pat would raise his hand against the priest, and they looked such strong men, both of them, that everyone wondered which would get the better of the other.

'You won't go home when I tell you to do so. We will see if I can't put you out of the door then.'

'If you weren't a priest,' said Pat, 'the divil a bit of you would put me out of the door.'

'If I weren't a priest I would break every bone in your body for talking to me like that. Now out you go,' he said, taking him by the collar, and he put him out.

'And now, Kate Kavanagh,' said the priest, coming back from the door, 'you said you didn't marry because no man would have you. Peter has been waiting for you ever since you were a girl of sixteen years old, and I may say it for him, since he doesn't say much himself, that you have nearly broken his heart.'

'I'm sure I never meant it. I like Pether.'

'You acted out of recklessness without knowing what you were doing.'

A continual smile floated round Peter's moustache, and he looked like a man to whom rebuffs made no difference. His eyes were patient and docile; and whether it was the presence of this great and true love by her side, or whether it was the presence of the priest, Kate did not know, but a great change came over her, and she said:

'I know that Pether has been very good, that he has a liking for me.... If he wishes to put the ring on me—'

When Kate gave him her hand there was a mist in his eyes, and he stood trembling before her.

PATCHWORK

NEXT morning, as Father Maguire was leaving the house, his servant handed him a letter. It was from an architect who had been down to examine the walls of the church, and the envelope that Father Maguire was tearing open contained his report; two hundred pounds would be required to make the walls secure. Well, he'd see if this were so, and he continued to read the report until he arrived at the church. The wedding party was waiting, but the architect's report was much more important than a wedding, and he wandered round the old walls examining the cracks as he went. He could see they were crumbling, and he believed the architect was right. It would be better to build a new church. But to build a new church three or four thousand pounds would be required, and the architect might as well suggest that he should collect three or four millions.... Meanwhile, Mary Byrne and Ned Kavanagh were going to be married.

And Ned and Mary noticed the dark look between the priest's eyes as he came out of the sacristy, and Ned regretted that his reverence should be out of his humour that morning, for he had spent three out of the five pounds he had saved to pay the priest for marrying him. He had cherished hopes that the priest would understand that he had had to buy some new clothes, but the priest looked so cross that it was with difficulty he summoned courage to tell him that he had only two pounds left.

'I want two hundred pounds to make the walls of the church safe. Where's the money to come from? All the money in Kilmore goes into drink, and,' he added bitterly, 'into blue trousers. No, I won't marry you for two pounds. I won't marry you for less than five. I will marry you for nothing or I will marry you for five pounds,' he added, and Ned looked round the wedding guests; he knew that none had five shillings in his pocket, and he did not dare to take the priest at his word and let him marry him for nothing.

Father Maguire felt that his temper had got the better of him, but it was too late to go back on what he said. Marry them for two pounds with the architect's letter in the pocket of his cassock! And

if he was to accept two pounds, who'd pay five to be married? If he
didn't stand out for his dues the marriage fee would be reduced
from five pounds to one pound.... And if he accepted Ned's two
pounds his authority would be weakened; he wouldn't be able to get
them to subscribe to have the church made safe. So on the whole he
thought he'd done right, and his servant was of the same opinion.

'They'd have the cassock off your back, your reverence, if they
could get it.'

'And the architect writing to me that the walls can't be made safe
under two hundred pounds, and the whole lot of them earning not
less than thirty shillings a week, and they can't pay the priest five
pounds for marrying them.'

In the course of the day he went to Dublin to see the architect;
and next morning it occurred to him that he might have to go to
America to get the money to build a new church, and as he sat
thinking the door was opened, and the servant said that Biddy
M'Hale wanted to see his reverence.

She came in curtseying; and before saying a word she took ten
sovereigns out of her pocket and put them upon the table. The priest
thought she had heard of the architect's report, and he said:

'Now, Biddy, I am glad to see you. I suppose you have brought
me this for my church. You have heard of the money it will cost to
make the walls safe?'

'No, your reverence, I did not hear any more than that there were
cracks in the walls.'

'But you have brought me this money to have the cracks
mended?'

'Well, no, your reverence. I have been thinking a long time of
doing something for the church, and I thought I should like to have
a window put up in the church with colours in it.'

Father Maguire was touched by Biddy's desire to do something
for the church, and told her her name would be put on the top of the
subscription list.

'A subscription from Miss M'Hale ten pounds.'

Biddy didn't answer, and it annoyed the priest to see her sitting in
his own chair stretching out her hand ready to take the money back.
He could see that her wish to benefit the church was merely a
pretext for the glorification of herself, and he began to argue with
the old woman. But he might have spared himself the trouble of
explaining that it was necessary to have a new church before you
could have a window. She understood well enough it was useless to
put a window up in a church that was going to fall down. But her

idea still was St. Joseph in a red cloak and the Virgin in blue with a crown of gold on her head, and forgetful of everything else, she asked him whether her window in the new church should be put over the high altar, or if it should be a window lighting a side altar.

'But, my good woman, ten pounds will not pay for a window. You couldn't get anything to speak of for less than fifty pounds.'

He had expected to astonish Biddy, but she did not seem astonished. She said that although fifty pounds was a great deal of money she would not mind spending all that money if she were to have her window all to herself. She had thought at first of only putting in part of the window, a round piece at the top, and she had thought that that could be bought for ten pounds. The priest could see that she had been thinking a good deal of this window, and she seemed to know more about it than he expected.

'It is extraordinary,' he said to himself, 'how a desire of immortality persecutes these voteens. A desire of temporal immortality,' he said, fearing he had been guilty of a heresy.

'If I could have the whole window to myself, I would give you fifty pounds, your reverence.'

The priest had no idea she had saved as much money as that.

'The hins have been very good to me, your reverence, and I'd like to put up the window in the new church better than in the old church.'

'But I've got no money, my good woman, to build the church.'

'Ah, won't your reverence go to America and get the money? Aren't all our own people over there, and always giving money for churches?'

The priest spoke to her about statues, and suggested that perhaps a statue would be a more permanent gift, but the old woman knew that stained glass could be secured from breakage by means of wire-netting.

'Do you know, Biddy, it will require three or four thousand pounds to build a new church? If I go to America and do my best to get the money, how much will you help me with?'

'Does your reverence mean for the window?'

'No, Biddy, I was thinking of the church itself.'

And Biddy said that she would give him five pounds to help to build the church and fifty pounds for her window, and, she added, 'if the best gilding and paint costs a little more I would be sorry to see the church short.'

'Well, you say, Biddy, you will give five pounds towards the church. Now, let us think how much money I could get in this parish.'

He had a taste for gossip, and she began by telling him she had met Kate Kavanagh on the road, and Kate had told her that there had been great dancing last night.

'But there was no wedding,' said the priest.

'I only know, your reverence, what Kate Kavanagh told me. There had been great dancing last night. The supper was ordered at Michael Dunne's and the cars were ordered, and they went to Enniskerry and back.'

'But Michael Dunne would not dare to serve supper to people who weren't married,' said the priest.

'The supper had been ordered, and they would have to pay for it whether they ate it or not. There was a pig's head, and the cake cost eighteen shillings, and it was iced.'

'Never mind the food,' said the priest, 'tell me what happened.'

'Kate said that after coming back from Enniskerry, Michael Dunne said, "Is this the wedding party?" and that Ned jumped off the car, and said: " To be sure. Ain't I the wedded man?" And they had half a barrel of porther.'

'Never mind the drink,' said the priest, 'what then?'

'There was dancing first and fighting after. Pat Connex and Peter M'Shane were both there. You know Pat plays the melodeon, and he asked Peter to sing, and Peter can't sing a bit, and he was laughed at. So he grabbed a bit of stick and hit Pat on the head, and hit him badly, too. I hear the doctor had to be sent for.'

'That is always the end of their dancing and drinking,' said the priest. 'And what happened then, what happened? After that they went home?'

'Yes, your reverence, they went home.'

'Mary Byrne went home with her own people, I suppose, and Ned went back to his home.'

'I don't know, your reverence, what they did.'

'Well, what else did Kate Kavanagh tell you?'

'She had just left her brother and Mary, and they were going towards the Peak. That is what Kate told me when I met her on the road.'

'Mary Byrne wouldn't go to live with a man to whom she was not married. But you told me that Kate said she had just left Mary Byrne and her brother.'

'Yes, they were just coming out of the cabin,' said Biddy. 'She passed them on the road.'

'Out of whose cabin?' said the priest.

'Out of Ned's cabin. I know it must have been out of Ned's cabin, because she said she met them at the crossroads'

He questioned the old woman, but she grew less and less explicit.

'I don't like to think this of Mary Byrne, but after so much dancing and drinking, it is impossible to say what mightn't have happened.'

'I suppose they forgot your reverence didn't marry them.'

'Forgot!' said the priest. 'A sin has been committed, and through my fault.'

'They will come to your reverence tomorrow when they are feeling a little better.'

The priest did not answer, and Biddy said:

'Am I to take away my money, or will your reverence keep it for the window?'

'The church is tumbling down, and before it is built up you want me to put up statues.'

'I'd like a window better.'

'I've got other things to think of now.'

'Your reverence is very busy. If I had known it I wouldn't have come disturbing you. But I'll take my money with me.'

'Yes, take your money,' he said. 'Go home quietly, and say nothing about what you have told me. I must think over what is best to be done.'

Biddy hurried away, gathering her shawl about her, and this great strong man who had taken Pat Connex by the collar and could have thrown him out of the schoolroom, fell on his knees and prayed that God might forgive him the avarice and anger that had caused him to refuse to marry Ned Kavanagh and Mary Byrne.

'Oh! my God, oh! my God,' he said, 'Thou knowest that it was not for myself that I wanted the money, it was to build up Thine Own House.'

He remembered that his uncle had warned him again and again against the sin of anger. He had thought lightly of his uncle's counsels, and he had not practised the virtue of humility, which, as St. Teresa said, was the surest virtue to seek in this treacherous world.

'Oh, my God, give me strength to conquer anger.'

The servant opened the door, but seeing the priest upon his knees, she closed it quietly, and the priest prayed that if sin had been committed he might bear the punishment.

And on rising from his knees he felt that his duty was to seek out the sinful couple. But how to speak to them of their sin? The sin was not theirs. He was the original wrongdoer. If Ned Kavanagh and Mary Byrne were to die and lose their immortal souls, how could the man who had been the cause of the loss of two immortal souls save his own? and the consequences of his refusal to marry Ned Kavanagh and Mary Byrne seemed to reach to the very ends of Eternity.

He walked to his uncle's with great swift steps, hardly seeing his parishioners as he passed them on the road.

'Is Father Stafford in?'

'Yes, your reverence.'

'Uncle John, I have come to consult you.'

The priest sat huddled in his armchair over the fire, and Father Maguire noticed the cassock covered with snuff, the fringe of reddish hair about the great bald head, and the fat, inert hands. He seemed to see his uncle more clearly than he had ever seen him before, and he fell to wondering why he observed him so explicitly, his mind being intent on a matter of great spiritual importance.

'I have come to ask you,' Father Tom said, 'regarding the blame attaching to a priest who refuses to marry a young man and a young woman, there being no impediment of consanguinity or other.'

'But have you refused to marry anyone because they couldn't pay you your dues?'

'Listen, the church is falling.'

'My dear Tom, you shouldn't have refused to marry them,' he said, as soon as his soul-stricken curate had laid the matter before him.

'Nothing can justify my action in refusing to marry them,' said Father Tom, 'nothing. Uncle John, I know that you can extenuate, that you are kind, but I don't see it is possible to look at it from any other side.'

'My dear Tom, you are not sure they remained together; the only knowledge you have of the circumstances you obtained from that old woman, Biddy M'Hale, who cannot tell a story properly. An old gossip, who manufactures stories out of the slightest materials.... but who sells excellent eggs; her eggs are always fresh. I had two this morning.'

'Uncle John, I didn't come here to be laughed at.'

'I am not laughing at you, my dear Tom; but really you know very little about this matter.'

'I know well enough that they remained together last night. I examined the old woman carefully, and she had just met Kate Kavanagh on the road. There can be no doubt about it,' he said.

'But,' said Father John, 'they intended to be married; the

intention was there.'

'Yes, but the intention is no use. We aren't living in a country where the edicts of the Council of Trent haven't been promulgated.'

'That's true,' said Father John. 'But how can I help you? What am I to do?'

'Are you feeling well enough for a walk this morning? Could you come up to Kilmore?'

'But it is two miles I really—'

'The walk will do you good. If you do this for me, Uncle John—'

'My dear Tom, I am, as you say, not feeling very well this morning, but—'

He looked at his nephew, and seeing that he was suffering, he said:

'I know what these scruples of conscience are; they are worse than physical suffering.'

But before he decided to go with his nephew to seek the sinners out, he could not help reading him a little lecture.

'I don't feel as sure as you do that a sin has been committed; but admitting that a sin has been committed, I think you ought to admit that you set your face against the pleasure of these poor people too resolutely.'

'Pleasure,' said Father Tom. 'Drinking and dancing, hugging and kissing each other about the lanes.'

'You said dancing now, I can see no harm in it.'

'There's no harm in dancing, but it leads to harm. If they only went back with their parents after the dance, but they linger in the lanes.'

'It was raining the other night, and I felt sorry, and I said, "Well, the boys and girls will have to stop at home tonight, there will be no courting tonight." If you don't let them walk about the lanes and make their own marriages, they marry for money. These walks at eventide represent all the aspiration that may come into their lives. After they get married, the work of the world grinds all the poetry out of them.'

'Walking under the moon,' said Father Tom, 'with their arms round each other's waists, sitting for hours saying stupid things to each other that isn't my idea of poetry. The Irish find poetry in other things than sex.'

'Mankind,' said Father John, 'is the same all the world over. The Irish aren't different from other races; do not think it. Woman represents all the poetry that the ordinary man is capable of appreciating.'

'And what about ourselves?'

'We're different. We have put this interest aside. I have never regretted it, and you have not regretted it either.'

'Celibacy has never been a trouble to me.'

'But Tom, your own temperament should not prevent you from sympathy with others. You aren't the whole of human nature; you should try to get a little outside yourself.'

'Can one ever do this?' said Father Tom.

'Well, you see what a difficulty your narrowmindedness has brought you into.'

'I know all that,' said Father Tom. 'It is no use insisting upon it. Will you come with me? They must be married this morning. Will you come with me? I want you to talk to them. You are kinder than I am. You sympathize with them more than I do, and it wasn't you who refused to marry them.'

Father John got out of his armchair and staggered about the room on his short fat legs, trying to find his hat. Father Tom said:

'Here it is. You don't want your umbrella. There's no sign of rain.'

'No,' said his uncle, 'but it will be very hot presently. My dear Tom, I can't walk fast.'

'I am sorry, I didn't know I was walking fast.'

'You are walking at the rate of four miles an hour at the least.'

'I am sorry, I will walk slower.'

At the crossroads inquiry was made, and the priests were told that the cabin Ned Kavanagh had taken was the last one.

'That's just another half-mile,' said Father John.

'If we don't hasten we shall be late.'

'We might rest here,' said Father John, 'for a moment,' and he leaned against a gate. 'My dear Tom, it seems to me you're agitating yourself a little unnecessarily about Ned Kavanagh and his wife I mean the girl he is going to marry.'

'I am quite sure. Ned Kavanagh brought Mary back to his cabin. There can be no doubt.'

'Even so,' said Father John. 'He may have thought he was married.'

'How could he have thought he was married unless he was drunk, and that cannot be put forward as an excuse. No, my dear uncle, you are inclined for subtleties this morning.'

'He may have thought he was married. Moreover, he intended to be married, and if through forgetfulness—'

'Forgetfulness!' cried Father Maguire. 'A pretty large measure of forgetfulness!'

'I shouldn't say that a mortal sin has been committed; a venial one.... If he intended to be married—'

'Oh, my dear uncle, we shall be late, we shall be late!'

Father Stafford repressed the smile that gathered in the corner of his lips, and he remembered how Father Tom had kept him out of bed till two o'clock in the morning, talking to him about St. Thomas Aquinas.

'If they're to be married today we must be getting on.' And Father Maguire's stride grew more impatient. 'I'll walk on in front.'

At last he spied a woman in a field, and she told him the married couple had gone for a walk most of the party were with them, but Pat Connex was in bed, and the doctor had been to see him.

'I've heard,' said Father Tom, 'of last night's drunkenness. Half a barrel of porter; there's what remains,' he said, pointing to some stains on the roadway. 'They were too drunk to turn off the tap.'

'I heard your reverence wouldn't marry them,' the woman said.

'I am going to bring them down to the church at once.'

'Well, if you do,' said the woman, 'you won't be a penny the poorer; you will have your money at the end of the week. And how do you do, your reverence?' The woman dropped a curtsey to Father Stafford. 'It's seldom we see you up here.'

'They've gone towards the Peak,' said Father Tom, for he saw his uncle would take advantage of the occasion to gossip. 'We shall catch them up there.'

'I am afraid I am not equal to it, Tom. I'd like to do this for you, but I am afraid I am not equal to another half-mile uphill.'

Father Maguire strove to hypnotize his parish priest.

'Uncle John, you're called upon to make this effort. I cannot speak to these people as I should like to.'

'If you spoke to them as you would like to, you would only make matters worse,' said Father John.

'Very likely, I'm not in a humour to contest these things with you. But I beseech you to come with me. Come,' he said, 'take my arm.'

They went a few hundred yards up the road, then there was another stoppage, and Father Maguire had again to exercise his power of will, and he was so successful that the last half-mile of the road was accomplished almost without a stop.

At Michael Dunne's, the priests learned that the wedding party had been there, and Father Stafford called for a lemonade.

'Don't fail me now, Uncle John. They are within a few hundred yards of us. I couldn't meet them without you. Think of it. If they were to tell me that I had refused to marry them for two pounds, my authority would be gone for ever. I should have to leave the parish.'

'My dear Tom, I would do it if I could, but I am completely exhausted.'

At that moment sounds of voices were heard.

'Listen to them, Uncle John.' And the curate took the glass from Father John. 'They aren't as far as I thought, they are sitting under these trees. Come,' he said.

And they walked some twenty yards, till they came to a spot where the light came pouring through the young leaves, and all the brown leaves of last year were spotted with light. There were light shadows amid the rocks and pleasant mosses, and the sounds of leaves and water falling, and from the top of a rock Kate listened while Peter told her they would rebuild his house.

'The priests are after us,' she said.

And she gave a low whistle, and the men and boys looked round, and seeing the priests coming, they dispersed, taking several paths, and none but Ned and Mary were left behind. Ned was dozing; Mary was sitting beside him fanning herself with her hat: they had not heard Kate's whistle, and they did not see the priests until they were by them.

'Now, Tom, don't lose your head; be quiet with them.'

'Will you speak to them, or shall I?' said Father Tom.

'You are too excited, and will—'

'I think you had better let me speak to them,' said Father John. 'You are Ned Kavanagh, and you are Mary Byrne, I believe. Now, I don't know you all, for I am getting an old man, and don't often come up this way. But notwithstanding my age, and the heat of the day, I have come up, for I've heard that you haven't acted as good Catholics should. I do not doubt for a moment that you intended to get married, but you have, I fear, been guilty of a great sin, and you've set a bad example.'

'We were on our way to your reverence now,' said Mary. 'I mean to his reverence.'

'Well,' said Father Tom, 'you are taking your time over it, lying here half asleep under the trees.'

'We hadn't the money,' Mary answered; 'it wasn't our fault.'

'Didn't I say I'd marry you for nothing?'

'But sure, your reverence, that's only a way of speaking.'

'There's no use lingering here,' said Father Tom. 'You took the pledge the day before yesterday, and yesterday you were tipsy.'

'Maybe I had a drop of drink in me, your reverence. Pat Connex passed me the mug of porther and I forgot myself.'

'And once,' said the priest, 'you tasted the porter you thought you could go on taking it.'

Ned did not answer, and the priests whispered together.

'We are halfway now,' said Father Tom; 'we can get there before twelve o'clock.'

'I don't think I'm equal to it. 'I really don't think—You see it is all uphill. See how the road ascends. I couldn't manage it.'

'The road is pretty flat at the top of the hill once you get to the top of the hill. You'll—'

The sound of wheels was heard, and a peasant driving a donkey-cart came up the road.

It seemed undignified to accept a lift, but his nephew's conscience was at stake, and the Vicar General allowed himself to be helped into the donkey-cart.

'Now walk on in front of us,' Father Tom said to the unmarried couple, 'and step out as quickly as you can.'

But no sooner were the words out of his mouth than Father Tom remembered he had caught sight of Kate standing at the top of the rock talking to Peter M'Shane: in a few days they would come to him to be married, and he hoped that Peter and Kate's marriage would make amends for this miserable patchwork, for Ned Kavanagh's and Mary Byrne's marriage was no better than patchwork.

THE WEDDING FEAST

AND everywhere Kate went her gown was being talked about the gown she was to be married in, a grey silk that had been bought at a rummage sale. They were all at her, and so persistently that she had begun to feel she was being driven into a trap, and on the morning of her wedding turned round to ask her sister if she thought she ought to marry Peter. Julia thought it would be a pity if she didn't, for her dress would be wasted, and Kate threw a look down the skirt that boded no good.

'I hate the both of them the priest and that old waddling sow of a mother-in-law of mine, or what is to be.'

After this speech Julia expected to hear Peter's name, but Kate was not thinking of him then nor did she think of him once during the ceremony; she seemed all the time to be absent from herself; and it was not till he got up beside her on the car that she remembered they were now one flesh. But Peter did not notice that she shrank from him; nor did the others. The distribution occupied all their attention. The fat were set beside the lean, and the bridal party drove away, amid a great waving of hands and hullabalu.

And when the last car passed out of sight, Mrs. M'Shane returned home like a goose, waddling slowly, a little overcome by the thought of the happiness that awaited her son. There would be no more lonely evenings in the cabin; Kate would be with him now, and later on there would be some children, and she waddled home thinking of the cradle, and the joy it would be to her to take her grandchildren upon her knee. Passing in at the door, she sat down, so that she might dream over her happiness a little longer. But she had not been sitting long when she had a thought of the work before her the cabin to be cleaned from end to end, the supper to be cooked, and she did not pause in her work till the pig's head was on the table, and the sheeps' tongues also; till the bread was baked and the barrel of porter rolled up in a corner. As she stood with her arms akimbo, expecting the piper every minute, thinking of the great evening it would be, she remembered that her old friend, Annie Connex, had refused to come to Peter's wedding, and that all the village was saying that Kate wouldn't have married Peter if she hadn't been driven to it by the priest and her mother.

'Poor boy!' she thought, 'his heart is so set upon her that he has no ears for any word against her. And aren't people ill-natured to be talking ill of a girl on her wedding-day, and Annie Connex preventing her son from coming to the dance? If she won't come herself, she might let Pat come round for an hour.' And if Annie would do this, all the gossips would have their tongues tied. Anyhow, she might try to persuade her. She locked her door and waddled up the road.

'I came round, Annie, to tell you they're married.'

'Well, come in, Mary,' she said, 'if you have the time.'

'If I have the time,' Mrs. M'Shane repeated to herself as she passed into the comfortable kitchen, with sides of bacon and home-cured hams hanging from the rafters. She had not prospered like Mrs. Connex, and she knew she would never have a beautiful closed range, but an open hearth, till the end of her days. She would never have a nice dresser with a pretty carved top. The dresser in her kitchen was deal, and had no nice shining brass knobs on it. She would never have a parlour, and this parlour had in it a mahogany table and a grandfather's clock that would show you the moon on it just the same as it was in the sky, and there was a glass over the fireplace. And this was Annie Connex's own parlour. The parlour on the other side of the house was even better furnished, for in the summer months Mrs. Connex bedded and boarded her lodgers for one pound or one pound five shillings a week.

'So she was married today, and Father Maguire married her after all. I never thought he would have brought her to it. Well, I'm glad she's married.' It rose to Mary's lips to say, 'You are glad she didn't marry your son,' but she put back the words. 'It comes upon me as a bit of surprise, for sure and all I could never see her settling down in the parish.'

'Them that are the wildest before marriage are often the best after, and I think it will be like that with Kate.'

'I hope so,' said Annie. 'And there is reason why it should be like that. She must have liked Peter better than we thought; you will never get me to believe that it was the priest's will or anybody's will but her own that brought Kate to do what she did.'

'I hope she'll make my boy a good wife.'

'I hope so, too,' said Annie, and the women sat over the fire thinking it out.

Annie Connex held the Kavanagh family in abomination; they

got two shillings a week off the rates, though every Saturday evening they bought a quarter barrel of porter, and Annie Connex could not believe in the future of a country that would tolerate such a thing. If her son had married a Kavanagh her life would have come to an end, and the twenty years she had worked for him would have been wasted years. Alert as a bee she sprang from her chair, for she was thinking of the work that was waiting for her as soon as she could rid herself of that bothering old slut Mary, who'd just as lief sit here all the morning talking of the Kavanaghs.

'You know Julia is doing well with her lacemaking?'

'Selling it, I haven't a doubt, above its market value.'

'She sells it for what she can get. Why shouldn't she?'

'And it looking like as if it was cut out of paper!'

To sell above the market value was abominable in Annie Connex's eyes. Her idea of life was order and administration. And Mary M'Shane seemed to her the very picture of the thriftless, idle village in which they lived.

'We never had anyone like Kate Kavanagh in the village before. I hear she turned round to her sister Julia, who was dressing her, and said, " Now am I to marry him, or shall I go to America?" And she putting on her grey dress at the time.'

'She looked fine in that grey dress; there was lace on the front of it, and there isn't a man in the parish that wouldn't be in Pether's place today if he only dared.'

'I don't catch your meaning, Mary.'

'Well, perhaps I oughtn't to have said it now that she's my own daughter, but I think many would have been a bit afraid of her after what she said to the priest three days ago.'

'She did have her tongue on him. People are telling all ends of stories.'

''Tis said that Father Maguire was up at the Kavanaghs' three days ago, and I heard that she hunted him. She called him a policeman, and a tax collector, and a landlord, and if she said this she said more to a priest than anyone ever said before, for there is plenty in the parish who believe he could turn them into rabbits if he liked, though I don't take it on myself to say if it be truth or lie. But I know for a fact that Patsy Rogan had promised to vote for the Unionist to please his landlord, but the priest had been to see his wife, who was going to be confined, and didn't he tell her that if Patsy voted for the wrong man there would be horns on the new baby, and Mrs. Rogan was so frightened that she wouldn't let her husband go when he came in that night till he had promised to vote as the priest wished.'

'Patsy Rogan is an ignorant man,' said Annie; 'there are many like him even here.'

'Ah, sure there will be always some like him. Don't we like to believe the priest can do all things?'

'Anyhow she's married, and there will be an end to all the work that has been going on.'

'That's true for you, Annie, and that's just what I came to talk to you about. I think now she's married we ought to give her a chance. Every girl ought to get her chance, and the way to put an end to all this talk about her will be for you to come round to the dance tonight.'

'I don't know that I can do that. I am not friends with the Kavanaghs, though I always bid them the time of day when I meet them on the road.'

'If you come in for a few minutes, or if Pat were to come in for a few minutes. If Pether and Pat aren't friends they'll be enemies. 'Maybe they'd be worse enemies if I don't keep Pat out of Kate's way. She's married Pether; but her mind isn't settled yet.'

'Yes, Annie, I've thought of all that; but they'll be meeting on the road, and, if they aren't friends, there will be quarrelling, and some bad deed may be done.'

Annie did not answer, and, thinking to convince her, Mary said:

'You wouldn't like to see a corpse right over your window.'

'It ill becomes you, Mary, to speak of corpses after the blow that Pether gave Pat with his stick at Ned Kavanagh's wedding. And I must stand by my son, and keep him out of the low Irish, and he won't be safe until I get him a good wife.'

'The low Irish! Indeed, it ill becomes you, Annie, to be talking in that way of your neighbours. Is it because none of us have brass knockers on our doors? I have seen this pride growing up in you, Annie Connex, this long while. There isn't one in the village that you've any respect for, except the grocer, that black Protestant, who sits behind his counter and makes money, and knows no enjoyment in life at all.'

'That's your way of looking at it; but it isn't mine. I set my face against my son marrying Kate Kavanagh, and you should have done the same.'

'Something will happen to you for the cruel words you have spoken to me this day.'

'Mary, you came to ask me to your son's wedding, and I had to tell you—'

'Yes, and you've told me that you won't come, and that you hate the Kavanaghs, and you've said all you could against them. I oughtn't to have listened to all you said; if I did, 'tis because we have known each other these twenty years. But don't I remember well the rags you'd on your back when you came to this village? It ill becomes—'

Annie followed her to the gate. The sounds of wheels and hooves were heard; it was the wedding party going by, and on the first car whom should they see but Kate sitting between Pat and Peter.

'Good-bye, Annie, and good luck to you. I see that Pat's coming to our dance after all,' and she could not speak for want of breath when she got to her door.

They were all there, Pat and the piper, and Kate and Peter, and all their friends: but she couldn't speak, and hadn't the strength to find the key, for she could only think of the black look that had come over Annie's face when she saw Pat sitting by Kate on the car, and Mrs M'Shane laughed as she searched for the key, thinking how quickly her punishment had come.

And all the while they were telling her how they had met Pat at Michael Dunne's.

'When he saw us he tried to sneak into the yard; but I went after him. And don't you think I did right?' Kate was heard to say; and as soon as they were inside she said: 'Now I'll get the biggest jug of porter, and Pether shall drink one half and Pat the other.'

Peter was fond of jugs, and there were large and small on the dresser: some white and brown, and some were gilt, with pink flowers.

'Now, Pether, you'll say something nice.'

'I'll say, then,' said Peter, 'this is the happiest day of my life, as it should be, indeed: for haven't I got the girl that I wanted, and hasn't Pat forgiven me for the blow I struck him? For he knows well I wouldn't hurt a hair of his head. Weren't we boys together? But I had a cross drop in me at the time, and that was how it was.'

Catching sight of Kate's black hair and rosy cheeks, which were all the world to him, he stopped speaking and stood looking at her, unheedful of everything; and at that moment he looked so good and foolish that more than one woman thought it would be a weary thing to live with him.

'Now, Pat, you must make a speech, too,' said Kate.

'I haven't any speech in me,' he said. 'I'm glad enough to be sitting here; but I'm sore afraid my mother saw me on the car, and I think I had better be going home and letting you finish this marriage.'

'What's that you're saying?' said Kate. 'You won't go out of this house till you've danced a reel with me, and now sit down at the table next to me; and, Pether, you sit on the other side of him, so that he won't run away to his mother.'

Her eyes were as bright as coals of fire, and she calling to her father, who was at the end of the table, to have another slice of pig's head, and to the piper, who was having his supper in the window, to have a bit more; and then turning to Pat, who said never a word, and laughing at him for having nothing to say.

It was afterwards they remembered that Kate had seemed to put Pat out of her mind suddenly, and had stood talking to her husband, saying he must dance with her, though it was no amusement to a girl to dance opposite Peter. It was afterwards that Mary, Ned's wife, remembered how Kate, though she had danced with Peter in the first reel, had not been able to keep her eyes from the corner where Pat sat sulking, and that, sudden-like, she had grown weary of Peter. Mary remembered, too, she had seen a wild look pass in Kate's eyes, and that she had gone over to Pat and pulled him out for a dance. And why shouldn't she? for it was a pleasure for a girl to dance opposite to Pat, so cleverly did his feet move to the pipes. Everyone was admiring them when Pat cried out:

'I'm going home. I bid you all good-night here; finish this wedding as you like.'

And before anyone could stop him he had run out of the house.

'Pether, go after him,' Kate said; 'bring him back. It would be ill luck on our wedding night for anyone to leave us like that.'

Peter went out of the door, and was away some time; but he came back without Pat.

'The night is that dark, I lost him,' he said.

Then Kate didn't seem to care what she said. Her black hair fell down, and she told Peter he was a fool, and that he should have run faster. And her mother said it was the porter that had been too much for her; but she said it was the priest's blessing, and this frightened everyone. But, after saying all this, she went to her husband, saying that he was very good to her, and she had no fault to find with him. But no sooner were the words out of her mouth than her mind seemed to wander, and everyone had expected her to run out of the house. But she went into the other room instead, and shut the door behind her. Everyone knew then there would be no more dancing that night; the piper packed up his pipes, and the wedding party left Peter by the fire, who seemed to be crying like. And they were all sorry to leave him like this; and, so that he might not remember what had happened, Ned drew a big jug of porter, and put it by him.

He took a sup out of it, but seemed to forget everything, and the jug fell out of his hand.

'Never mind the pieces, Pether,' his mother said. 'You can't put them together; and it would be better for you not to drink any more porther. Go to your bed. There's been too much drinking this night, I'm thinking.'

'Mother, I want to know why she said I didn't run fast enough after Pat. And didn't she know that if I hit Pat so hard it was because there were knobs on his stick; and didn't I pick up his stick by mistake for my own?'

'Sure, Peter, it wasn't your fault; we all know that, and Kate knows it too. Now let there be no more talking or drinking. No, Pether, you've had enough porther for tonight'

He looked round the kitchen, and seeing that Kate was not there, he said:

'She's in the other room, I think; mother, you'll be wantin' to go to your bed.'

And Peter got on his feet and stumbled against the wall, and his mother had to help him towards the door.

'Is it drunk I am, mother? Will you open the door for me?'

But Mrs. M'Shane couldn't open the door, and she said:

'I think she's put a bit of stick in it.'

'A bit of stick in the door? And didn't she say that she didn't want to marry me? Didn't she say something about the priest's blessing?'

And then Peter was sore afraid that he would not get sight of his wife that night, and he said:

'Won't she acquie-esh-sh?'

And Kate said:

'No, I won't.'

And then he said:

'We were married in church today, you acquieshed.'

And she said:

'I'll not open the door to you. You're drunk, Pether, and not fit to enter a decent woman's room.'

'It isn't because I've a drop too much in me that you should have fastened the door on me; it is because you're thinking of the blow I gave Pat. But, Kate, it was because I loved you so much that I struck him. Now will you open the door?'

'No, I'll not open the door tonight,' she said. 'I'm tired and want to go to sleep.'

And when he said he would break open the door, she said:

'You're too drunk, Pether, and sorra bit of good it will do you. I'll be no wife to you tonight, and that's as true as God's in heaven.'

'Pether,' said his mother, 'don't trouble her tonight. There has been too much dancing and drinking.'

'It's a hard thing.... shut out of me wife's room.'

'Pether, don't vex her tonight. Don't hammer her door any more.'

'Didn't she acquie-esh? Mother, you have always been agin me. Didn't she acquie-esh?'

'Oh, Pether, why do you say I'm agin you?'

'Did you hear her say that I was drunk. If you tell me I'm drunk I'll say no more. I'll acquie-esh.'

'Pether, you must go to sleep.'

'Yes, go to sleep.... I want to go to sleep, but she won't open the door.'

'Pether, never mind her.'

'It isn't that I mind; I'm getting sleepy, but what I want to know, mother, before I go to bed, is if I'm drunk. Tell me I'm not drunk on my wedding night, and, though Kate—and I'll acquie-esh in all that may be put upon me.'

He covered his face with his hands and his mother begged him not to cry. He became helpless, she put a blanket under his head and covered him with another blanket, and went up the ladder and lay down in the hay. She asked herself what had she done to deserve this trouble, and cried a great deal. And the poor, hapless old woman was asleep in the morning when Peter stumbled to his feet and found his way into the yard. As soon as he had dipped his head in a pail of water, he remembered the horses were waiting for him in the farm, and walked off to his work, staggering a little. Kate must have been watching for his going, for as soon as he was gone she drew back the bolt of the door and came into the kitchen.

'I'm going, mother,' she called up to the loft.

'Wait a minute, Kate,' said Mrs. M'Shane, and she was halfway down the ladder when Kate said:

'I can't wait, I'm going.' And she walked up the road to her mother's all the chairs were out in the pathway, for the rector was coming down that afternoon, and she wanted to show him how beautifully clean she kept the cabin.

'I've come, mother, to give you this,' and she took the wedding ring off her finger and threw it on the ground. 'I shut the door on him last night, and I'm going to America today. You see how well the marriage that you and the priest made up together has turned out.'

'Going to America,' said Mrs. Kavanagh. 'Now, is Pat going with you? and for pity sake—'

Kate stood looking at the bushes that grew between their cottage and the next one, remembering that elder-flower water is good for the complexion.

'I'm going,' she said suddenly, 'there's nothing more to say. Good-bye.'

And her mother said, 'She's going with Pat Connex.' But Kate had no thought of going to America with him or of seeing him that day. But she met him at the crossroads, out with one of his carts, and she thought he looked a nice boy; but her second thoughts were, 'He's better suited to Ireland.' And on this thought he and the country she had lived in always seemed to escape from her like a dream.

'I'm going to America, Pat.'

'You were married yesterday.'

'Yes, that was the priest's doing and mother's, and I thought they knew best. But I'm thinking one must go one's own way, and there's no judging for oneself here. That's why I'm going. You'll find some other girl, Pat.'

'There's not another girl like you in the village. We're a dead and alive lot. You stood up to the priest.'

'I didn't stand up to him enough. You're waiting for someone. Who are you waiting for?'

'I don't like to tell you, Kate.'

She pressed him to answer her, and he told her he was waiting for the priest. His mother had said he must marry, and the priest was coming to make up a marriage for him.

'Everything's mother's.'

'That's true, Pat, and you'll give a message for me. Tell my mother-in-law that I've gone.'

'She'll be asking me questions, and I'll be sore set for an answer.'

She looked at him steadily, but she left him without speaking, and he stood thinking. He had had good times with her, and all such times were ended for him for ever. He was going to be married and he didn't know to whom.

Suddenly he remembered he had a message to deliver, and went down to the M'Shanes' cabin.

'Ah, Mrs. M'Shane, it was a bad day for me when she married Pether. But this is a worse one, for we've both lost her.'

'My poor boy will feel it sorely.'

And when Peter came in for his dinner his mother said:

'Pether, she's gone, she's gone to America, and you're well rid of her.'

'Don't say that, mother, I am not well rid of her, for there's no other woman in the world for me except her that's gone. Has she gone with Pat Connex?'

'No, he said nothing about that, and it was he who brought the message.'

'I've no one to blame but myself, mother. Wasn't I drunk last night, and how could she be letting a drunken fellow like me into her bed?'

And out he went into the backyard, and didn't his mother hear him crying there till it was time for him to go back to work?

THE WINDOW

AND it was on getting up to go to his work that he caught sight of Biddy M'Hale.

'And for what will she be coming up here at this time in the morning,' he said, 'but to be asking if the news is true?'

'And away he goes past me like a madman,' said Biddy, as she turned into the cabin.

'Ah, well may you ask bad work surely,' said Mrs. M'Shane, 'and you'll be telling the priest the true story as I'm telling it to you that the devil a bit of her would let as much as her husband's foot into her bed last night. You're on your way to him, and it would be ill-befitting the truth should remain unbeknownst to him.'

'If she won't do the duties of a wife towards him, it is a fine penance for her sin that she will be getting when she goes to confession—'

'When she goes to confession! Don't ye know, then, that she took the train this morning for America and flaunted Pat Connex on the road, saying he wasn't a man at all?'

'And you'd be disgracing his reverence's ears with such a story as that! Let Pat tell it to him in his confession.'

'Whether he hears it in the confession or in the daylight, isn't it the same?'

'Now it is I that am sorry to hear you speaking like a Protestant . . . no betther,' she added under her breath as she hurried away.

She would have liked to have heard if Pat had danced with Kate at the wedding, but the priest was expecting her, and she daren't keep him waiting.

'But sorra penny of my money will he be getting all the same to build the walls of his old church. He'll go to America for it and come home and build a new church with a fine spire and a big bell in it, that can be heard for miles and then we'll see what I'll be doing for him!' And on these words her dream began again of the saints and angels she hoped she'd see one day looking down upon her, and the sun setting behind them to the great glory of God, and His Virgin Mother. And so immersed was she in her dream that she did not see the priest watching her all the while, his arms leaning over the paling that divided his strip of garden from the road.

'The stupid old woman!' he was saying to himself. 'The divil a bit of her will understand that the church must come before her window.'

'Sure, your reverence, there's terrible work going on in the village, and I hope I haven't been keeping your reverence waiting, for I had to stop to listen to Mrs. M'Shane, and she telling me that Kate Kavanagh that was, is gone to America after shutting the door on her husband last night because he was drunk.'

'What's this you're telling me, Biddy M'Hale?'

'If your reverence will listen to me—'

'I'm listening to you. Amn't I always listening to you? Go on with your story.'

At last all the facts seemed clear, and he said: 'I made up this marriage so that she mightn't go away with Pat Connex.'

'Well, we've been saved that,' said Biddy.

'Ned Kavanagh's marriage was bad enough, but this is worse. 'Tis no marriage at all.'

'Ah, your reverence, you mustn't be taking it to heart, for if the marriage didn't turn out all right it was the drink.'

'Ah, the drink the drink,' said the priest, and he declared that the brewer and the distiller were the ruin of Ireland.

'That's true for you; at the same time we mustn't forget they have put up many a fine church.'

A cloud came into the priest's face, for his brother was a publican and had promised a large subscription.

'Now, Biddy, what are you going to give me to make the walls safe? I don't want you all to be killed while I am away.'

'There's no fear of that, your reverence; a church never fell down on anyone.'

'Even so, if it falls down when nobody's in it where are the people to hear Mass?'

'Ah, won't they be going down to hear Mass at Father Stafford's?'

'If you don't wish to give anything, say so.'

'Your reverence, ain't I—?'

'We don't want to hear about that window. And Biddy began to fear she would have to give him a few pounds to quiet him. But fortunately Pat Connex came up the road, and, turning from Biddy, the priest said:

'I hear you were dancing with Kate Kavanagh she that went

away to America this morning. Have you heard that?'

'I have, your reverence. She passed me on the road this morning.'

'And you weren't thinking you might stop her?'

'Stop her!' said Pat. 'Mightn't she be asking me to sin with her if I did?'

'And now your mother writes to me, Pat Connex, to ask if I will get Lennon's daughter for you.'

'I see your reverence has private business with Pat Connex. I'll be going,' said Biddy.

'Now, Biddy M'Hale, don't you be going!' But Biddy pretended not to hear him.

'Will I be running after her,' said Pat, 'and bringing her back?'

'No, let her go. If she doesn't want to help to make the walls safe I'm not going to go on my knees to her.... You'll have to walk to Father Stafford's to hear Mass. Have you heard your mother say what she's going to give towards the new church, Pat Connex?'

'I think she said, your reverence, she was going to send you ten pounds.'

'That's very good of her.' And this proof that a public and religious spirit was not yet dead in his parish softened the priest's temper, and, thinking to please him and perhaps escape a scolding, Pat began to calculate how much Biddy had saved.

'She must be worth, I'm thinking, close on one hundred pounds today' As the priest did not answer, he said: 'I wouldn't be surprised if she was worth another fifty!'

'Hardly as much as that,' said the priest.

'Hadn't her aunt the house we're living in before mother came to Kilmore, and it full of lodgers all the summer? It's true her aunt kept her working for nothing, but when she died she left her one hundred pounds, and she's been making money ever since.'

'Her poultry you're thinking of,' said the priest. 'They're the best in the county.' And the thought of Biddy's accident crossed his mind how one day when carrying an exceptionally heavy tray she had slipped on the stairs, and for two years afterwards was on her back, everyone saying she'd never do a hand's-turn, but be looking out of the window ever afterwards. Yet it was while looking out of the window that the thought of poultry had been put into her mind; seeing the fowls pecking in the yard, she had said to herself: 'Now if it be the will of God for me to get about again, I'll see what I can do with chickens, and if I do well with them I'll do something for Him afterwards.' It was herself that had dropped these words to the priest, and he remembered her eyes as she spoke them the pathetic eyes of the hunchback. Hunchback is perhaps too strong a word, but her shoulders were higher than shoulders usually are; she was jerked forward from the waist, and by her side hung the long thin arms of the hunchback. 'It was God's will,' she said, 'that I should mend.... Before my accident there wasn't a girl in the village that could keep ahead of me when we went blackberrying.' A light came into her eyes. 'We used to run all over the hills,' was all she said; but she stood at gaze, lost in remembrances of the country underneath the hills, the plain lost in blue vapour, and on either side the blue sea spitting foam over the rocks of Braehead. 'I was the only one of the girls that could keep up with the boys.'

'But after her accident she was no good for anything except minding fowls.' The priest threw his eye over Pat Connex and wondered if he'd ever be able to make a steady fellow of him now that Kate was out of the country; she was better in America, and by her flight made atonement in a measure for her conduct towards Peter.

'We'll go to Mrs. M'Shane. I shall want to hear her story.'

'Sure, what story can she be telling of me, for didn't I run out of the house away from Kate when I saw what she was thinking of? What more could I do?'

'If Mrs. M'Shane tells the same story as you do, we'll go to your mother's, and afterwards I'll go to see Lennon about his daughter. Why, here is Ned. You've heard the news, Ned, haven't you?'

'Your reverence, I have.'

And all the morning was spent between the priest and Ned Lennon, who was not inclined for the match; but at last he made show of giving in to the priest, after reducing his daughter's dowry to about half.

'Nor would yourself be able to get me to do that much, your reverence, if Kate had remained in the country. But she's gone from us, bad cess to her. But if your reverence is going to America you may be meeting her, and 'tis a fine fistful of money she should be giving. But if you're going at once she won't be.... And God speed your reverence, and bring ye back safe to us with a fine lump of money for building the entire church.'

'I think I shall be able to bring you back the money for the church if that woman—' His sentence did not finish: he was thinking of Biddy. But there were many other things to think of now; further negotiations for Pat's marriage, his packing, the payment of bills and a letter to the bishop, fully occupied the last three weeks.

'I'd like to stop for a minute, Pat,' he said, on his way to the station.

'Well, if you do, your reverence, we shall be missing your train.'

'Then go on with you!' said the priest.

The image of the old woman walking up and down telling her beads, followed by Buff Orpingtons, often rose up in his mind while he was trying to persuade a loafer to give him fifty dollars. 'Now, if Biddy could be dealt with like this man!' If the loafer refused him he said: 'He is another such a one as Biddy.' As the money piled up he said to himself: 'I am bringing Biddy back her window,' and on his way from the station on his return the first person he saw was Biddy telling her beads, followed by her poultry. Much impressed by the coincidence he called to the driver to stop.

'Then how are ye, Biddy M'Hale?' he cried out.

'So you're back again, your reverence, and I hope you've been lucky in America.'

'I've brought some money home, and who knows, Biddy, but one of these days you'll be telling your beads under beautiful panes full of saints and angels?'

'Your reverence is very good to me, and God is very good,' she answered, and stood looking after him, thinking how she had brought him round to her way of thinking. 'And all of them singing,' she said, 'with harps in their hands. And to think that 'tis the birds themselves that will be bringing the window to do honour to God and Kilmore!' She began calling, 'Bea-bea-beaby!' And the Buff Orpingtons and the Plymouth Rocks gathered round her. 'Not a church twenty miles of Kilmore that I haven't been in.... Bea-bea-beaby! And they mustn't be sparing of their reds and yallers; and there must be angels with wings spread out. Bea-bea-beaby!' And when all the food was gone she put aside the basin, and began telling her beads once more.

A few days after she was at the priest's door.

'He has a gentleman with him, Miss M'Hale.'

'Isn't it the architect he has with him? And haven't I need to be seeing him, since it is me that's paying for the saints and angels.'

'To be sure,' the priest called from his parlour. 'Show her in, Margaret.' He drew forth his armchair for Miss M'Hale, and the architect laid his pencil aside and leaned his chin on his hand, so that he might better understand the kind of window she wished to give to her church; and encouraged by his complacency, she rambled on, an unbearable loquacity, all about herself and her neighbours.

'I think I understand,' said the architect, interrupting, 'and we'll do everything to meet your views, Miss M'Hale.'

'Perhaps it is a little premature to discuss the window,' said the priest, 'but you shall choose the subjects you would like to see represented, and as for the colours, the architect and designer will advise you. I am sorry, Biddy, this gentleman sags that the four thousand pounds the Americans were good enough to give me will not do much more than build the walls.'

'They're waiting for me to offer them my money, but I won't say a word,' Biddy said to herself; and she sat fidgeting with her shawl, coughing from time to time, until the priest lost his patience.

'Well, Biddy, we're very busy here, and I'm sure you want to get back to your fowls. When the church is finished we'll see if we want your window.'

The priest had hoped to frighten her, but her faith in her money was abundant; as long as she had her money the priest would come to her for it on one pretext or another, sooner or later; and she was as well pleased that nothing should be settled at present, for she was not quite decided whether she would like to see Christ sitting in judgment, or Christ crowning His Virgin Mother; and during the next six months she pondered on the pictures; the design and the colours grew clearer, and every morning, as soon as she had fed her chickens, she went up to Kilmore to watch the workmen.

She was up there when the first spadeful of earth was thrown up, and as soon as the walls showed above the ground she began to ask the workmen how long it would take them to reach the windows, and if a workman put down his trowel and wandered from his work, she would tell him it was God he was cheating; and later on, when the priest's money began to come to an end and he could not pay the workmen full wages, she told them they were working for God's Own House, and that He would reward them in the next world.

'Hold your tongue,' said a mason. 'If you want the church built why don't you give the priest the money you're saving, and let him pay us?'

'Keep a civil tongue in your head, Pat Murphy. 'Tisn't for myself I am keeping it back, and isn't it all going to be spent?'

The walls were now built, and amid the clatter of the slaters' hammers Biddy began to tell the plasterers of the beautiful pictures that would be seen in her window, gabbling on and mixing up her memories of the different panes she had seen, until at last her chatter grew wearisome, and they threw bits of mortar, laughing at her for a crazy old woman, or the priest would suddenly come upon them and they would scatter in all directions, leaving him with Biddy.

'What were they saying to you, Biddy?'

'They were saying, your reverence, that America is a great place.'

'You spend a great deal of your time here, Biddy, and I suppose you are beginning to see that it takes a long time to build a church. But you're not listening to what I am saying. You are thinking about your window; but as I have often told you, you must have a house before you can have a window.'

'I know that very well, your reverence; but, you see, God has given us the house.'

'God's House consists of something more than walls and a roof.'

'Indeed it does, your reverence; and ain't I saving up all my money for the window?'

'But, my good Biddy, there's hardly any plastering done yet. The laths have come in, and there isn't sufficient to fill that end of the church, and I've no more money.'

'Won't your reverence be getting the rest of the money in America? And ain't I thinking a bazaar would be a good thing? We'd all be making scapulars, and your reverence might get medals that the Pope had blessed.'

Eventually he drove her out of the church with his umbrella. But as his anger cooled he began to think that perhaps Biddy was right a bazaar might be a good thing, and a distribution of medals and scapulars might induce his workmen to do some overtime. He went to Dublin to talk over this matter with some pious Catholics, and an old lady wrote a cheque for fifty pounds, two or three others subscribed smaller sums, and the plasterers were busy all next week. But these subscriptions did not go nearly as far towards completing the work as he had expected. The architect had led him astray, and he looked round the vast barn that he had built, and despaired. It seemed to him it would never be finished in his lifetime. A few weeks after he was speaking to his workmen one Saturday afternoon, telling them how they could obtain a plenary indulgence by subscribing so much towards the building of the church, and by going to Confession and Communion on the first Sunday of the month. If they could not give money they could give their work. 'And he would see that none would be the loser,' he was saying, when Biddy suddenly appeared, and, standing in front of the men, she raised up her hands and said they should not pass by her until they had pledged themselves to come to work on Monday.

'But haven't we got wives and little ones? and we must be thinking of them.'

'Ah, one can live on very little when one is doing the work of

God,' said Biddy.

The men called her a vain old woman, who was starving herself so that she might put up a window, and they pushed her aside and went away, repeating they had their wives and children to feed.

The priest turned upon her angrily and asked her what she meant by interfering between him and his workmen.

'Now, don't be angry with me, your reverence. I will say a prayer, and you will say a word or two in your sermon tomorrow'

And he spoke in his sermon of the disgrace it would be to Kilmore if the church remained unfinished. The news would go over to America, and what priest would be ever able to get money there again to build a church?

'Do you think a priest likes to go about the bar-rooms asking for dollars and half-dollars? And if I have to go to America again, what answer shall I make if they cry after me down the bar: "They don't want churches at Kilmore. If they did your workmen wouldn't have left you?" You'll be disgracing Kilmore for ever if you don't come to work; and if any of you should chance to go to America, let him not say he comes from Kilmore, for he won't be thought much of.'

A murmur went up from the body of the church, the people not liking the threat, and there was great talking that night in Michael Dunne's; and everyone was agreed that it would be a disgrace to Kilmore if the church were not finished, there was no doubt about that; but no one could see that he could work for less wages than he was in the habit of getting, and as the evening wore on the question of indulgences was raised.

'The divil a bit of use going against the priest,' said Ned Kavanagh, 'and the indulgences will do us no harm.'

'The devil a bit, but maybe a great deal of good,' said Peter M'Shane, and an hour later they were staggering down the road swearing they would stand by the priest till death.

But on Monday morning nearly all were in their beds; only half a dozen came to the work, and the priest sent them all away, except one; one plasterer, he thought, could stand on the scaffold.

'If I were to fall I'd go straight to Heaven,' the plasterer said, and he stood so near the edge, and his knees seemed so weak under him, that Biddy thought he was going to fall.

'It would be betther for you to finish what you are doing; the Holy Virgin will be more thankful to you.'

'Aye, maybe she would,' he said, and he continued working on the clustered columns about the window Biddy had chosen for her stained glass, and she never taking her eyes off him. A little before twelve o'clock the priest returned, as the plasterer was going to his dinner, and he asked the plasterer if he were feeling better.

'I'm all right, your reverence, and it won't occur agin.'

'I hope he won't go down to Michael Dunne's during his dinner hour,' the priest said to Biddy. 'If you see any further sign of drink upon him when he comes back you must tell me.'

'He is safe enough, your reverence. Wasn't he telling me while your reverence was having your breakfast that if he fell down he would go straight to Heaven, and opening his shirt and showing me he was wearing the scapular of the Holy Virgin?'

Biddy began to advocate a sale of scapulars.

'A sale of scapulars won't finish my church. You're all a miserly lot here, you want everything done for you.'

'Weren't you telling me, your reverence, that a pious lady in Dublin—?'

'The work is at a standstill. If I were to go to America tomorrow it would be no use unless I could tell them it was progressing.'

'Sure they don't ask any questions in America, they just give their money.'

'If they do, that's more than you're doing at home. Come, Biddy, you've been talking long enough about what you are going to do for this church. Come, now, out with it! How much?'

'Well, now, your reverence, aren't you very hard on me? Haven't I often said I'd begin with a pound? and that much you've had from me, and—'

'You don't seem to understand, Biddy, that you can't put up your window until the plastering is finished.'

'I think I understand that well enough, but the church will be finished.'

'How will it be finished? When will it be finished?'

She didn't answer, and nothing was heard in the still church but her irritating little cough.

'You're very obstinate. Well, tell me where you would like to have your window.'

'It is there I do be kneeling, and I'd like to see the Virgin and St. John with her. And don't you think, your reverence, we might have St. Joseph as well, with Our Lord in the Virgin's arms? And I think, your reverence, I'd like Our Lord coming down to judge us, and Him on His throne on the day of Judgment up at the top of the window.'

'I can see you've been thinking a good deal about this window,' the priest said.

She began again, and the priest heard the names of the different saints she would like to see in stained glass, and he let her prattle on. But his temper boiled up suddenly, and she ran away shrinking like a dog, and the priest walked up and down the unfinished church. 'She tries my temper more than anyone I ever met,' he said to himself. At that moment he heard some loose boards clanking, and, thinking it was the old woman coming back, he looked round, his eyes flaming. It was not Biddy, but a short and square-set man, of the type that one sees in Germany, and he introduced himself as an agent of a firm of stained-glass manufacturers. 'I met an old woman on the road, and she told me that I would find you in the church considering the best place for the window she is going to put up. But she looks very poor.'

'She's not as poor as she looks; she's been saving money all her life for this window; and like people of one idea, she's apt to become a little tiresome.'

'I don't quite understand.'

'Well, this is the way it is,' and seeing the German was interested in the old woman, he began to acquire an interest in her himself an unpremeditated interest; for he had not suspected Biddy's mediae-valism till the German said she reminded him of the quaint sculpture of Nuremburg; and talking of St. Tharagolinda, mediaevalism, and Gothic art, the priest and the agent for the manufacture of stained glass in Munich walked up and down the unfinished church till the return of the plasterer to his lonely labour reminded the German that it would be well to inquire when the church would be finished. The priest hesitated, and at last decided to take the German into his confidence.

'These embarrassments always occur,' said the agent, 'but there is no such thing as an unfinished church in Ireland; if you were to let her put up the window subscriptions would pour in.'

'How is that?'

'A paragraph in the newspaper describing the window the gift of a local saint. I think you told me her name was M'Hale, and that she lives in the village.'

'Yes, you pass her house on the way to the station.'

The German took his leave abruptly, and when he was halfway down the hill he asked some children to direct him.

'Is it Biddy M'Hale, that has all the hins, that you are looking for?'

The German said that that was the woman he was seeking.

'You will see her feeding her chickens over beyant, and you must call to her over the hedge.'

He did as he was bidden.

'Madam.... The priest has sent me to show you some designs for a stained-glass window.'

No one had ever addressed Biddy as Madam before, and, very pleased, she wiped the table clean so that he could spread the designs upon it, and the first he showed her were the four Evangelists, but he said he would like a woman's present to the church to be in a somewhat lighter style, and produced a picture of St. Cecilia. As Biddy seemed doubtful, he suggested a group of figures would look handsomer than a single figure. She was fascinated by what she saw, but unable to put aside the idea of the window that had grown up in her mind, she began her relation.

At the top of the picture, where the window narrowed to a point, Our Lord must sit dressed in white on a throne, placing a golden crown on the head of the Virgin kneeling before Him, and all around the women that had loved Him; and with tears rolling over her eyelids the old woman said she was sorry she was not a nun, but perhaps God in His goodness might not think less of her; it couldn't be helped now; for as far as a mortal sin she could say truly she had never committed one. 'And 'tis only them that do be dying in mortal sin that go into boiling pots.' The cauldrons that Biddy wished to see them in, the agent said, would be difficult to introduce the suffering of the souls could be more artistically indicated by flames.

'I shall have great joy,' she said, 'seeing the blessed women standing about Our Divine Lord, singing hymns in His praise, and the sight of sinners broiling will make me be sorrowful.'

She did not notice that he was turning over his designs and referring to his notebook while she was talking. Suddenly he said:

'Excuse me, but I think we have got the greater part of the window you wish for in stock, and the rest can be easily made up. Now the only question that remains is the question of the colours you care about.'

'I've always thought there's no colour like blue. I'd like the Virgin to wear a blue cloak.'

She did not know why she had chosen that colour, but the agent told her that she was quite right that blue signified chastity; and when the German had gone she sat thinking of the Virgin and her cloak, oblivious of the cackling of the Minorcas, Buff Orpingtons, and Plymouth Rocks waiting to be fed. And while feeding them she sat, her eyes fixed on the beautiful evening sky, wondering if the blue in the picture would be as pale, or if it would be a deeper blue.

She used to wear a blue ribbon when she went blackberrying among the hills; and finding it in an old box, she tied it round her neck; and her mind was lighted up with memories of the saints and the miracles they had performed, and she went to Father Maguire to tell him of the miracle. That the agent should have in stock the very window she had imagined seemed a miracle, and she was encouraged to think some miraculous thing had happened when the priest asked her to tell him exactly what her window was like. She had often told him before, but he had never listened to her. But now he recognized her window as an adaptation of Fra Angelico's picture, and he told her how the saint had wandered from monastery to monastery painting pictures on the walls, and promised to procure a small biography of the saint for her. She received it a few days after, and as she turned over the leaves the children were out in the road coming home from school; and taking it out to them, they read bits of it aloud, for her sight was failing. She frightened them by dropping on her knees and crying out that God had been very good to her. Soon after she took to wandering over the country visiting churches, returning to Kilmore suddenly. She was seen as usual at sunrise and at sunset feeding her poultry, and then she went away again, and the next time she was heard of was in a church near Dublin celebrated for its stained glass. A few days after Ned Kavanagh met her hurrying up the road from the station, and she told him she had just received a letter from the Munich agent saying he had forwarded her window.

It was to arrive tomorrow some time about midday, but Biddy's patience was exhausted long before, and she walked a great part of the way to Dublin, returning with the dray, walking with the draymen till within three miles of Kilmore, when she was so tired that she could walk no longer; they put her on the top of the boxes, and a cheer went up from the villagers when she was lifted down. As soon as she reached the ground she called to the workmen to be careful in unpacking the glass; and when they were putting the window in she went down on her knees and prayed that no accident might happen.

At sunset the church had to be closed, and it was with difficulty she was persuaded to leave it. Next morning at sunrise she was knocking at the door of the woman who was charged with the cleaning of the church, asking for the key; and from that day she was hardly ever out of the church, preventing the charwoman from getting on with her work, saying she would show her things in the window she had not seen before. One day, as the priest and the charwoman were talking, Biddy came in. She seemed a little astray, a little exalted, and Father Maguire watched her as she knelt with uplifted face, telling her beads. He noticed that she held the same bead a long time between her fingers. Minutes passed, but her lips did not move; and her look was so enraptured that he began to wonder if Paradise were being revealed to her.

And while the priest wondered, Biddy listened to music inconceivably tender. She had been awakened from her prayers by the sound of a harp-string touched very gently; the note floated down the aisle, and all the vibrations were not dead when the same note was repeated. Biddy listened, anxious to hear it a third time. Once more she heard it, and the third time she saw the saint's fingers moving over the strings; she played a little tune of six notes. And it was at the end of the second playing of the tune that the priest touched Biddy on the shoulder. She looked up and it was a long while before she saw him, and she was greatly grieved that she had been awakened from her dream. It was the priest that said it was a dream, not she; though he was a priest, she couldn't believe he was right in this, and looking at him, she wondered what would have happened if he had not awakened her.

Next day was Sunday, and she was in the church at sunrise listening for the music. But she heard and saw nothing until the priest had reached the middle of the Mass. The acolyte had rung the bell to prepare the people for the Elevation, and it was then that she heard the faint low sound that the light wire emitted when the saint touched her harp, and she noticed that it was the same saint that had played yesterday, the tall saint with the long fair hair who stood apart from the others, looking more intently at Our Blessed Lord than the others. The saint touched her harp again and the note vibrated for a long while, and when the last vibrations died she touched the string again. The note was sweet and languid and intense, and it pierced to the very core of Biddy. The saint's hand passed over the strings, producing faint exquisite sounds, so faint that Biddy felt no surprise they were not heard by anyone else; it was only by listening intently that she could hear them. Yesterday's little tune appeared again, a little tune of six notes, and it seemed to Biddy even more exquisite than it had seemed when she first heard it. The only difference between today and yesterday was, that today all the saints struck their harps, and after playing for some time the music grew white like snow and remote as star-fire, and yet Biddy heard it more clearly than she had heard anything before, and she saw Our Lord more clearly than she had ever seen anybody else.

She saw Him look up when He had placed the crown on His mother's head; she heard Him sing a few notes, and then the saints began to sing. Biddy was lifted into their heavenly life, and among them she was beautiful and clad in shining garments. She praised God with them, and when the priest raised the host, Biddy saw Our Lord look at her, and His eyes brightened as if with love of her. He seemed to have forgotten the saints that sang His praises so beautifully, and when He bent towards her and she felt His presence about her, she cried out: 'He is coming to take me in His arms!' and fell out of her place, pale as a dead woman. The clerk went to her, but she lay rigid as one who had been dead a long while.

'He is coming to put the gold crown on my head,' she cried, and swooned again.

It was a long time before she seemed conscious of those around her. She was carried to the porch and sprinkled with holy water, and little by little she regained consciousness; she was helped to her feet, and tottered out of the church and followed the road without seeing it or the people whom she met on the road. At last a woman took her by the arm and led her into her cabin and spoke to her. She could not answer at first, but she awoke gradually, and began to remember that she had heard music in the window and that Our Lord had been very good to her. The neighbour left her babbling. She began to feed her chickens, and was glad when she had fed them, for she wanted to think of all the great and wonderful sights she had seen. Her craving for ecstasy grew more intense; and striving to forget her poor cabin, she placed her thought in her window and waited for Sunday to come round again. The priest's mutterings were indifferent to her; tremulous and expectant, she knelt, and the signal was the same as before. The note from the harp-string floated down the aisles, and when it had been repeated three times the saintly fingers moved over the strings, and she heard the beautiful little tune.

Every eye was upon her, and forgetful of the fact that the priest was celebrating Mass, they said, 'Look, she hears the saints singing about her. She sees Christ coming.' The priest heard Biddy cry out 'Christ is coming,' and she fell prone and none dared to raise her up, and she lay there till the Mass was finished. When the priest left the altar she was still lying at length, and the people were about her; and knowing how much she would feel the slightest reproof, he did not say a word that would throw doubt on her statement. He did not like to impugn a popular belief, but he felt himself obliged to exercise clerical control.

'Now, Biddy, I know you to be a pious woman, but I cannot allow you to interrupt the Mass.'

'If the Lord comes to me ain't I to receive Him, your reverence?'

'In the first place I object to your dress; you are not properly dressed.'

She wore a bright blue cloak she seemed to wear hardly anything else, and tresses of dirty hair hung over her shoulders.

'The Lord has not said anything to me about my dress, your reverence, and He put His gold crown on my head today'

'Biddy, is all this true?'

'As true as you're standing there.'

'I'm not asking if your visions are true: I have my opinion about that. I'm asking if they are true to you.'

'True to me, your reverence? I don't rightly understand.'

'I want to know if you think Our Lord put a gold crown on your head today'

'To be sure He did, your reverence.'

'If He did, where is it?'

'Where is it, your reverence? It is with Him, to be sure. He wouldn't be leaving it on my head and me walking about the parish that wouldn't be reasonable at all, I'm thinking. He doesn't want me to be robbed.'

'There is no one in the parish who'd rob you.'

'Maybe someone would come out of another parish, if I had a gold crown on my head. And such a crown as He put upon it! I'm sorry you didn't see it, but your reverence was saying the holy Mass at the time.'

And she fell on her knees and clung to his cassock.

'And you saw the crown, Biddy?'

'I had it on my head, your reverence.'

'And you heard the saints singing?'

'Yes, and I'll tell you what they were singing,' and she began crooning. 'Something like that, your reverence. You don't believe me, but we have only our ears and our eyes to guide us.'

'I don't say I don't believe you, Biddy, but you may be deceived.'

'Sorra deceiving, your reverence, or I've been deceived all my life. And now, your reverence, if you've no more business with me I will go, for they do be waiting in the chapel yard to hear me tell them about the crown that was put upon my head.'

'Well, Biddy, I want you to understand that I cannot have you interrupting the Mass. I cannot permit it. The visions may be true, or not true, but you must not interrupt the Mass.'

The acolyte opened the door of the sacristy, Biddy slipped through, and the priest took off his cassock. As he did so, he noticed that the acolyte's eyes were at the window watching, and when the priest looked he saw the people gathering about Biddy, and when he came out of the sacristy no one noticed him; everyone was listening to Biddy.

'She's out of her mind,' he said. 'She's as good as mad. What did she tell me that Our Lord put a crown on her head?'

One parishioner withdrew without answering. Another went away saying, 'Well, I suppose your reverence knows best.' He heard another say, 'Well, after all, doesn't she hear the saints singing?'

And next day there were people from Dublin asking after Biddy, and Father Maguire had to send for her, though he feared all the honour that was being shown to her would turn her head and lead her into further extravagances. On the other hand, subscriptions were coming in and he could not close his mind to the fact that it was Biddy who enabled him to furnish his church with varnished pews and holy pictures. He received two fine statues of Our Lady and St. Joseph in different coloured cloaks St. Joseph in a purple, Our Lady in a blue, and there were gold stars on it. He placed these two statues on the two side altars, and fell to thinking of the many things he wanted and that he could get through Biddy. For the sake of these things he must let her remain in Kilmore; but she could not be allowed to interrupt the Mass, and he must be allowed to pass in and out of his church without extravagant salutation.

Now he was going home to his breakfast, and a young man extremely interested in ecclesiastical art was coming to breakfast with him; and as soon as they entered the church they would be accosted by this old woman, who would follow them about asking them to look at her window, telling them her visions, which might or might not be true. She had a knack of hiding herself he often came upon her suddenly behind the pillars, and sometimes he found her in the confessional. 'Now, shall I tell him about Biddy or shall I take my chance that she may not be in the church this morning?' He remembered that the young man was very learned in Walter Pater and Chartres Cathedral, and Father Maguire feared he would cut a poor figure in the discussion, for he could not fix his attention; he could think only of Biddy, and when he and his visitor walked down to the new church he thought he had done well to keep his own counsel. He could not see the old woman anywhere; his fears subsided, and he called the young man's attention to the altar that had been specially designed for his church. The young man was interested in it, and had begun to tell the priest of the altars he had seen in Italy, when a hand was laid upon his shoulder suddenly.

'Your honour will be well rewarded if you'll come to my window. Now why should I be telling him a lie, your reverence?'

She threw herself at the priest's feet and besought him to believe that the saints had been with her, and that every word she was speaking was the truth.

'Biddy, if you don't go away at once, I'll not allow you inside the church tomorrow'

The young man looked at the priest, surprised at his sternness, and the priest said:

'She has become a great trial to us at Kilmore. Come aside and I'll tell you about her.'

And when the priest had told the young man about the window the young man asked if Biddy would have to be sent away.

'I hope not, for if she were separated from her window she would certainly die. It came out of her savings, out of the money she made out of chickens.'

'And what has become of the chickens?'

'She has forgotten all about them, and they've wandered away or died. She has been evicted, and lives now in an outdoes on the bits of bread and the potatoes the neighbours give her. The things of this world are no longer realities to her. Her realities are what she sees and hears in that window. Last night she told me a saint knocked at her door. I don't like to encourage her to talk, but if you would like to hear her Biddy, come here!'

The old woman came back as a dog comes to its master, joyful, and with brightening eyes.

'Tell us what you saw last night.'

'Well, your reverence, I was asleep, and there suddenly came a knocking at the door, and I got up, and then I heard a voice saying, "Open the door." A beautiful young man was outside, his hair was yellow and curly, and he was dressed in white. He came into the room first, and he was followed by other saints, and they all had harps in their hands, and they sang for a long while. Come to the window, and you will hear it for yourselves. Someone is always singing it in the window, but not always as clearly as they did last night.'

'We'll go to see your window presently.'

The old woman crept back to her place, and the priest and the young man began to talk about the possibilities of miracles in modern times; and they talked on, until the sudden sight of Biddy gave them pause.

'Look at her,' said the young man. 'Can you doubt that she sees heaven quite plainly, and that the saints visited her just as she told us?'

'No doubt, no doubt. But she's a great trial to us at Mass.... The Mass mustn't be interrupted.'

'I suppose even miracles are inconvenient at times, Father Maguire. Be patient with her: let her enjoy her happiness.'

And the two men stood looking at her, trying vainly to imagine what her happiness might be.

A LETTER TO ROME

ONE morning the priest's housekeeper mentioned, as she gathered up the breakfast things, that Mike Mulhare had refused to let his daughter Catherine marry James Murdoch until he had earned the price of a pig.

'This is bad news,' said the priest, and he laid down the newspaper.

'And he waiting for her all the summer! Wasn't it in February last that he came out of the poorhouse? And the fine cabin he has built for her! He'll be so lonesome in it that he'll be going—'

'To America!' said the priest.

'Maybe it will be going back to the poorhouse he'll be, for he'll never earn the price of his passage at the relief works.'

The priest looked at her for a moment as if he did not catch her meaning. A knock came at the door, and he said:

'The inspector is here, and there are people waiting for me.' And while he was distributing the clothes he had received from Manchester, he argued with the inspector as to the direction the new road should take; and when he came back from the relief works, his dinner was waiting. He was busy writing letters all the afternoon; and it was not until he had handed them to the postmistress that he was free to go to poor James Murdoch, who had built a cabin at the end of one of the famine roads in a hollow out of the way of the wind.

From a long way off the priest could see him digging his patch of bog.

And when he caught sight of the priest he stuck his spade in the ground and came to meet him, almost as naked as an animal, bare feet protruding from ragged trousers; there was a shirt, but it was buttonless, and the breast-hair trembled in the wind a likely creature to come out of the hovel behind him.

'It has been dry enough,' he said, 'all the summer; and I had a thought to make a drain. But 'tis hard luck, your reverence, and after building this house for her. There's a bit of smoke in the house now, but if I got Catherine I wouldn't be long making a chimney. I

85

told Mike he should give Catherine a pig for her fortune, but he said he would give her a calf when I bought the pig, and I said, "Haven't I built a fine house, and wouldn't it be a fine one to rear him in?"'

And together they walked through the bog, James talking to the priest all the way, for it was seldom he had anyone to talk to.

'Now I mustn't take you any further from your digging.'

'Sure there's time enough,' said James. 'Amn't I there all day?'

'I'll go and see Mike Mulhare myself,' said the priest.

'Long life to your reverence.'

'And I will try to get you the price of the pig.'

'Ah, 'tis your reverence that's good to us.'

The priest stood looking after him, wondering if he would give up life as a bad job and go back to the poorhouse; and while thinking of James Murdoch he became conscious that the time was coming for the priests to save Ireland. Catholic Ireland was passing away; in five-and-twenty years Ireland would be a Protestant country if—(he hardly dared to formulate the thought)—if the priests did not marry. The Greek priests had been allowed to retain their wives in order to avert a schism. Rome had always known how to adapt herself to circumstances; there was no doubt that if Rome knew Ireland's need of children she would consider the revocation of the decree of celibacy, and he returned home remembering that celibacy had only been made obligatory in Ireland in the twelfth century.

Ireland was becoming a Protestant country! He drank his tea mechanically, and it was a long time before he took up his knitting. But he could not knit, and laid the stocking aside. Of what good would his letter be? A letter from a poor parish priest asking that one of the most ancient decrees should be revoked! It would be thrown into the wastepaper basket. The cardinals are men whose thoughts move up and down certain narrow ways, clever men no doubt, but clever men are often the dupes of conventions. All men who live in the world accept the conventions as truths. It is only in the wilderness that the truth is revealed to man. 'I must write the letter! Instinct,' he said, 'is a surer guide than logic, and my letter to Rome was a sudden revelation.'

As he sat knitting by his own fireside his idea seemed to come out of the corners of the room. 'When you were at Rathowen,' his idea said, 'you heard the clergy lament that the people were leaving the country. You heard the bishop and many eloquent men speak on the subject. Words, words, but on the bog road the remedy was revealed to you.

'That if each priest were to take a wife about four thousand children would be born within the year, forty thousand children would be added to the birthrate in ten years. Ireland can be saved by her priesthood!'

The truth of this estimate seemed beyond question, and yet,

Father MacTurnan found it difficult to reconcile himself to the idea of a married clergy. 'One is always the dupe of prejudice,' he said to himself and went on thinking. 'The priests live in the best houses, eat the best food, wear the best clothes; they are indeed the flower of the nation, and would produce magnificent sons and daughters. And who could bring up their children according to the teaching of our holy church as well as priests?'

So did his idea unfold itself, and very soon he realized that other advantages would accrue, beyond the addition of forty thousand children to the birthrate, and one advantage that seemed to him to exceed the original advantage would be the nationalization of religion, the formation of an Irish Catholicism suited to the ideas and needs of the Irish people.

In the beginning of the century the Irish lost their language, in the middle of the century the characteristic aspects of their religion. It was Cardinal Cullen who had denationalized religion in Ireland. But everyone recognized his mistake. How could a church be nationalized better than by the rescission of the decree of celibacy ? The begetting of children would attach the priests to the soil of Ireland; and it could not be said that anyone loved his country who did not contribute to its maintenance. The priests leave Ireland on foreign missions, and every Catholic who leaves Ireland, he said, helps to bring about the very thing that Ireland has been struggling against for centuries—Protestantism.

His idea talked to him every evening, and, one evening, it said, 'Religion, like everything else, must be national,' and it led him to contrast cosmopolitanism with parochialism. 'Religion, like art, came out of parishes,' he said. He felt a great force to be behind him. He must write! He must write....

He dropped the ink over the table and over the paper, he jotted down his ideas in the first words that came to him until midnight; and when he slept his letter floated through his sleep.

'I must have a clear copy of it before I begin the Latin translation.'

He had written the English text thinking of the Latin that would come after, very conscious of the fact that he had written no Latin since he had left Maynooth, and that a bad translation would discredit his ideas in the eyes of the Pope's secretary, who was doubtless a great Latin scholar.

'The Irish priests have always been good Latinists,' he murmured, as he hunted through the dictionary.

The table was littered with books, for he had found it necessary to create a Latin atmosphere, and one morning he finished his translation and walked to the whitening window to rest his eyes before reading it over. But he was too tired to do any more, and he laid his manuscript on the table by his bedside.

'This is very poor Latin,' he said to himself some hours later, and the manuscript lay on the floor while he dressed. It was his servant who brought it to him when he had finished his breakfast, and, taking it from her, he looked at it again.

'It is as tasteless,' he said, 'as the gruel that poor James Murdoch is eating.' He picked up St. Augustine's Confessions. 'Here is idiom,' he muttered, and he continued reading till he was interrupted by the wheels of a car stopping at his door. It was Meehan! None had written such good Latin at Maynooth as Meehan.

'My dear Meehan, this is indeed a pleasant surprise.'

'I thought I'd like to see you. I drove over. But—I am not disturbing you.... You've taken to reading again. St. Augustine! And you're writing in Latin!'

Father James's face grew red, and he took the manuscript out of his friend's hand.

'No, you mustn't look at that.'

And then the temptation to ask him to overlook certain passages made him change his mind.

'I was never much of a Latin scholar.'

'And you want me to overlook your Latin for you. But why are you writing Latin?'

'Because I am writing to the Pope. I was at first a little doubtful, but the more I thought of this letter the more necessary it seemed to me.'

'And what are you writing to the Pope about?'

'You see Ireland is going to become a Protestant country.'

'Is it?' said Father Meehan, and he listened a little while. Then, interrupting his friend, he said:

'I've heard enough. Now, I strongly advise you not to send this letter. We have known each other all our lives. Now, my dear MacTurnan—'

Father Michael talked eagerly, and Father MacTurnan sat listening. At last Father Meehan saw that his arguments were producing no effect, and he said: 'You don't agree with me.'

'It isn't that I don't agree with you. You have spoken admirably from your point of view, but our points of view are different.'

'Take your papers away, burn them!'

Then, thinking his words were harsh, he laid his hand on his friend's shoulder and said:

'My dear MacTurnan, I beg of you not to send this letter.'

Father James did not answer; the silence grew painful, and Father Michael asked Father James to show him the relief works that the Government had ordered.

But important as these works were, the letter to Rome seemed more important to Father Michael, and he said:

'My good friend, there isn't a girl that would marry us; now is there? There isn't a girl in Ireland who would touch us with a forty-foot pole. Would you have the Pope release the nuns from their vows?'

'I think exceptions should be made in favour of those in

Orders. But I think it would be for the good of Ireland if the secular clergy were married.'

'That's not my point. My point is that even if the decree were rescinded we shouldn't be able to get wives. You've been living too long in the waste, my dear friend. You've lost yourself in dreams. We shouldn't get a penny. "Why should we support that fellow and his family?" is what they'd be saying.'

'We should be poor, no doubt,' said Father James, 'But not so poor as our parishioners. My parishioners eat yellow meal, and I eat eggs and live in a good house.'

'We are educated men, and should live in better houses than our parishioners.'

'The greatest saints lived in deserts.'

And so the argument went on until the time came to say good-bye, and then Father James said:

'I shall be glad if you will give me a lift on your car. I want to go to the post-office.'

'To post your letter?'

'The idea came to me—it came swiftly like a lightning-flash, and I can't believe that it was an accident. If it had fallen into your mind with the suddenness that it fell into mine, you would believe that it was an inspiration.'

'It would take a good deal to make me believe I was inspired,' said Father Michael, and he watched Father James go into the post-office to register his letter.

At that hour a long string of peasants returning from their work went by. The last was Norah Flynn, and the priest blushed deeply for it was the first time he had looked on one of his parishioners in the light of a possible spouse; and he entered his house frightened; and when he looked round his parlour he asked himself if the day would come when he should see Norah Flynn sitting opposite to him in his armchair. His face flushed deeper when he looked towards the bedroom door, and he fell on his knees and prayed that God's will might be made known to him.

During the night he awoke many times, and the dream that had awakened him continued when he had left his bed, and he wandered round and round the room in the darkness, seeking a way. At last he reached the window and drew the curtain, and saw the dim dawn opening out over the bog.

'Thank God,' he said, 'it was only a dream—only a dream.'

And lying down he fell asleep, but immediately another dream as horrible as the first appeared, and his housekeeper heard him beating on the walls.

'Only a dream, only a dream,' he said.

He lay awake, not daring to sleep lest he might dream. And it was about seven o'clock when he heard his housekeeper telling him that the inspector had come to tell him they must decide what direction the new road should take. In the inspector's opinion it should run parallel with the old road. To continue the old road two miles further would involve extra labour; the people would have to go further to their work, and the stones would have to be drawn further. The priest held that the extra labour was of secondary importance. He said that to make two roads running parallel with each other would be a wanton humiliation to the people.

But the inspector could not appreciate the priest's arguments. He held that the people were thinking only how they might earn enough money to fill their bellies.

'I don't agree with you, I don't agree with you,' said the priest.

'Better go in the opposite direction and make a road to the sea.'

'You see, your reverence, the Government don't wish to engage upon any work that will benefit any special class. These are my instructions.'

'A road to the sea will benefit no one.... I see you are thinking of the landlord. But there isn't a harbour; no boat ever comes into that flat, waste sea.'

'Well, your reverence, one of these days a harbour may be made. An arch would look well in the middle of the bog, and the people wouldn't have to go far to their work.'

'No, no. A road to the sea will be quite useless; but its futility will not be apparent—at least, not so apparent—and the people's hearts won't be broken.'

The inspector seemed a little doubtful, but the priest assured him that the futility of the road would satisfy English ministers.

'And yet these English ministers,' the priest reflected, 'are not stupid men; they're merely men blinded by theory and prejudice, as all men are who live in the world. Their folly will be apparent to the next generation, and so on and so on for ever and ever, world without end.'

'And the worst of it is,' the priest said, 'while the people are earning their living on these roads, their fields will be lying idle, and there will be no crops next year.'

'We can't help that,' the inspector answered, and Father MacTurnan began to think of the cardinals and the transaction of business in the Vatican; cardinals and ministers alike are the dupes of convention. Only those who are estranged from habits and customs can think straightforwardly.

'If, instead of insisting on these absurd roads, the Government would give me the money, I'd be able to feed the people at a cost of about a penny a day, and they'd be able to sow their potatoes. And if only the cardinals would consider the rescission of the decree on its merits, Ireland would be saved from Protestantism.'

Some cardinal was preparing an answer—an answer might be even in the post. Rome might not think his letter worthy of an answer.

A few days afterwards the inspector called to show him a letter he had just received from the Board of Works. Father James had to go to Dublin, and in the excitement of these philanthropic activities the emigration question was forgotten. Six weeks must have gone by when the postman handed him a letter. 'This is a letter from Father Moran,' he said to the inspector who was with him at the time. 'The Bishop wishes to see me. We will continue the conversation tomorrow. It is eight miles to Rathowen, and how much further is the Palace?'

'A good seven,' said the inspector. 'You're not going to walk it, your reverence?'

'Why not? In four hours I shall be there.' He looked at his boots first, and hoped they would hold together; and then he looked at the sky, and hoped it would not rain.

There was no likelihood of rain; no rain would fall today out of that soft dove-coloured sky full of sun; ravishing little breezes lifted the long heather, the rose-coloured hair of the knolls, and over the cutaway bog wild white cotton was blowing. Now and then a yellow-hammer rose out of the coarse grass and flew in front of the priest, and once a pair of grouse left the sunny hillside where they were nesting with a great whirr; they did not go far, but alighted in a hollow, and the priest could see their heads above the heather watching him.

'The moment I'm gone they'll return to their nest.'

He walked on, and when he had walked six miles he sat down and took a piece of bread out of his pocket. As he ate it his eyes wandered over the undulating bog, brown and rose, marked here and there by a black streak where the peasants had been cutting turf. The sky changed very little; it was still a pale, dove colour; now and then a little blue showed through the grey, and sometimes the light lessened; but a few minutes after the sunlight fluttered out of the sky again and dozed among the heather.

'I must be getting on,' he said, and he looked into the brown water, fearing he would find none other to slake his thirst. But just as he stooped he caught sight of a woman driving an ass who had come to the bog for turf, and she told him where he would find a spring, and he thought he had never drunk anything so sweet as this water.

'I've got a good long way to go yet,' he said, and he walked studying the lines of the mountains, thinking he could distinguish one hill from the other; and that in another mile or two he would be out of the bog. The road ascended, and on the other side there were a few pines. Some hundred yards further on there was a green sod. But the heather appeared again, and he had walked ten miles before he was clear of whins and heather.

As he walked he thought of his interview with the Bishop, and was nearly at the end of his journey when he stopped at a cabin to mend his shoe. And while the woman was looking for a needle and thread, he mopped his face with a great red handkerchief that he kept in the pocket of his threadbare coat—a coat that had once been black, but had grown green with age and weather. He had outwalked himself, and would not be able to answer the points that the Bishop would raise. The woman found him a scrap of leather, and it took him an hour to patch his shoe under the hawthorn tree.

He was still two miles from the Palace, and arrived footsore, covered with dust, and so tired that he could hardly rise from the chair to receive Father Moran when he came into the parlour.

'You seem to have walked a long way, Father MacTurnan.'

'I shall be all right presently. I suppose his Grace doesn't want to see me at once.'

'Well, that's just it. His Grace sent me to say he would see you at once. He expected you earlier.'

'I started the moment I received his Grace's letter. I suppose his Grace wishes to see me regarding my letter to Rome.'

The secretary hesitated, coughed, and went out, and Father MacTurnan wondered why Father Moran looked at him so intently. He returned in a few minutes, saying his Grace was sorry that Father MacTurnan had had so long a walk, and he hoped he would rest awhile and partake of some refreshment... The servant brought in some wine and sandwiches, and the secretary returned in half an hour. His Grace was now ready to receive him....

Father Moran opened the library door, and Father MacTurnan saw the Bishop—a short, alert man, about fifty-five, with a sharp nose and grey eyes and bushy eyebrows. He popped about the room giving his secretary many orders, and Father MacTurnan wondered if the Bishop would ever finish talking to his secretary. He seemed to have finished, but a thought suddenly struck him, and he followed his secretary to the door, and Father MacTurnan began to fear that the Pope had not decided to place the Irish clergy on the same footing as the Greek. If he had, the Bishop's interest in these many various matters would have subsided: his mind would be engrossed by the larger issue.

As he returned from the door his Grace passed Father MacTurnan without speaking to him, and going to his writing-table he began to search amid his papers. At last Father MacTurnan said:

'Maybe your Grace is looking for my letter to Rome?'

'Yes,' said his Grace, 'do you see it?'

'It's under your Grace's hand, those blue papers.'

'Ah, yes,' and his Grace leaned back in his armchair, leaving Father MacTurnan standing.

'Won't you sit down, Father MacTurnan?' he said casually. 'You've been writing to Rome, I see, advocating the revocation of the decree of celibacy. There's no doubt the emigration of Catholics is a very serious question. So far you have got the sympathy of Rome, and I may say of myself; but am I to understand that it was your fear for the religious safety of Ireland that prompted you to write this letter?'

'What other reason could there be?'

Nothing was said for a long while, and then the Bishop's meaning began to break in on his mind; his face flushed, and he grew confused.

'I hope your Grace doesn't think for a moment that—'

'I only want to know if there is anyone—if your eyes ever went in a certain direction, if your thoughts ever said, "Well, if the decree were revoked—"'

'No, your Grace, no. Celibacy has been no burden for me—far from it. Sometimes I feared that it was celibacy that attracted me to the priesthood. Celibacy was a gratification rather that a sacrifice.'

'I am glad,' said the Bishop, and he spoke slowly and emphatically, 'that this letter was prompted by such impersonal motives.'

'Surely, your Grace, His Holiness didn't suspect—'

The Bishop murmured an euphonious Italian name, and Father MacTurnan understood that he was speaking of one of the Pope's secretaries.

'More than once,' said Father MacTurnan, 'I feared if the decree were revoked, I shouldn't have had sufficient courage to comply with it.'

And then he told the Bishop how he had met Norah Flynn on the road. An amused expression stole into the Bishop's face, and his voice changed.

'I presume you do not contemplate making marriage obligatory; you do not contemplate the suspension of the faculties of those who do not take wives?'

'It seems to me that exception should be made in favour of those in Orders, and of course in favour of those who have reached a certain age like your Grace.'

The Bishop coughed, and pretended to look for some paper which he had mislaid.

'This was one of the many points that I discussed with Father Michael Meehan.'

'Oh, so you consulted Father Meehan,' the Bishop said, looking up.

'He came in the day I was reading over my Latin translation before posting it. I'm afraid the ideas that I submitted to the consideration of His Holiness have been degraded by my very poor Latin. I should have wished Father Meehan to overlook my Latin, but he refused. He begged of me not to send the letter.'

'Father Meehan,' said his Grace, 'is a great friend of yours. Yet nothing he could say could shake your resolution to write to Rome?'

'Nothing,' said Father MacTurnan. 'The call I received was too distinct and too clear for me to hesitate.'

'Tell me about this call.'

Father MacTurnan told the Bishop that the poor man had come out of the workhouse because he wanted to be married, and that Mike Mulhare would not give him his daughter until he had earned the price of a pig. 'And as I was talking to him I heard my conscience say, "No one can afford to marry in Ireland but the clergy." We all live better than our parishioners.'

And then, forgetting the Bishop, and talking as if he were alone with his God, he described how the conviction had taken possession of him that Ireland would become a Protestant country if the Catholic emigration did not cease. And he told how this conviction had left him little peace until he had written his letter.

The priest talked on until he was interrupted by Father Moran.

'I have some business to transact with Father Moran now,' the Bishop said, 'but you must stay to dinner. You've walked a long way, and you are tired and hungry.'

'But, your Grace, if I don't start now, I shan't get home until nightfall.'

'A car will take you back, Father MacTurnan. I will see to that. I must have some exact information about your poor people. We must do something for them.'

Father MacTurnan and the Bishop were talking together when the car came to take Father MacTurnan home, and the Bishop said:

'Father MacTurnan, you have borne the loneliness of your parish a long while.'

'Loneliness is only a matter of habit. I think, your Grace, I'm better suited to the place than I am for any other. I don't wish any change, if your Grace is satisfied with me.'

'No one will look after the poor people better than yourself, Father MacTurnan. But,' he said, 'it seems to me there is one thing we have forgotten. You haven't told me if you have succeeded in getting the money to buy the pig.'

Father MacTurnan grew very red.... 'I had forgotten it. The relief works—'

'It's not too late. Here's five pounds, and this will buy him a pig.'

'It will indeed,' said the priest, 'it will buy him two!'

He had left the Palace without having asked the Bishop how his letter had been received at Rome, and he stopped the car, and was about to tell the driver to go back. But no matter, he would hear about his letter some other time. He was bringing happiness to two poor people, and he could not persuade himself to delay their happiness by one minute. He was not bringing one pig, but two pigs, and now Mike Mulhare would have to give him Norah and a calf; and the priest remembered that James Murdoch had said— 'What a fine house this will be to rear them in.' There were many who thought that human beings and animals should not live together; but after all, what did it matter if they were happy ? And the priest forgot his letter to Rome in the thought of the happiness he was bringing to two poor people. He could not see Norah Mulhare that night; but he drove down to the famine road, and he and the driver called till they awoke James Murdoch. The poor man came stumbling across the bog, and the priest told him the news.

A PLAY-HOUSE IN
THE WASTE

'IT'S a closed mouth that can hold a good story,' as the saying goes, and very soon it got about that Father MacTurnan had written to Rome saying he was willing to take a wife to his bosom for patriotic reasons, if the Pope would relieve him of his vow of celibacy. And many phrases and words from his letter (translated by whom by the Bishop or Father Meehan? Nobody ever knew) were related over the Dublin firesides, till at last out of the talk a tall gaunt man emerged, in an old overcoat green from weather and wear, the tails of it flapping as he rode his bicycle through the great waste bog that lies between Belmullet and Crossmolina. His name! We liked it. It appealed to our imagination. MacTurnan! It conveyed something from afar like Hamlet or Don Quixote. He seemed as near and as far from us as they, till Pat Comer, one of the organizers of the I.A.O.S., came in and said, after listening to the talk that was going round:

'Is it of the priest that rides in the great Mayo bog you are speaking? If it is, you haven't got the story rightly.' As he told us the story, so it is printed in this book. And we sat wondering greatly, for we seemed to see a soul on its way to heaven. But round a fire there is always one who cannot get off the subject of women and blasphemy a papist generally he is; and it was Quinn that evening who kept plaguing us with jokes, whether it would be a fat girl or a thin that the priest would choose if the Pope gave him leave to marry, until at last, losing all patience with him, I bade him be silent, and asked Pat Comer to tell us if the priest was meditating a new plan for Ireland's salvation.

'For a mind like his,' I said, 'would not stand still and problems such as ours waiting to be solved.'

'You're wrong there! He thinks no more of Ireland, and neither reads nor plans, but knits stockings ever since the wind took his play-house away.'

'Took his play-house away!' said several.

97

'And why would he be building a play-house,' somebody asked, 'and he living in a waste?'

'A queer idea surely!' said another. 'A play-house in the waste!'

'Yes, a queer idea,' said Pat, 'but a true one all the same, for I have seen it with my own eyes or the ruins of it, and not later back than three weeks ago, when I was staying with the priest himself. You know the road, all of you how it straggles from Foxford through the bog alongside of bogholes deep enough to drown one, and into which the jarvey and myself seemed in great likelihood of pitching, for the car went down into great ruts, and the horse was shying from one side of the road to the other, and at nothing so far as we could see.'

'There's nothing to be afeared of, yer honour; only once was he near leaving the road, the day before Christmas, and I driving the doctor. It was here he saw it a white thing gliding, and the wheel of the car must have gone within an inch of the boghole.'

'And the doctor. Did he see it?' I said.

'He saw it too, and so scared was he that the hair rose up and went through his cap.'

'Did the jarvey laugh when he said that?' we asked Pat Comer; and Pat answered: 'Not he! Them fellows just speak as the words come to them without thinking. Let me get on with my story. We drove on for about a mile, and it was to stop him from clicking his tongue at the horse that I asked him if the bog was Father MacTurnan's parish.'

'Every mile of it, sir,' he said, 'every mile of it, and we do be seeing him buttoned up in his old coat riding along the roads on his bicycle going to sick calls.'

'Do you often be coming this road?' says I.

'Not very often, sir. No one lives here except the poor people, and the priest and the doctor. Faith! there isn't a poorer parish in Ireland, and every one of them would have been dead long ago if it had not been for Father James.'

'And how does he help them?'

'Isn't he always writing letters to the Government asking for relief works? Do you see those bits of roads?'

'Where do those roads lead to?'

'Nowhere. Them roads stops in the middle of the bog when the money is out.'

'But,' I said, 'surely it would be better if the money were spent upon permanent improvements on drainage, for instance.'

The jarvey didn't answer; he called to his horse, and not being able to stand the clicking of his tongue, I kept on about the drainage.

'There's no fall, sir.'

'And the bog is too big,' I added, in hope of encouraging conversation.

'Faith it is, sir.'

'But we aren't very far from the sea, are we?'

'About a couple of miles.'

'Well then,' I said, 'couldn't a harbour be made?'

'They were thinking about that, but there's no depth of water, and everyone's against emigration now.'

'Ah! the harbour would encourage emigration.'

'So it would, your honour.'

'But is there no talk about home industries, weaving, lace-making?'

'I won't say that.'

'But has it been tried?'

'The candle do be burning in the priest's window till one in the morning, and he sitting up thinking of plans to keep the people at home. Now, do ye see that house, sir, fornint my whip at the top of the hill? Well, that's the play-house he built.'

'A play-house?'

'Yes, yer honour. Father James hoped the people might come from Dublin to see it, for no play like it had ever been acted in Ireland before, sir!'

'And was the play performed?'

'No, yer honour. The priest had been learning them all the summer, but the autumn was on them before they had got it by rote, and a wind came and blew down one of the walls.'

'And couldn't Father MacTurnan get the money to build it up?'

'Sure, he might have got the money, but where'd be the use when there was no luck in it?'

'And who were to act the play?'

'The girls and the boys in the parish, and the prettiest girl in all the parish was to play Good Deeds.'

'So it was a miracle play,' I said.

'Do you see that man? It's the priest coming out of Tom Burke's cabin, and I warrant he do be bringing him the Sacrament, and he having the holy oils with him, for Tom won't pass the day; we had the worst news of him last night.'

'And I can tell you,' said Pat Comer, dropping his story for a moment and looking round the circle, 'it was a sad story the jarvey told me. He told it well, for I can see the one-roomed hovel full of

peat smoke, the black iron pot with traces of the yellow stirabout in
it on the hearth, and the sick man on the pallet bed, and the priest by
his side mumbling prayers together. Faith! these jarveys can tell a
story none better.'

'As well as yourself, Pat,' one of us said. And Pat began to tell of
the miles of bog on either side of the straggling road, of the hilltop
to the left, with the play-house showing against the dark and
changing clouds; of a woman in a red petticoat, a handkerchief tied
round her head, who had flung down her spade the moment she
caught sight of the car, of the man who appeared on the brow and
blew a horn. 'For she mistook us for bailiffs,' said Pat, 'and two
little sheep hardly bigger than geese were driven away.'

'A play-house in the waste for these people,' I was saying to
myself all the time, till my meditations were interrupted by the
jarvey telling that the rocky river we crossed was called the
Greyhound a not inappropriate name, for it ran swiftly.... Away
down the long road a white cottage appeared, and the jarvey said to
me, 'That is the priest's house.' It stood on the hillside some little
way from the road, and all the way to the door I wondered how his
days passed in the great loneliness of the bog.

'His reverence isn't at home, yer honour he's gone to attend a
sick call.'

'Yes, I know Tom Burke.'

'And is Tom better, Mike?'

'The devil a bether he'll be this side of Jordan,' the jarvey
answered, and the housekeeper showed me into the priest's parlour.
It was lined with books, and I looked forward to a pleasant chat
when we had finished our business. At that time I was on a relief
committee, and the people were starving in the poor parts of the
country.

'I think he'll be back in about an hour's time, yer honour.' But
the priest seemed to be detained longer than his housekeeper
expected, and the moaning of the wind round the cottage reminded
me of the small white thing the horse and the doctor had seen
gliding along the road. 'The priest knows the story he will tell me,' I
said, and piled more turf on the fire fine sods of hard black turf they
were, and well do I remember seeing them melting away. But all of
a sudden my eyes closed. I couldn't have been asleep more than a
few minutes when it seemed to me a great crowd of men and
women had gathered about the house, and a moment after the door
was flung open, and a tall, gaunt man faced me.

'I've just come,' he said, 'from a deathbed, and they that have followed me aren't far from death if we don't succeed in getting help.'

I don't know how I can tell you of the crowd I saw round the house that day. We are accustomed to see poor people in towns cowering under arches, but it is more pitiful to see people starving in the fields on the mountain side. I don't know why it should be so, but it is. But I call to mind two men in ragged trousers and shirts as ragged, with brown beards on faces yellow with famine; and the words of one of them are not easily forgotten: 'The white sun of Heaven doesn't shine upon two poorer men than upon this man and myself.' I can tell you I didn't envy the priest his job, living all his life in the waste listening to tales of starvation, looking into famished faces. There were some women among them, kept back by the men, who wanted to get their word in first. They seemed to like to talk about their misery.... and I said:

'They are tired of seeing each other. I am a spectacle, a show, an amusement for them. I don't know if you can catch my meaning?'

'I think I do,' Father James answered. And I asked him to come for a walk up the hill and show me the play-house.

Again he hesitated, and I said: 'You must come, Father MacTurnan, for a walk. You must forget the misfortunes of those people for a while.' He yielded, and we spoke of the excellence of the road under our feet, and he told me that when he conceived the idea of a play-house, he had already succeeded in persuading the inspector to agree that the road they were making should go to the top of the hill. 'The policy of the Government,' he said, 'from the first was that relief works should benefit nobody except the workers, and it is sometimes very difficult to think out a project for work that will be perfectly useless. Arches have been built on the top of hills, and roads that lead nowhere. A strange sight to the stranger a road must be that stops suddenly in the middle of a bog. One wonders at first how a Government could be so foolish, but when one thinks of it, it is easy to understand that the Government doesn't wish to spend money on works that will benefit a class. But the road that leads nowhere is difficult to make, even though starving men are employed upon it; for a man to work well there must be an end in view, and I can tell you it is difficult to bring even starving men to engage on a road that leads nowhere. If I'd told everything I am telling you to the inspector, he wouldn't have agreed to let the road run to the top of the hill; but I said to him: "The road leads nowhere; as well let it end at the top of the hill as down in the valley." So I got the money for my road and some money for my play-house, for of course the play-house was as useless as the road; a play-house in the waste can neither interest or benefit anybody! But there was an idea at the back of my mind all the time that when the road and the play-house were finished, I might be able to induce the Government to build a harbour.'

'But the harbour would be of use?'

'Of very little,' he answered. 'For the harbour to be of use a great deal of dredging would have to be done.'

'And the Government needn't undertake the dredging. How very ingenious! I suppose you often come here to read your breviary?'

'During the building of the play-house I often used to be up here, and during the rehearsals I was here every day.'

'If there was a rehearsal,' I said to myself, 'there must have been a play.' And I affected interest in the grey shallow sea and the erosion of the low lying land a salt marsh filled with pools.

'I thought once,' said the priest, 'that if the play were a great success, a line of flat-bottomed steamers might be built.'

'Sitting here in the quiet evenings,' I said to myself, 'reading his breviary, dreaming of a line of steamships crowded with visitors! He has been reading about the Oberammergau performances.' So that was his game the road, the play-house, the harbour and I agreed with him that no one would have dared to predict that visitors would have come from all sides of Europe to see a few peasants performing a miracle play in the Tyrol.

'Come,' I said, 'into the play-house and let me see how you built it.'

Half a wall and some of the roof had fallen, and the rubble had not been cleared away, and I said:

'It will cost many pounds to repair the damage, but having gone so far you should give the play a chance.'

'I don't think it would be advisable,' he muttered, half to himself, half to me.

As you may well imagine, I was anxious to hear if he had discovered any aptitude for acting among the girls and the boys who lived in the cabins.

'I think,' he answered me, 'that the play would have been fairly acted; I think that, with a little practice, we might have done as well as they did at Oberammergau.'

An odd man, more willing to discuss the play that he had chosen than the talents of those who were going to perform it, and he told me that it had been written in the fourteenth century in Latin, and that he had translated it into Irish.

I asked him if it would have been possible to organize an excursion from Dublin—'Oberammergau in the West.'

'I used to think so. But it is eight miles from Rathowen, and the road is a bad one, and when they got here there would be no place for them to stay; they would have to go all the way back again, and that would be sixteen miles.'

'Yet you did well, Father James, to build the play-house, for the people could work better while they thought they were accomplishing something. Let me start a subscription for you in Dublin.'

'I don't think that it would be possible—'

'Not for me to get fifty pounds?'

'You might get the money, but I don't think we could ever get a performance of the play.'

'And why not?' I said.

'You see, the wind came and blew down the wall. The people are very pious; I think they felt that the time they spent rehearsing might have been better spent. The play-house disturbed them in their ideas. They hear Mass on Sundays, and there are the Sacraments, and they remember they have to die. It used to seem to me a very sad thing to see all the people going to America; the poor Celt disappearing in America, leaving his own country, leaving his language, and very often his religion.'

'And does it no longer seem to you sad that such a thing should happen?'

'No, not if it is the will of God. God has specially chosen the Irish race to convert the world. No race has provided so many missionaries, no race has preached the Gospel more frequently to the heathen; and once we realize that we have to die, and very soon, and that the Catholic Church is the only true Church, our ideas about race and nationality fade from us. We are here, not to make life successful and triumphant, but to gain heaven. That is the truth, and it is to the honour of the Irish people that they have been selected by God to preach the truth, even though they lose their nationality in preaching it. I do not expect you to accept these opinions. I know that you think very differently, but living here I have learned to acquiesce in the will of God.'

He stopped speaking suddenly, like one ashamed of having expressed himself too openly, and soon after we were met by a number of peasants, and the priest's attention was engaged; the inspector of the relief works had to speak to him; and I didn't see him again until dinner-time.

'You have given them hope,' he said.

This was gratifying to hear, and the priest sat listening while I told him of the looms already established in different parts of the country. We talked about half an hour, and then like one who suddenly remembers, the priest got up and fetched his knitting.

'Do you knit every evening?'

'I have got into the way of knitting lately it passes the time.'

'But do you never read?' I asked, and my eyes went towards the bookshelves.

'I used to read a great deal. But there wasn't a woman in the parish that could turn a heel properly, so I had to learn to knit.'

'Do you like knitting better than reading?' I asked, feeling ashamed of my curiosity.

'I have constantly to attend sick calls, and if one is absorbed in a book one doesn't like to put it aside.'

'I see you have two volumes of miracle plays!'

'Yes, and that's another danger: a book begets all kinds of ideas and notions into one's head. The idea of that play-house came out of those books.'

'But,' I said, 'you don't think that God sent the storm because He didn't wish a play to be performed?'

'One cannot judge God's designs. Whether God sent the storm or whether it was accident must remain a matter for conjecture; but it is not a matter of conjecture that one is doing certain good by devoting oneself to one's daily task, getting the Government to start new relief works, establishing schools for weaving. The people are entirely dependent upon me, and when I'm attending to their wants I know I'm doing right.'

The play-house interested me more than the priest's ideas of right and wrong, and I tried to get him back to it; but the subject seemed a painful one, and I said to myself: 'The jarvey will tell me all about it tomorrow. I can rely on him to find out the whole story from the housekeeper in the kitchen.' And sure enough, we hadn't got to the Greyhound River before he was leaning across the well of the car talking to me and asking if the priest was thinking of putting up the wall of the play-house.

'The wall of the play-house?' I said.

'Yes, yer honour. Didn't I see both of you going up the hill in the evening time?'

'I don't think we shall ever see a play in the play-house.'

'Why would we, since it was God that sent the wind that blew it down?'

'How do you know it was God that sent the wind? It might have been the devil himself, or somebody's curse.'

'Sure it is of Mrs. Sheridan you do be thinking, yer honour, and of her daughter she that was to be playing Good Deeds in the play, yer honour; and wasn't she wake coming home from the learning of the play? And when the signs of her wakeness began to show, the widow Sheridan took a halter off the cow and tied Margaret to the wall, and she was in the stable till the child was born. Then didn't her mother take a bit of string and tie it round the child's throat, and bury it near the play-house; and it was three nights after that the storm rose, and the child pulled the thatch out of the roof.'

'But did she murder the child?'

'Sorra wan of me knows. She sent for the priest when she was dying, and told him what she had done.'

'But the priest wouldn't tell what he heard in the confessional,' I said.

'Mrs. Sheridan didn't die that night; not till the end of the week, and the neighbours heard her talking of the child she had buried, and then they all knew what the white thing was they had seen by the roadside. The night the priest left her he saw the white thing standing in front of him, and if he hadn't been a priest he'd have dropped down dead; so he took some water from the boghole and dashed it over it, saying, "I baptize thee in the name of the Father, and of the Son, and of the Holy Ghost!"'

The driver told his story like one saying his prayers, and he seemed to have forgotten that he had a listener.

'It must have been a great shock to the priest.'

'Faith it was, sir, to meet an unbaptized child on the roadside, and that child the only bastard that was ever born in the parish so Tom Mulhare says, and he's the oldest man in the county.'

'It was altogether a very queer idea this play-house.'

'It was indeed, sir, a quare idea, but you see he's a quare man. He has been always thinking of something to do good, and it is said that he thinks too much. Father James is a very quare man, your honour.'

JULIA CAHILL'S CURSE

'AND what has become of Margaret?'

'Ah, didn't her mother send her to America as soon as the baby was born? Once a woman is wake here she has to go. Hadn't Julia to go in the end, and she the only one that ever said she didn't mind the priest?'

'Julia who?' said I.

'Julia Cahill.'

The name struck my fancy, and I asked the driver to tell me her story.

'Wasn't it Father Madden who had her put out of the parish, but she put her curse on it, and it's on it to this day.'

'Do you believe in curses?'

'Bedad I do, sir. It's a terrible thing to put a curse on a man, and the curse that Julia put on Father Madden's parish was a bad one, the divil a worse. The sun was up at the time, and she on the hilltop raising both her hands. And the curse she put on the parish was that every year a roof must fall in and a family go to America. That was the curse, your honour and every word of it has come true. You'll see for yourself as soon as we cross the mearing.'

'And what became of Julia's baby?'

'I never heard she had one, sir.'

He flicked his horse pensively with his whip, and it seemed to me that the disbelief I had expressed in the power of the curse disinclined him for further conversation.

'But,' I said, 'who is Julia Cahill, and how did she get the power to put a curse upon the village?'

'Didn't she go into the mountains every night to meet the fairies, and who else could've given her the power to put a curse on the village?'

'But she couldn't walk so far in one evening.'

'Them that's in league with the fairies can walk that far and as much farther in an evening, your honour. A shepherd saw her; and you'll see the ruins of the cabins for yourself as soon as we cross the mearing, and I'll show you the cabin of the blind woman that

Julia lived with before she went away.'

'And how long is it since she went?'

'About twenty year, and there hasn't been a girl the like of her in these parts since. I was only a gossoon at the time, but I've heard tell she was as tall as I'm myself, and as straight as a poplar. She walked with a little swing in her walk, so that all the boys used to be looking after her, and she had fine black eyes, sir, and she was nearly always laughing. Father Madden had just come to the parish; and there was courting in these parts then, for aren't we the same as other people we'd like to go out with a girl well enough if it was the custom of the country. Father Madden put down the ball alley because he said the boys stayed there instead of going into Mass, and he put down the cross-road dances because he said dancing was the cause of many a bastard, and he wanted none in his parish. Now there was no dancer like Julia; the boys used to gather about to see her dance, and who ever walked with her under the hedges in the summer could never think about another woman. The village was cracked about her. There was fighting, so I suppose the priest was right: he had to get rid of her. But I think he mightn't have been as hard on her as he was.

'One evening he went down to the house. Julia's people were well-to-do people, they kept a grocery store in the village; and when he came into the shop who should be there but the richest farmer in the country, Michael Moran by name, trying to get Julia for his wife. He didn't go straight to Julia, and that's what swept him. There are two counters in that shop, and Julia was at the one on the left hand as you go in. And many's the pound she had made for her parents at that counter. Michael Moran says to the father, "Now, what fortune are you going to give with Julia?" And the father says there was many a man who would take her without any; and that's how they spoke, and Julia listening quietly all the while at the opposite counter. For Michael didn't know what a spirited girl she was, but went on arguing till he got the father to say fifty pounds, and thinking he had got him so far he said, "I'll never drop a flap to her unless you give the two heifers." Julia never said a word, she just sat listening. It was then that the priest came in. And over he goes to Julia; "And now," says he, "aren't you proud to hear that you'll have such a fine fortune, and it's I that'll be glad to see you married, for I can't have any more of your goings-on in my parish. You're the encouragement of the dancing and courting here; but I'm going to put an end to it." Julia didn't answer a word, and he went over to them that were arguing about the sixty pounds. "Now why not make it fifty-five?" says he. So the father agreed to that since the priest had said it. And all three of them thought the marriage was settled. "Now what will you be taking, Father Tom?" says Cahill, "and you, Michael?" Sorra one of them thought of asking her if she was pleased with Michael; but little did they know what was passing in her mind, and when they came over to the counter to tell her what they had settled, she said, "Well, I've just been listening to you, and 'tis well for you to be wasting your time talking about me," and she tossed her head, saying she would just pick the boy out of the parish that pleased her best. And what angered the priest most of all was her way of saying it that the boy that would marry her would be marrying herself and not the money that would be paid when the book was signed or when the first baby was born. Now it was agin girls marrying according to their fancy that Father Madden had set himself. He had said in his sermon the Sunday before that young people shouldn't be allowed out by themselves at all, but that the parents should make up the marriages for them. And he went fairly wild when Julia told him the example she was going to set. He tried to keep his temper, sir, but it was getting the better of him all the while, and Julia said, "My boy isn't in the parish now, but maybe he is on his way here, and he may be here tomorrow or the next day." And when Julia's father heard her speak like that he knew that no one would turn her from what she was saying, and he said, "Michael Moran, my good man, you may go your way: you'll never get her." Then he went back to hear what Julia was saying to the priest, but it was the priest that was talking. "Do you think," says he, "I am going to let you go on turning the head of every boy in the parish? Do you think," says he, "I'm going to see you gallavanting with one and then with the other? Do you think I'm going to see fighting and quarrelling for your like? Do you think I'm going to hear stories like I heard last week about poor Patsy Carey, who has gone out of his mind, they say, on account of your treatment? No," says he, "I'll have no more of that. I'll have you out of my parish, or I'll have you married." Julia didn't answer the priest; she tossed her head, and went on making up parcels of tea and sugar and getting the steps and taking down candles, though she didn't want them, just to show the priest that she didn't mind what he was saying. And all the while her father trembling, not knowing what would happen, for the priest had a big stick, and there was no saying that he wouldn't strike her. Cahill tried to quiet the priest, he promising him that Julia shouldn't go out any more in the evenings, and bedad, sir, she was out the same evening with a young man and the priest saw them, and the next evening she was out with another and the priest saw them, nor was she minded at the end of the month to marry any of them. Then the priest went down to the shop to speak to her a second time, and he went down again a third time, though what he said the third time no one knows, no one being there at the time. And next Sunday he spoke out, saying that a disobedient daughter would have the worst devil in hell to attend on her. I've heard tell that he called her the evil spirit that set men mad. But most of the people that were there are dead or gone to America, and no one rightly knows what he did say, only that the words came pouring out of his mouth, and the people when they saw Julia crossed themselves, and even the boys who were most mad after Julia were afraid to speak to her. Cahill had to put her out.'

'Do you mean to say that the father put his daughter out?'

'Sure, didn't the priest threaten to turn him into a rabbit if he didn't, and no one in the parish would speak to Julia, they were so afraid of Father Madden, and if it hadn't been for the blind woman that I was speaking about a while ago, sir, it is to the Poor House she'd have to go. The blind woman has a little cabin at the edge of the bog I'll point it out to you, sir; we do be passing it by and she was with the blind woman for nearly two years disowned by her own father. Her clothes wore out, but she was as beautiful without them as with them. The boys were told not to look back, but sure they couldn't help it.

'Ah, it was a long while before Father Madden could get shut of her. The blind woman said she wouldn't see Julia thrown out on the roadside, and she was as good as her word for wellnigh two years, till Julia went to America, so some do be saying, sir, whilst others do be saying she joined the fairies. But 'tis for sure, sir, that the day she left the parish Pat Quinn heard a knocking at his window and somebody asking if he would lend his cart to go to the railway station. Pat was a heavy sleeper and he didn't get up, and it is thought that it was Julia who wanted Pat's cart to take her to the station; it's a good ten mile; but she got there all the same!'

'You said something about a curse?'

'Yes, sir. You'll see the hill presently. A man who was taking some sheep to the fair saw her there. The sun was just getting up and he saw her cursing the village, raising both her hands, sir, up to the sun, and since that curse was spoken every year a roof has fallen in, sometimes two or three.'

I could see he believed the story, and for the moment I, too, believed in an outcast Venus becoming the evil spirit of a village that would not accept her as divine.

'Look, sir, the woman coming down the road is Bridget Coyne. And that's her house,' he said, and we passed a house built of loose stones without mortar, but a little better than the mud cabins I had seen in Father MacTurnan's parish.

'And now, sir, you will see the loneliest parish in Ireland.' And I noticed that though the land was good, there seemed to be few people on it, and what was more significant than the untilled fields were the ruins for they were not the cold ruins of twenty, or thirty, or forty years ago when the people were evicted and their tillage turned into pasture the ruins I saw were the ruins of cabins that had been lately abandoned, and I said:

'It wasn't the landlord who evicted these people.'

'Ah, it's the landlord who would be glad to have them back, but there's no getting them back. Everyone here will have to go, and 'tis said that the priest will say Mass in an empty chapel, sorra a one will be there but Bridget, and she'll be the last he'll give communion to. It's said, your honour, that Julia has been seen in America, and I'm going there this autumn. You may be sure I'll keep a lookout for her.'

'But all this is twenty years ago. You won't know her. A woman changes a good deal in twenty years.'

'There will be no change in her, your honour. Sure hasn't she been with the fairies?'

THE WEDDING GOWN

IT was said, but with what truth I cannot say, that the Roche property had been owned by the O'Dwyers many years ago, several generations past, some time in the eighteenth century. Only a faint legend of this ownership remained; only once had young Mr. Roche heard of it, and it was from his mother he had heard it; among the country people it was forgotten. His mother had told him that his great-great-grandfather, who had made large sums of money abroad, had increased his property by purchase from the O'Dwyers, who then owned, as well as farmed, the hillside on which the Big House stood. The O'Dwyers themselves had forgotten that they were once much greater people than they now were, but the master never spoke to them without remembering it, for though they only thought of themselves as small farmers, dependents on the squire, every one of them, boys and girls alike, retained an air of high birth, which at the first glance distinguished them from the other tenants of the estate. Though they were not aware of it, some sense of their remote origin must have survived in them, and I think that in a still more obscure way some sense of it survived in the countryside, for the villagers did not think worse of the O'Dwyers because they kept themselves aloof from the pleasures of the village and its squabbles. The O'Dwyers kept themselves apart from their fellows without any show of pride, without wounding anyone's feelings.

The head of the family was a man of forty, and he was the trusted servant, almost the friend, of the young master. He was his bailiff and his steward and he lived in a pretty cottage by the edge of the lake. O'Dwyer's aunts they were old women of sixty-eight and seventy lived in the Big House; the elder had been cook, and the younger housemaid, and both were now past their work, and they lived full of gratitude to the young master, to whom they thought they owed a great deal. He believed the debt to be all on his side, and when he was away he often thought of them, and when he returned home he went to greet them as he might go to the members of his own family. The family of the O'Dwyers was longlived, and Betty and Mary had a sister far older than themselves, Margaret

Kirwin, 'Granny Kirwin,' as she was called, and she lived in the cottage by the lake with her nephew, Alec O'Dwyer. She was over eighty it was said that she was nearly ninety but her age was not known exactly. Mary O'Dwyer said that Margaret was nearly twenty years older than she, but neither Betty nor Mary remembered the exact date of their sister's birth. They did not know much about her, for though she was their sister, she was almost a stranger to them. She had married when she was sixteen, and had gone away to another part of the country, and they had hardly heard of her for thirty years. It was said that she had been a very pretty girl, and that many men had been in love with her, and it was known for certain that she had gone away with the son of the gamekeeper of the grandfather of the present Mr. Roche, so you can understand what a very long while ago it was, and how little of the story of her life had come to the knowledge of those living now.

It was certainly sixty years since she had gone away with this young man; she had lived with him in Meath for some years, nobody knew exactly how many years, maybe some nine or ten years, and then he had died suddenly, and his death, it appears, had taken away from her some part of her reason. It was known for certain that she left Meath after his death, and had remained away many years. She had returned to Meath about twenty years ago, though not to the place she had lived in before. Some said she had experienced misfortunes so great that they had unsettled her mind. She herself had forgotten her story, and one day news had come to Galway news, but it was sad news, that she was living in some very poor cottage on the edge of Navan town where her strange behaviour and her strange life had made a scandal of her. The priest had to inquire out her relations, and it took him some time to do this, for the old woman's answers were incoherent, but he at length discovered she came from Galway, and he had written to the O'Dwyers. And immediately on receiving the priest's letter, Alec sent his wife to Navan, and she had come back with the old woman.

'And it was time indeed that I went to fetch her,' she said. 'The boys in the town used to make game of her, and follow her, and throw things at her, and they nearly lost the poor thing the little reason that was left to her. The rain was coming through the thatch, there was hardly a dry place in the cabin, and she had nothing to eat but a few scraps that the neighbours gave her. Latterly she had forgotten how to make a fire, and she ate the potatoes the neighbours gave her raw, and on her back there were only a few dirty rags. She had no care for anything except for her wedding gown. She kept that in a box covered over with paper so that no damp should get to it, and she was always folding it and seeing that the moth didn't touch it, and she was talking of it when I came in at the door. She thought that I had come to steal it from her. The neighbours told me that that was the way she always was, thinking that someone had come to steal her wedding gown.'

And this was all the news of Margaret Kirwin that Alec O'Dwyer's wife brought back with her. The old woman was given a room in the cottage, and though with food and warmth and kind treatment she became a little less bewildered, a little less like a wild, hunted creature, she never got back her memory sufficiently to tell them all that had happened to her after her husband's death. Nor did she seem as if she wanted to try to remember: she was garrulous only of her early days when the parish bells rang for her wedding, and the furze was in bloom. This was before the Big House on the hill had been built. The hill was then a fine pasture for sheep, and Margaret would often describe the tinkling of the sheep-bells in the valley, and the yellow furze, and the bells that were ringing for her wedding. She always spoke of the bells, though no one could understand where the bells came from. It was not customary to ring the parish bell for weddings, and there was no other bell, so that it was impossible to say how Margaret could have got the idea into her head that bells were ringing for her when she crossed the hill on her way to the church, dressed in the beautiful gown, which the grandmother of the present Mr. Roche had dressed her in, for she had always been the favourite, she said, with the old mistress, a much greater favourite than even her two sisters had ever been. Betty and Mary were then little children and hardly remembered the wedding, and could say nothing about the bells.

Margaret Kirwin walked with a short stick, her head lifted hardly higher than the handle, and when the family were talking round the kitchen fire she would come among them for a while and say something to them, and then go away, and they felt they had seen someone from another world. She hobbled now and then as far as the garden-gate, and she frightened the peasantry, so strange did she seem among the flowers so old and forlorn, almost cut off from this world, with only one memory to link her to it. It was the spectral look in her eyes that frightened them, for Margaret was not ugly. In spite of all her wrinkles the form of the face remained, and it was easy, especially when her little grandniece was by, to see that sixty-five years ago she must have had a long and pleasant face, such as one sees in a fox, and red hair like Molly.

Molly was sixteen, and her grey dress reached only to her ankles. Everyone was fond of the poor old woman; but it was only Molly who had no fear of her at all, and one would often see them standing together beside the pretty paling that separated the steward's garden from the high road. Chestnut trees grew about the house, and China roses over the walls, and in the course of the summer there would be lilies in the garden, and in the autumn hollyhocks and sunflowers. There were a few fruit trees a little further on, and, lower down, a stream. A little bridge led over the stream into the meadow, and Molly and her grandaunt used to go as far as the bridge, and everyone wondered what the child and the old woman had to say to each other. Molly was never able to give any clear account of what the old woman said to her during the time they spent by the stream. She had tried once to give Molly an account of one long winter when the lake was frozen from side to side. Then there was something running in her mind about the transport of pillars in front of the Big House how they had been drawn across the lake by oxen, and how one of the pillars was now lying at the bottom of the lake. That was how Molly took up the story from her, but she understood little of it. Molly's solicitude for the old woman was a subject of admiration, and Molly did not like to take the credit for a kindness and pity which she did not altogether feel. She had never seen anyone dead, and her secret fear was that the old woman might die before she went away to service. Her parents had promised to allow her to go away when she was eighteen, and she lived in the hope that her aunt would live two years longer, and that she would be saved the terror of seeing a dead body. And it was in this intention that she served her aunt, that she carefully minced the old woman's food and insisted on her eating often, and that she darted from her place to fetch the old woman her stick when she rose to go. When Margaret Kirwin was not in the kitchen Molly was always laughing and talking, and her father and mother often thought it was her voice that brought the old woman out of her room. So the day Molly was grieving because she could not go to the dance the old woman remained in her room, and not seeing her at teatime they began to be afraid, and Molly was asked to go to fetch her aunt.

'Something may have happened to her, mother. I daren't go.'

And when old Margaret came into the kitchen towards evening she surprised everyone by her question:

'Why is Molly crying?'

No one else had heard Molly sob, if she had sobbed, but everyone knew the reason of her grief; indeed, she had been reproved for it many times that day.

'I will not hear any more about it,' said Mrs. O'Dwyer; 'she has been very tiresome all day. Is it my fault if I cannot give her a gown to go to the dance?' And then, forgetting that old Margaret could not understand her, she told her that the servants were having a dance at the Big House, and had asked Molly to come to it. 'But what can I do? She has got no gown to go in. Even if I had the money there wouldn't be time to send for one now, nor to make one. And there are a number of English servants stopping at the house; there are people from all parts of the country, they have brought their servants with them, and I am not going to see my girl worse dressed than the others, so she cannot go. She has heard all this, she knows it.... I've never seen her so tiresome before.' Mrs. O'Dwyer continued to chide her daughter; but her mother's reasons for not allowing her to go to the ball, though unanswerable, did not seem to console Molly, and she sat looking very miserable. 'She has been sitting like that all day,' said Mrs. O'Dwyer, 'and I wish that it were tomorrow, for she will not be better until it is all over.'

'But, mother, I am saying nothing; I'll go to bed. I don't know why you're blaming me. I'm saying nothing. I can't help feeling miserable.'

'No, she don't look a bit cheerful,' the old woman said, 'and I don't like her to be disappointed.' This was the first time that old Margaret had seemed to understand since she came to live with them what was passing about her, and they all looked at her, Mrs. O'Dwyer and Alec and Molly. They stood waiting for her to speak again, wondering if the old woman's speech was an accident, or if she had recovered her mind. 'It is a hard thing for a child at her age not to be able to go to the dance at the Big House, now that she has been asked. No wonder there is not a smile on her face. I remember the time that I should have been crying too for a dance, and isn't she the very same?'

'But, Granny, she can't go in the clothes she is wearing, and she has only got one other frock, the one she goes to Mass in. I can't let my daughter—'

But seeing the old woman was about to speak Alec stopped his wife.

'Let's hear what she has to say,' he whispered.

'There's my wedding gown, it's beautiful enough for anyone to wear. It hasn't been worn since the day I wore it, when the bells were ringing, and I went over the hill to be married; and I've taken such care of it that it is the same as it was that day. Molly will look very nice in it, she will look just as I looked on my wedding day.'

And they stood astonished father, mother, and daughter for the old woman, ever since she had come to live with them, had kept her wedding gown sacred from their eyes and hands, closing her door before taking it out to give it the air and strew it with camphor. Only once they had seen it. She had brought it out one day and shown it to them as a child might show a toy; but the moment Mrs. Dwyer put out her hand to touch it, Granny had gone away with her gown, and they had heard her shutting the box it was in. Now she was going to lend it to Molly, so she said, but they fully expected her to turn away and to go to her room, forgetful of what she had said. Even if she were to let Molly put the dress on, she would not let her go out of the house with it. She would change her mind at the last minute.

'When does this dancing begin' she asked, and when they told her she said there would be just time for her to dress Molly, and asked the girl to come into her room. Mrs. O'Dwyer feared the girl would be put to a bitter disappointment, but if Molly once had the gown on she would not oblige her to take it off.

'In my gown you will be just like what I was when the bells were ringing.'

She took the gown out of its box herself, the petticoat and the stockings and the shoes.

'The old mistress gave me all these. Molly has gotten the hair I used to have, and will look like myself. Aren't they beautiful shoes? Look at the buckles, and they'll fit her, for her feet are the same size as mine were.'

Molly's feet went into the shoes just as if they had been made for her, and the gown fitted as well as the shoes, and Molly's hair was arranged according to the old woman's fancy, as she used to wear her own hair when it was thick and red like a fox's.

The girl thought that Granny would regret her gifts, and she expected the old woman to follow her into the kitchen and ask her to give back the gown as she was going out of the house. As she stood on the threshold her mother offered her the key; the ball would not be over till five, and Granny said she'd stay up for her.

'I'll doze a bit upon a chair. If I am tired I'll lie down upon my bed. I shall hear Molly; I shan't sleep much. She'll not be able to enter the house without my hearing her.'

It was extraordinary to hear her speak like this, and, a little frightened by her sudden sanity, they tried to persuade her to allow them to lock up the house; but she sat looking into the fire, seemingly so contented that they left her, and for an hour she sat dreaming, seeing Molly young and beautifully dressed in the wedding gown of more than sixty years ago.

Dream after dream went by, the fire had burned low, the sods were falling into white ashes, and the moonlight began to stream into the room. It was the chilliness that had come into the air that awoke her, and she threw several sods of turf on to the fire.

An hour passed, and old Margaret awoke. 'The bells are ringing, the bells are ringing,' she said, and went to the kitchen door; she opened it, and under the rays of the moon she stood lost in memories, for the night of her marriage was just such a night as this one, and she had stood in the garden amid the summer flowers, just as she did now.

'The day is beginning,' she said, mistaking the moonlight for the dawn, and, listening, it seemed to her that she heard once more the sound of bells coming across the hill. 'Yes, the bells are ringing,' she said; 'I can hear them quite clearly, and must hurry and get dressed I must not keep him waiting.'

And, returning to the house, she went to her box, where her gown had lain so many years; and though no gown was there it seemed to her that there was one, and one more beautiful than the gown she had cherished. It was the same gown, only grown more beautiful. It had passed into softer silk, into a more delicate colour; it had become more beautiful, and holding the dream-gown in her hands, she sat with it in the moonlight thinking how fair he would find her in it. Once her hands went to her hair, and then she dropped them again.

'I must begin to dress myself; I mustn't keep him waiting.'

The moonlight lay still upon her knees, but little by little the moon moved up the sky, leaving her in the shadow.

It was at this moment, as the shadows grew denser about old Margaret, that the child who was dancing at the ball came to think of her who had given her her gown, and who was waiting for her. It was in the middle of a reel she was dancing, and she was dancing it with Mr. Roche, that she felt that something had happened to her aunt.

'Mr. Roche,' she said, 'you must let me go away; I cannot dance any more tonight. I am sure that something has happened to my aunt, the old woman, Margaret Kirwin, who lives with us in the Lodge. It was she who lent me this gown. This was her wedding gown, and for sixty-five years it has never been out of her possession. She has hardly allowed anyone to see it; but she said that I was like her, and she heard me crying because I had no gown to go to the ball, and so she lent me her wedding gown.'

'You look very nice, Molly, in the wedding gown, and this is only a fancy.' Seeing the girl was frightened and wanted to go, he said: 'But why do you think that anything has happened to your aunt?'

'She is very old.'

'But she isn't much older than she was when you left her.'

'Let me go, Mr. Roche; I think I must go. I feel sure that something has happened to her. I never had such a feeling before, and I couldn't have that feeling if there was no reason for it.'

'Well, if you must go.'

She glanced to where the moon was shining and ran down the drive, leaving Mr. Roche looking after her, wondering if after all she might have had a warning of the old woman's death. The night was one of those beautiful nights in May, when the moon soars high in the sky, and all the woods and fields are clothed in the green of spring. But the stillness of the night frightened Molly, and when she stopped to pick up her dress she heard the ducks chattering in the reeds. The world seemed divided into darkness and light. The hawthorn trees threw black shadows that reached into the hollows, and Molly did not dare to go by the path that led through a little wood, lest she should meet Death there. For now it seemed to her that she was running a race with Death, and that she must get to the cottage before him. She did not dare to take the short cut, but she ran till her breath failed her. She ran on again, but when she went through the wicket she knew that Death had been before her. She knocked twice; receiving no answer she tried the latch, and was surprised to find the door unlocked. There was a little fire among the ashes, and after blowing the sod for some time she managed to light the candle, and holding it high she looked about the kitchen.

'Auntie, are you asleep? Have the others gone to bed?'

She approached a few steps, and then a strange curiosity came over her, and though she had always feared death she now looked curiously upon death, and she thought that she saw the likeness which her aunt had often noticed.

'Yes,' she said, 'she is like me. I shall be like that some day if I live long enough.'

And then she knocked at the door of the room where her parents were sleeping.

THE CLERK'S QUEST

FOR thirty years Edward Dempsey had worked low down in the list of clerks in the firm of Quin and Wee. He did his work so well that he seemed born to do it, and it was felt that any change in which Dempsey was concerned would be unlucky. Managers had looked at Dempsey doubtingly and had left him in his habits. New partners had come into the business, but Dempsey showed no sign of interest. He was interested only in his desk. There it was by the dim window there were his pens, there was his penwiper, there was the ruler, there was the blotting-pad. Dempsey was always the first to arrive and the last to leave. Once in thirty years of service he had accepted a holiday; it had been a topic of conversation all the morning, and the clerks tittered when he came into the bank in the afternoon saying he had been looking into the shop windows, and had come down to the bank to see how they were getting on.

An obscure, clandestine, taciturn little man occupying in life only the space necessary to bend over a desk, and whose conical head leaned to one side as if in token of his humility.

It seemed that Dempsey had no other ambition than to be allowed to stagnate at a desk to the end of his life, and this modest ambition would have been realized had it not been for a slight accident the single accident that had found its way into Dempsey's well-ordered and closely-guarded life. One summer's day, when the heat of the areas was rising and filling the open window, Dempsey's somnolescent senses were moved by a soft and suave perfume. At first he was puzzled to say whence it came; then he perceived that it had come from the bundle of cheques which he held in his hand; and then that the odoriferous paper was a pale pink cheque in the middle of the bundle. He had hardly seen a flower for thirty years, and could not determine whether the odour was that of mignonette, or honeysuckle, or violet. But at that moment the cheques were called for; he handed them to his superior, and with cool hand and clear brain continued to make entries in the ledger until the bank closed.

But that night, just as he was falling asleep, a remembrance of the insinuating perfume returned to him. He wondered whose cheque it

121

was, and regretted not having looked at the signature, and many times during the succeeding weeks he paused as he was making entries in the ledger to think if the haunting perfume were rose, lavender, or mignonette. It was not the scent of rose, he was sure of that. And a vague swaying of hope began. Dreams that had died or had never been born floated up like things from the depths of the sea, and many old things that he had dreamed about or had never dreamed at all drifted about. Out of the depths of life a hope that he had never known, or that the severe rule of his daily life had checked long ago, began its struggle for life; and when the same sweet odour came again he knew now it was the scent of heliotrope his heart was lifted and he was overcome in a sweet, possessive trouble. He sought for the cheque amid the bundle of cheques, and finding it, he pressed the paper to his face. The cheque was written in a thin, feminine handwriting, and was signed 'Henrietta Brown,' and the name and handwriting were pregnant with occult significances in Dempsey's disturbed mind. His hand paused amid the entries, and he grew suddenly aware of some dim, shadowy form, gracile and sweet-smelling as the spring moist shadow of wandering cloud, emanation of earth, or woman herself? Dempsey pondered, and his absent-mindedness was noticed, and occasioned comment among the clerks.

For the first time in his life he was glad when the office hours were over. He wanted to be alone, he wanted to think, he felt he must abandon himself to the new influence that had so suddenly and unexpectedly entered his life. Henrietta Brown! the name persisted in his mind like a half-forgotten, half-remembered tune; and in his efforts to realize her beauty he stopped before the photographic displays in the shop windows; but none of the famous or the infamous celebrities there helped him in the least. He could only realize Henrietta Brown by turning his thoughts from without and seeking the intimate sense of her perfumed cheques. The end of every month brought a cheque from Henrietta Brown, and for a few moments the clerk was transported and lived beyond himself.

An idea had fixed itself in his mind. He knew not if Henrietta Brown was young or old, pretty or ugly, married or single; the perfume and the name were sufficient, and could no longer be separated from the idea, now forcing its way through the fissures in the failing brain of this poor little bachelor clerk that idea of light and love and grace so inherent in man, but which rigorous circumstance had compelled Dempsey to banish from his life.

Dempsey had had a mother to support for many years, and had found it impossible to economize. But since her death he had laid by about a hundred and fifty pounds; he thought of this money with awe, and, awed by his good fortune, he thought how much more he might save before he was forced to leave his employment; and to have touched a penny of his savings would have seemed to him a sin near to sacrilege. Yet he did not hesitate for a single moment to send Henrietta Brown, whose address he had been able to obtain through the bank books, a diamond brooch which had cost twenty pounds. He omitted to say whence it had come, and for days he lived in warm wonderment, satisfied in the thought that she was wearing something that he had seen and touched.

His ideal was now by him and always, and its dominion was so complete that he neglected his duties at the bank, and was censured by the amazed manager. The change of his condition was so obvious that it became the subject for gossip, and jokes were now beginning to pass into serious conjecturing. Dempsey took no notice, and his plans matured amid jokes and theories. The desire to write and reveal himself to his beloved had become imperative; and after some very slight hesitation for he was moved more by instinct than by reason he wrote a letter urging the fatality of the circumstances that separated them, and explaining rather than excusing this revelation of his identity. His letter was full of deference, but at the same time it left no doubt as to the nature of his attachments and hopes. The answer to this letter was a polite note begging him not to persist in this correspondence, and warning him that if he did it would become necessary to write to the manager of the bank. But the return of his brooch did not dissuade Dempsey from the pursuit of his ideal; and as time went by it became more and more impossible for him to refrain from writing love-letters and sending occasional presents of jewellery. When the letters and jewellery were returned to him he put them away carelessly, and he bought the first sparkle of diamonds that caught his fancy, and forwarded ring, bracelet, and ear-ring, with whatever words of rapturous love that came up in his mind.

One day he was called into the manager's room, severely reprimanded, and eventually pardoned in consideration of his long and faithful services. But the reprimands of his employers were of no use, and he continued to write to Henrietta Brown, growing more and more careless of his secret, dropping brooches about the office, and letters. At last the story was whispered from desk to desk. Dempsey's dismissal was the only course open to the firm; and it was with much regret that the partners told their old servant that his services were no longer required.

To their surprise Dempsey seemed quite unaffected by his dismissal; he even seemed relieved, and left the bank smiling, thinking of Henrietta, bestowing no thought on his want of means. He did not even think of providing himself with money by the sale of some of the jewellery he had about him, nor of going to his lodging and packing up his clothes, he did not think how he should get to Edinburgh it was there that she lived. He thought of her even to the exclusion of the simplest means of reaching her, and was content to walk about the fields in happy mood, watching for glimpses of some evanescent phantom at the wood's edge wearing a star on her forehead, or catching sight in the wood's depths of a glistening shoulder and feet flying towards the reeds. Full of happy aspiration he wandered, seeking the country through the many straggling villages that hang like children round the skirts of Dublin, and passing through one of these at nightfall, and feeling tired, he turned into the bar of an inn, and asked for a bit to eat.

'You look as if you'd come a long way, Mister.'

'I have come a good twenty miles, and I'll have to go a good few more before I reach Edinburgh.'

'And what might you be going to Edinburgh for if you'll excuse me asking?'

'I am going to the lady I love, and I am taking her beautiful presents of jewellery.'

The two rough fellows exchanged glances; and it is easy to imagine how Dempsey was induced to let them have his diamonds, so that inquiries might be made of a friend round the corner regarding their value. After waiting a little while, Dempsey paid for his bread and cheese, and went in search of the thieves. But the face of Henrietta Brown obliterated all remembrance of thieves and diamonds, and he wandered for a few days, sustained by his dream and the crusts that his appearance drew from the pitiful. At last he even neglected to ask for a crust, and, foodless, followed the beckoning vision, from sunrise to sundown.

It was a soft, quiet summer's night when Dempsey lay down to sleep for the last time. He was very tired, he had been wandering all day, and threw himself on the grass by the roadside. He lay there looking up at the stars, thinking of Henrietta, knowing that everything was slipping away, and he passing into a diviner sense. Henrietta seemed to be coming nearer to him and revealing herself more clearly; and when the word of death was in his throat, and his eyes opened for the last time, it seemed to him that one of the stars came down from the sky and laid its bright face upon his shoulder.

ALMS-GIVING

AS I searched for a penny it began to rain. The blind man opened a parcel, and I saw that it contained a small tarpaulin cape. But the several coats I wore made it difficult to find my change; I thought I had better forego my charity that day, and walked quickly away.

'Eight or nine hours a day waiting for alms is his earthly lot,' I said, and walking towards the river, and leaning on the parapet, I wondered if he recognized the passing steps if he recognized my steps and associated them with a penny. Of what use that he should know the different steps? If he knew them there would be anticipation and disappointments. But a dog would make life comprehensible, and I imagined a companionship, a mingling of muteness and blindness, and the joy that would brighten the darkness when the dog leaped eagerly upon the blind man's knees. I imagined the joy of warm feet and limb, and the sudden poke of the muzzle. A dog would be a link to bind the blind beggar to the friendship of life. Now why has this small blind man, with a face as pale as a plant that never sees the sun, not a dog? A dog is the natural link, and the only link, that binds the blind beggar to the friendship of life.

Looking round, I could see that he was taking off his little cape, for it had ceased raining. But in a few weeks it would rain every day, and the wind would blow from the river in great gusts. 'Will he brave another winter?' I asked myself. 'Iron blasts will sweep through the passage; they will find him through the torn shirt and the poor grey trousers, the torn waistcoat, the black jacket, and the threadbare overcoat someone's cast-off garment. But he may have been born blind, or he may have become blind; in any case he has been blind for many years, and if he persists in living he will have to brave many winters in that passage, for he is not an old man. What instinct compels him to bear his dark life? Is he afraid to kill himself? Does this fear spring from physical or from religious motives? Fear of hell? Surely no other motive would enable him to endure his life.'

In my intolerance for all life but my own I thought I could

estimate the value of the Great Mockery, and I asked myself angrily why he persisted in living. I asked myself why I helped him to live. It would be better that he should throw himself at once into the river. And this was reason talking to me, and it told me that the most charitable act I could do would be to help him over the parapet. But behind reason there is instinct, and in obedience to an impulse, which I could not weigh or appreciate, I went to the blind man and put money into his hand; the small coin slipped through his fingers; they were so cold that he could not retain it, and I had to pick it from the ground.

'Thankee, sir. Can you tell, sir, what time it is?'

This little question was my recompense. He and I wanted to know the time of day. I asked him why he wanted to know the time, and he told me because that evening a friend was coming to fetch him. And, wondering who that friend might be, and hoping he might tell me, I asked him about his case of pencils, expressing a hope that he sold them. He answered that he was doing a nice bit of trading.

'The boys about here are a trouble,' he said, 'but the policeman on the beat is a friend of mine, and he watches them and makes them count the pencils they take. The other day they robbed me, and he gave them such a cuffing that I don't think they'll take my pencils again. You see, sir, I keep the money I take for the pencils in the left pocket, and the money that is given to me I keep in the right pocket. In this way I know if my accounts are right when I make them up in the evening.'

Now where, in what lonely room, does he sit making up his accounts? But, not wishing to seem inquisitorial, I turned the conversation.

'I suppose you know some of the passers-by.'

'Yes, I know a tidy few. There's one gentleman who gives me a penny every day, but he's gone abroad, I hear, and sixpence a week is a big drop.'

As I had given him a penny a day all the summer, I assumed he was speaking of me. And my sixpence a week meant a day's dinner, perhaps two days' dinner! It was only necessary for me to withhold my charity to give him ease. He would hardly be able to live without my charity, and if one of his other patrons were to do likewise the world would be freed from a life that I could not feel to be of any value.

So do we judge the world if we rely on our reason, but instinct clings like a child and begs like a child, and my instinct begged me to succour this poor man, to give him a penny every day, to find out what his condition was, and to stop for a chat every time I gave him my penny. I had obeyed my instinct all the summer, and now reason had intervened, reason was in rebellion, and for a long time I avoided, or seemed to avoid, the passage where the blind man sat for eight or nine hours, glad to receive, but never asking for alms.

I think I forgot the blind man for several months. I only remembered him when I was sitting at home, or when I was at the other side of the town, and sometimes I thought I made myself little excuses not to pass through the passage. Our motives are vague, complex, and many, and one is never quite sure why one does a thing, and if I were to say that I did not give the blind man pennies that winter because I believed it better to deprive him of his means of livelihood and force him out of life than to help him to remain in life and suffer, I should be saying what was certainly untrue, yet the idea was in my mind, and I experienced more than one twinge of conscience when I passed through the passage. I experienced remorse when I hurried past him, too selfish to unbutton my coat, for every time I happened to pass him it was raining or blowing very hard, and every time I hurried away trying to find reasons why he bore his miserable life. I hurried to my business, my head full of chatter about St. Simon Stylites, telling myself that he saw God far away at the end of the sky, His immortal hands filled with immortal recompenses; reason chattered about the compensation of celestial choirs, but instinct told me that the blind man standing in the stone passage knew of no such miraculous consolations.

As the winter advanced, as the winds grew harsher, my avoidance of the passage grew more marked, and one day I stopped to think, and ask myself why I avoided it.

There was a faint warmth in the sky, and I heard my heart speaking quite distinctly, and it said:

'Go to the blind man what matter about your ten minutes' delay; you have been unhappy since you refrained from alms-giving, and the blind beggar can feel the new year beginning.'

'You see, sir, I have added some shirt buttons and studs to the pencils. I don't know how they will go, but one never knows till one tries.'

Then he told me it was smallpox that destroyed his eyes, and he was only eighteen at the time.

'You must have suffered very much when they told you your sight was going?'

'Yes, sir. I had the hump for six weeks.'

'What do you mean?'

'It doubled me up, that it did. I sat with my head in my hands for six weeks.'

'And after that?'

'I didn't think any more about it what was the good?'

'Yes, but it must be difficult not to think, sitting here all alone.'

'One mustn't allow oneself to give way. One would break down altogether if one did. I've some friends, and in the evening I get plenty of exercise.'

'What do you do in the evenings?'

'I turn a hay-cutting machine in a stable.'

'And you're quite contented?'

'I don't think, sir, a happier man than I passes through this gateway once a month.'

He told me his little boy came to fetch him in the evening.

'You're married?'

'Yes, sir, and I've got four children. They're going away for their holidays next week.'

'Where are they going?'

'To the sea. It will do them good; a blow on the beach will do them a power of good.'

'And when they come back they will tell you about it?'

'Yes.'

'And do you ever go away for a holiday?'

'Last year I went with a policeman. A gentleman who passes this way, one of my friends, paid four shillings for me. We had a nice dinner in a public-house for a shilling, and then we went for a walk.'

'And this year are you going with the policeman?'

'I hope so, a friend of mine gave me half-a-crown towards it.'

'I'll give you the rest.'

'Thankee, sir.'

A soft south wind was blowing, and an instinct as soft and as gentle filled my heart, and I went towards some trees. The new leaves were beginning in the high branches. I was sitting where sparrows were building their nests, and very soon I seemed to see farther into life than I had ever seen before. 'We're here,' I said, 'for the purpose of learning what life is, and the blind beggar has taught me a great deal, something that I could not have learnt out of a book, a deeper truth than any book contains....' And then I ceased to think, for thinking is a folly when a soft south wind is blowing and an instinct as soft and as gentle fills the heart.

SO ON HE FARES

HIS mother had forbidden him to stray about the roads and, standing at the garden gate, little Ulick Burke often thought he would like to run down to the canal and watch the boats passing. His father used to take him for walks along the towing path, but his father had gone away to the wars two years ago, and standing by the garden gate he remembered how his father used to stop to talk to the lock-keepers. Their talk turned often upon the canals and its business, and Ulick remembered that the canal ended in the Shannon, and that the barges met ships coming up from the sea.

He was a pretty child with bright blue eyes, soft curls, and a shy winning manner, and he stood at the garden gate thinking how the boats rose up in the locks, how the gate opened and let the boats free, and he wondered if his father had gone away to the war in one of the barges. He felt sure if he were going away to the war he would go in a barge. And he wondered if the barge went as far as the war or only as far as the Shannon. He would like to ask his mother, but she would say he was troubling her with foolish questions, or she would begin to think again that he wanted to run away from home. He wondered if he were to hide himself in one of the barges whether it would take him to a battlefield where he would meet his father walking about with a gun upon his shoulder.

And leaning against the gatepost, he swung one foot across the other, though he had been told by his mother that he was like one of the village children when he did it. But his mother was always telling him not to do something, and he could not remember everything he must not do. He had been told not to go to the canal lest he should fall in, nor into the field lest he should tear his trousers. He had been told he must not run about in the garden lest he should tread on the flowers, and his mother was always telling him he was not to talk to the school children as they came back from school, though he did not want to talk to them. There was a time when he would have liked to talk to them: now he ran to the other side of the garden when they were coming home from school; but there was no place in the garden where he could hide himself

129

from them, unless he got into the dry ditch. The school children were very naughty children; they climbed up the bank, and, holding on to the paling, they mocked at him; and their mockery was to ask him the way to 'Hill Cottage'; for his mother had had the name painted on the gate, and no one else in the parish had given their cottage a name.

However, he liked the dry ditch, and under the branches, where the wren had built her nest, Ulick was out of his mother's way, and out of the way of the boys; and lying among the dead leaves he could think of the barges floating away, and of his tall father who wore a red coat and let him pull his moustache. He was content to lie in the ditch for hours, thinking he was a bargeman and that he would like to use a sail. His father had told him that the boats had sails on the Shannon if so it would be easy to sail to the war; and, breaking off in the middle of some wonderful war adventure, some tale about his father and his father's soldiers, he would grow interested in the life of the ditch, in the coming and going of the wren, in the chirrup of a bird in the tall larches that grew beyond the paling.

Beyond the paling there was a wood full of mossgrown stones and trees overgrown with ivy, and Ulick thought that if he only dared to get over the paling and face the darkness of the hollow on the other side of the paling, he could run across the meadow and call from the bank to a steersman. The steersman might take him away! But he was afraid his mother might follow him on the next barge, and he dreamed a story of barges drawn by the swiftest horses in Ireland.

But dreams are but a makeshift life. He was very unhappy, and though he knew it was wrong he could not help laying plans for escape. Sometimes he thought that the best plan would be to set fire to the house; for while his mother was carrying pails of water from the backyard, he would run away; but he did not dare to think out his plan of setting fire to the house, lest one of the spirits which dwelt in the hollow beyond the paling should come and drag him down a hole.

One day he forgot to hide himself in the ditch, and the big boy climbed up the bank, and asked him to give him some gooseberries, and though Ulick would have feared to gather gooseberries for himself, he did not like to refuse the boy, and he gave him some, hoping that the big boy would not laugh at him again. And they became friends, and very soon he was friends with them all, and they had many talks clustered in the corner, the children holding on to the palings, and Ulick hiding behind the hollyhocks ready to warn them.

'It's all right, she's gone to the village,' Ulick said. One day the big boy asked him to come with them; they were going to spear eels in the brook, and he was emboldened to get over the fence, and to follow across the meadow, through the hazels, and very soon it seemed to him that they had wandered to the world's end. At last they came to the brook and the big boy turned up his trousers, and Ulick saw him lifting the stones with his left hand and plunging a fork into the water with his right. When he brought up a struggling eel at the end of the fork, Ulick clapped his hands and laughed, and he had never been so happy in his life before.

After a time there were no more stones to raise, and sitting on the bank they began to tell stories. His companions asked him when his father was coming back from the wars, and he told them how his father used to take him for walks up the canal, and how they used to meet a man who had a tame rat in his pocket. Suddenly the boys and girls started up, crying, 'Here's the farmer,' and they ran wildly across the fields. However, they got to the high road long before the farmer could catch them, and his escape enchanted Ulick. Then the children went their different ways, the big boy staying with Ulick, who thought he must offer him some gooseberries. So they crossed the fence together and crouched under the bushes, and ate the gooseberries till they wearied of them. Afterwards they went to look at the bees, and while looking at the insects crawling in and out of their little door, Ulick caught sight of his mother, and she coming towards them. Ulick cried out, but the big boy was caught before he could reach the fence, and Ulick saw that, big as the boy was, he could not save himself from a slapping. He kicked out, and then blubbered, and at last got away. In a moment it would be Ulick's turn, and he feared she would beat him more than she had beaten the boy, for she hated him, whereas she was only vexed with the boy; she would give him bread and water; he had often had a beating and bread and water for a lesser wickedness than the bringing of one of the village boys into the garden to eat gooseberries.

He put up his right hand and saved his right cheek, and then she tried to slap him on the left, but he put up his left hand, and this went on until she grew so angry that Ulick thought he had better allow her to slap him, for if she did not slap him at once she might kill him.

'Down with your hands, sir, down with your hands, sir,' she

cried, but before he had time to let her slap him, she said, 'I will give you enough of bees,' and she caught one that had just rested on a flower and put it down his neck. The bee stung him in the neck where the flesh is softest, and he ran away screaming, unable to rid himself of the bee. He broke through the hedges of sweet pea, and he dashed through the poppies, trampling through the flower beds, until he reached the dry ditch.

There is something frightful in feeling a stinging insect in one's back, and Ulick lay in the dry ditch, rolling among the leaves in anguish. He thought he was stung all over; he heard his mother laughing and she called him a coward through an opening in the bushes, but he knew she could not follow him down the ditch. His neck had already begun to swell, but he forgot the pain of the sting in hatred. He felt he must hate his mother, however wicked it might be to do so. His mother had often slapped him; he had heard of boys being slapped, but no one had ever put a bee down a boy's back before; he felt he must always hate her, and creeping up through the brambles to where he could get a view of the garden, he waited until he saw her walk up the path into the house; and then, stealing back to the bottom of the ditch, he resolved to get over the paling. A few minutes after he heard her calling him, and then he climbed the paling, and he crossed the dreaded hollow, stumbling over the old stones.

As he crossed the meadow he caught sight of a boat coming through the lock, but the lock-keeper knew him by sight, and would tell the bargeman where he came from, and he would be sent home to his mother. He ran on, trying to get ahead of the boat, creeping through hedges, frightened lest he should not be able to find the canal! Now he stopped, sure that he had lost it; his brain seemed to be giving way, and he ran like a mad child up the bank. Oh, what joy! The canal flowed underneath the bank. The horse had just passed, the barge was coming, and Ulick ran down the bank calling to the bargeman. He plunged into the water, getting through the bulrushes. Half of the barge had passed him, and he held out his hands. The ground gave way and he went under the water; green light took the place of day, and when he struggled to the surface he saw the rudder moving. He went under again, and remembered no more until he opened his eyes and saw the bargeman leaning over him.

'Now, what ails you to be throwing yourself into the water in that way?'

Ulick closed his eyes; he had no strength for answering him, and a little while after he heard someone come on board the barge, and he guessed it must be the man who drove the horse. He lay with his eyes closed, hearing the men talking of what they should do with him. He heard a third voice, and guessed it must be a man come up from the cabin. This man said it would be better to take him back to the last lock, and they began to argue about who should carry him. Ulick was terribly frightened, and he was just going to beg of them not to bring him back when he heard one of them say, 'It will be easier to leave him at the next lock.' Soon after, he felt the boat start again, and when Ulick opened his eyes, he saw hedges gliding past, and he hoped the next lock was a long way off.

'Now,' said the steersman, 'since you are awaking out of your faint, you'll be telling us where you come from, because we want to send you home again.'

'Oh,' he said, 'from a long way off, the Shannon.'

'The Shannon!' said the bargeman. 'Why, that is more than seventy miles away. How did you come up here?'

It was a dreadful moment. Ulick knew he must give some good answer or he would find himself in his mother's keeping very soon. But what answer was he to give? It was half accident, half cunning that made him speak of the Shannon. The steersman said again, 'The Shannon is seventy miles away, how did you get up here?' and by this time Ulick was aware that he must make the bargemen believe he had hidden himself on one of the boats coming up from the Shannon, and that he had given the bargeman some money, and then he burst into tears and told them he had been very unhappy at home; and when they asked him why he had been unhappy, he did not answer, but he promised he would not be a naughty boy any more if they would take him back to the Shannon. He would be a good boy and not run away again. His pretty face and speech persuaded the bargemen to bring him back to the Shannon; it was decided to say nothing about him to the lock-keeper, and he was carried down to the cabin. He had often asked his father if he might see the bargeman's cabin; and his father had promised him that the next time they went to the canal he should go on board a barge and see the cabin; but his father had gone away to the wars. Now he was in the bargeman's cabin, and he wondered if they were going to give him supper and if he would be a bargeman himself when he grew up to be a man.

Some miles farther the boat bumped the edge of the bridge, and on the other side of the bridge there was the lock, and he heard the lock gate shut behind the boat and the water pour into the lock; the lock seemed a long time filling, and he was frightened lest the lock-man might come down to the cabin, for there was no place where he could hide. After passing through the lock one of the men came down to see him, and he was taken on deck, and in the calm of the evening Ulick came to look upon the bargemen as his good angels. They gave him some of their supper, and when they arrived at the next lock they made their beds on the deck, the night being so warm. It seemed to Ulick that he had never seen the night before, and he watched the sunset fading streak by streak, and imagined he was the captain of a ship sailing in the Shannon. The stars were so bright that he could not sleep, and it amused him to make up a long story about the bargemen snoring by his side. The story ended with the sunset and then the night was blue all over, and raising himself out of his blanket he watched the moonlight rippling down the canal. Then the night grew grey. He began to feel very cold, and wrapped himself in his blanket tightly, and the world got so white that Ulick grew afraid, and he was not certain whether it would not be better to escape from the boat and run away while everybody slept.

He lay awake maturing his little plan, seeing the greyness pass away and the sky fill up with pink and fleecy clouds.

One of the men roused, and, without saying a word, went to fetch a horse from the stables, and another went to boil the kettle in the cabin, and Ulick asked if he might help him; and while he blew the fire he heard the water running into the lock, and thought what a fool they were making of the lock-keeper, and when the boat was well on its way towards the next lock the steersman called him to come up, and they breakfasted together. Ulick would have wished this life to go on for ever, but the following day the steersman said:

'There is only one lock more between this and our last stopping-place. Keep a lookout for your mother's cottage.'

He promised he would, and he beguiled them all the evening with pretended discoveries. That cabin was his mother's cabin. No, it was farther on, he remembered those willow trees. Ulick's object was to get as far away from his home as possible; to get as near to the Shannon as he could.

'There's not a mile between us and the Shannon now,' said the steersman. 'I believe you've been telling us a lot of lies, my young man.'

Ulick said his mother lived just outside the town, they would see the house when they passed through the last lock, and he planned to escape that night, and about an hour before the dawn he got up, and, glancing at the sleeping men, he stepped ashore and ran until he felt very tired. And when he could go no farther he lay down in the hay in an outhouse.

A woman found him in the hay some hours after, and he told her his story, and as the woman seemed very kind he laid some stress on his mother's cruelty. He mentioned that his mother had put a bee down his neck, and bending down his head he showed her where the bee had stung him. She stroked his pretty curls and looked into his blue eyes, and she said that anyone who could put a bee down a boy's neck must be a she-devil.

She was a lone widow longing for someone to look after, and in a very short time Ulick was as much loved by his chance mother as he had been hated by his real mother.

Three years afterwards she died, and Ulick had to leave the cottage.

He was now a little over thirteen, and knew the ships and their sailors, and he went away in one of the ships that came up the river, and sailed many times round the coast of Ireland, and up all the harbours of Ireland. He led a wild, rough life, and his flight from home was remembered like a tale heard in infancy, until one day, as he was steering his ship up the Shannon, a desire to see what they were doing at home came over him. The ship dropped anchor, and he went to the canal to watch the boats going home. And it was not long before he was asking one of the bargemen if he would take him on board. He knew what the rules were, and he knew they could be broken, and how, and he said if they would take him he would be careful the lockmen did not see him, and the journey began.

The month was July, so the days were as endless and the country was as green and as full of grass as they were when he had come down the canal, and the horse strained along the path, sticking his toes into it just as he had done ten years ago; and when they came to a dangerous place Ulick saw the man who was driving the horse take hold of his tail, just as he had seen him do ten years ago.

'I think those are the rushes, only there are no trees, and the bank doesn't seem so high.' And then he said as the bargeman was going to stop his horse, 'No, I am wrong. It isn't there.'

They went on a few miles farther, and the same thing happened again. At last he said, 'Now I am sure it is there.'

And the bargeman called to the man who was driving the horse and stopped him, and Ulick jumped from the boat to the bank.

'That was a big leap you took,' said a small boy who was standing on the bank. 'It is well you didn't fall in.'

'Why did you say that?' said Ulick, 'is your mother telling you not to go down to the canal?'

'Look at the frog! he's going to jump into the water,' said the little boy. He was the same age as Ulick was when Ulick ran away, and he was dressed in the same little trousers and little boots and socks, and he had a little grey cap. Ulick's hair had grown darker now, but it had been as fair and as curly as this little boy's, and he asked him if his mother forbade him to go down to the canal.

'Are you a bargeman? Do you steer the barge or do you drive the horse?'

'I'll tell you about the barge if you'll tell me about your mother. Does she tell you not to come down to the canal?'

The boy turned away his head and nodded it:

'Does she beat you if she catches you here?'

'Oh, no, mother never beats me.'

'Is she kind to you?'

'Yes, she's very kind, she lives up there, and there's a garden to our cottage, and the name "Hill Cottage" is painted up on the gatepost'

'Now,' said Ulick, 'tell me your name.'

'My name is Ulick.'

'Ulick! And what's your other name?'

'Ulick Burke.'

'Ulick Burke!' said the big Ulick. 'Well, my name is the same. And I used to live at Hill Cottage too.'

The boy did not answer.

'Whom do you live with?'

'I live with mother.'

'And what's her name?'

'Well, Burke is her name,' said the boy.

'But her front name?'

'Catherine.'

'And where's your father?'

'Oh, father's a soldier; he's away.'

'But my father was a soldier too, and I used to live in that cottage.'

'And where have you been ever since?'

'Oh,' he said, 'I've been a sailor. I think I will go in the cottage with you.'

'Yes,' said little Ulick, 'come up and see mother, and you'll tell me where you've been sailing,' and he put his hand into the seafarer's.

And now the seafarer began to lose his reckoning; the compass no longer pointed north. He had been away for ten years, and coming back he had found his own self, the self that had jumped into the water at this place ten years ago. Why had not the little boy done as he had done, and been pulled into the barge and gone away. If this had happened Ulick would have believed he was dreaming or that he was mad. But the little boy was leading him, yes, he remembered the way, there was the cottage, and its paling, and its hollyhocks. And there was his mother coming out of the house, and very little changed.

'Ulick, where have you been? Oh, you naughty boy,' and she caught the little boy up and kissed him. And so engrossed was her attention in her little son that she had not noticed the man he had brought home with him.

'Now who is this?' she said.

'Oh, mother, he jumped from the boat to the bank, and he will tell you, mother, that I was not near the bank.'

'Yes, mother, he was ten yards from the bank; and now tell me, do you think you ever saw me before?....'

She looked at him.

'Oh, it's you! Why we thought you were drowned.'

'I was picked up by a bargeman.'

'Well, come into the house and tell us what you've been doing.'

'I've been seafaring,' he said, taking a chair. 'But what about this Ulick?'

'He's your brother, that's all.'

His mother asked him of what he was thinking, and Ulick told her how greatly astonished he had been to find a little boy exactly like himself, waiting at the same place.

'And father?'

'Your father is away.'

'So,' he said, 'this little boy is my brother. I should like to see father. When is he coming back?'

'Oh,' she said, 'he won't be back for another three years. He enlisted again.'

'Mother,' said Ulick, 'you don't seem very glad to see me.'

'I shall never forget the evening we spent when you threw yourself into the canal. You were a wicked child.'

'And why did you think I was drowned?'

'Well, your cap was picked up in the bulrushes.'

He thought that whatever wickedness he had been guilty of might have been forgiven, and he began to feel that if he had known how his mother would receive him he would not have come home.

'Well, the dinner is nearly ready. You'll stay and have some with us, and we can make you up a bed in the kitchen.'

He could see that his mother wished to welcome him, but her heart was set against him now as it had always been. Her dislike had survived ten years of absence. He had gone away and had met with a mother who loved him, and had done ten years' hard seafaring. He had forgotten his real mother forgotten everything except the bee and the hatred that gathered in her eyes when she put it down his back; and that same ugly look he could now see gathering in her eyes, and it grew deeper every hour he remained in the cottage. His little brother asked him to tell him tales about the sailing ships, and he wanted to go down to the canal with Ulick, but their mother said he was to bide here with her. The day had begun to decline, his brother was crying, and he had to tell him a sea-story to stop his crying. 'But mother hates to hear my voice,' he said to himself, and he went out into the garden when the story was done. It would be better to go away, and he took one turn round the garden and got over the paling at the end of the dry ditch, at the place he had got over it before, and he walked through the old wood, where the trees were overgrown with ivy, and the stones with moss. In this second experience there was neither terror nor mystery only bitterness. It seemed to him a pity that he had ever been taken out of the canal, and he thought how easy it would be to throw himself in again, but only children drown themselves because their mothers do not love them; life had taken a hold upon him, and he stood watching the canal, though not waiting for a boat. But when a boat appeared he called to the man who was driving the horse to stop, for it was the same boat that had brought him from the Shannon.

'Well, was it all right?' the steersman said. 'Did you find the house? How were they at home?'

'They're all right at home,' he said; 'but father is still away. I am going back. Can you take me?'

The evening sky opened calm and benedictive, and the green country flowed on, the boat passed by ruins, castles and churches, and every day was alike until they reached the Shannon.

THE WILD GOOSE

'OUR barbaric ancestors built for posterity. Three thousand years have not changed a single stone, and three thousand years hence this shrine will be the same as it is today. A shrine outlasts its creed,' he added, rising to his feet, and whilst feasting his eyes on the beautiful green country dozing under the sunny sky, he asked himself how it was that he had lived so long out of Ireland unstirred by a single longing for things of long ago. 'In America we think it better to be than to have been. But what is being?' and unable to find an answer to this question, he decided that the readers of his paper would require something more actual than his dreams of the distant peoples that had come to New Grange to worship. And thinking how he might convey his first impressions of his native land in a series of articles, he stopped at every gate to talk with herdsmen; and after every talk he strolled on interested in Ireland's slattern life, touched by the kindness and simplicity of the people. 'The art of verbal expression has been denied to them,' he muttered; 'they tell themselves better in stone;' his thoughts had gone back to New Grange, but they returned quickly from thence to admire an iron gate opening on to a long elm avenue.

'To what manor-house does this long, straight avenue lead?' he asked himself, and followed a rutted track to a stead built out of huge stones, only one degree removed from a Norman keep, so it seemed to him; and it was whilst peeping into the deep areas that would almost serve as a moat were they filled with water that the young man became aware of the presence of somebody above him. An elderly woman had come out of the house in the midst of her cleaning, and was watching him from the top of a high flight of steps.

'I have dropped nothing into your area,' he said apologetically, 'but have lost my heart to your house.'

'You are a stranger in these parts,' she replied, and whilst he confessed himself an American travelling in Ireland, he could see that his braided coat and his wide trousers that fell into folds quite naturally were attracting the housewife's admiration.

139

'I am glad you like my house, and perhaps my rooms would suit if you are looking for rooms.'

'I was not looking for rooms, for I did not expect to find any here; I was admiring the masonry. But if you have rooms to let I'd like to live here for a while.'

'I am not certain the rooms would suit you, but you are welcome to come and look at them.'

As she showed him from room to room the impression she gathered was of a young man of sunny smiles and hair, who talked delightfully about her house, praising the proportions and the height of the rooms, enlarging on the beauty of the eighteenth-century grates, designed, he said, for the burning of turf rather than coal.

'We burn coal,' she answered; 'seaborne coal is cheaper. But if you'd like to burn turf in your room we could get a creel or two in Dublin.'

He would have preferred the creel of turf to come from a bog, but as there didn't seem to be any bogs in this part of the country, he said, he must not be too exacting; he would be content to burn coal; and he listened with excessive politeness to Mrs. Grattan adorning her descriptions of the country with the names of those who had shootings to let on the mountains and the rights of fishing in the rivers.

'Salmon,' she said, 'come up the Liffey.'

'I am sorry; I neither shoot nor fish. I am a writer, or, to speak more exactly, a journalist.'

'An editor?' she asked.

'No; a contributor.' And he began to give his reasons for preferring the valley of the Liffey to the plains of Meath, saying that no landscape was altogether sympathetic to him without a river in it. As he had already said he was not a fisherman, she failed to understand, and she was not less puzzled by the remark that whereas County Meath was all meat, County Dublin was all milk. His reluctance to go to Dublin to fetch his trunk and his proposal to pay her a month in advance would have been easier to understand if he had offered her a cheque; but his pocket-book was full of notes, and he handed her one and said he would like to dine and sleep that night at Fir House.

'It will be time enough tomorrow to go to Dublin for my trunk.'

'But I have nothing in the house, sir, except a mutton chop.'

'Could you have anything better?' he answered.

'Do you eat cheese, Mrs. Grattan?' he asked, when she brought in the mutton chop.

'Not very often, sir; we are not great cheese eaters in Ireland.'

'Not of late years, I believe, but in the old stories cheese is often mentioned. You are the herdsmen of modern times. Your fairs—'

'If you are writing about the country, sir, you should go to see one of our fairs. The fair at Corrie is one of the biggest about here.'

'When is it?'

'Next week, sir.'

And at six o'clock next Monday morning he was making his way to Corrie convinced that it was a mistake to interfere with the genius of the Irish people. 'Which is herding cattle today as it was when Finn McColl drank the drugged wine at Tara. But we Americans are so superficial. We would set up industries in this pretty, pastoral country; we would teach them smelting, an art which they would have invented for themselves had it been in their nature; whereas—'

He stopped to admire, for though he was still some distance from the village the fair had already begun, buyers having advanced far out into the country so as to anticipate rivals. 'The finest herdsmen and the finest horsemen,' he muttered to himself when a gate was held across the road, and a boy rode a horse barebacked over it with a rope in his jaws for a bridle. 'What they like is a horse in their own pronunciation a harse and a bad rider is as rare in Ireland as a bad cook is in France.' The jumping of the gate was acclaimed by a great clapping of hands, which suddenly ceased.

'The Angelus, sir,' a peasant said.

As soon as the prayer was over everybody bought a pipe from an old woman sitting behind a cocklestall, and the two incidents the prayer to the Virgin in heaven and the buying of a pipe from the old woman on earth seemed to Ned Carmady to have come out of the same impulse as he pursued his way through the filth of the main street. There were but two streets in Corrie, the main street and another street, and up and down the Y-shaped village herdsmen shouted and whacked their beasts, forcing them backwards till their tails hung over the half-doors of the houses, or forcing them forwards till their noses pressed against the windows; and not knowing whither to go, bullock strove against bullock, getting up on each other's backs. To avoid the passing hooves, dogs and cats had been gathered into the houses, but a Buff Orpington, and a very nice chicken, too, not happening to escape in time, was trodden on, and thinking no one was watching him, a man picked up the bird and hid it within the lining of his coat. He started shouting immediately afterwards, and up went his stick and down it came on a white steer.

'One gets a chicken and the other a blow,' said Ned; 'such is the way of the world. But who are they?' he asked.

Three boon companions evidently they were, three well-known characters he judged them to be; and applying to a passer-by for information, he learnt that the giant was Michael Moran. And his eyes followed a great bulk, twenty stone in weight and six feet in height, accoutred in tarpaulins; for though the sun shone frequently, the showers were heavy. Ned reckoned the giant's boots to be several pounds in weight; the tarpaulin hat was like a small haycock; and he liked the great round funny face under it, the mouth turning up like a new moon. As if aware of the admiration he excited, Michael Moran walked talking and laughing between his disciples, the biggest stick in the fair in the hand of little Patsy Flynn, a face as curious as a ferret's, with bunches of red whiskers.

'And for sartin, the best joke in Connaught at the end of his tongue at this moment!'

'And who did you say the third man was?'

'Is it Jimmy Welsh you are asking the podgeen at the other side of Michael?'

'I didn't see him rightly,' Ned answered. 'But who is Michael?'

'So you never heard of Michael?'

'I'm a stranger in these parts home from America on a holiday.'

'Well, then, when you go back you'll be able to be telling them of Michael, the biggest pigjobber in Connaught, he that buys pigs on one side of the county and sells on the other, making a fine profit! Now, as they'll be wanting to hear of Patsy Flynn and Jimmy Welsh, I'll tell you a story—'

At that moment Ned's attention was drawn to a woman, tall and strong as a man, dressed in thick skirts, and wearing great boots like a drover. She went about brandishing a stick, cursing all those who laughed at her cow, a poor skeleton beast, which she had been driving unmercifully up and down the fair since eight in the morning. The tired beast hardly responded to her stick, and everybody was laughing. The cattle-dealers and herdsmen gathered round her, teasing her with threepenny bits. 'The value of the hide,' they said; and the success of the fair was when a man asked the woman if she would share a bet with him. He would bet any gentleman present half a crown that he could read a newspaper through the cow. Would any gentleman oblige him with the loan of a newspaper? A friend pulled one from his pocket, and the woman struck at her tormentors and chased them round the cow, her invective so vehement and so picturesque that Ned could not help wondering. 'As well as the gift of herding, they possess the gift of blasphemy,' he said; and he began to wonder at the patience with which the sellers waited for the buyers, keeping their animals back with raised sticks and shouts when they showed any tendency to stray. But it did not seem to him that much business was being done; he caught sight of the same animals in the same places as he passed up and down, and it was a relief to see a herd of bullocks driven under an archway. 'These have undoubtedly changed hands;' and he admired the obstinacy of a red steer that would not enter the yard. 'The animal possibly suspects he is required for beefsteaks.' Soon after he came upon a dozen fat sheep, with two men, butchers, no doubt, feeling for their ribs through the fleece. 'The sheep are less suspicious,' he said, and wandered on in search of new material for an article, coming at the end of the town upon two men in a tilt-cart vaunting the merits of old clothes.

'Down with the landlords!' cried one, catching sight of Ned, who, feeling he could give back an answer as well as another man, said:

'Now, where would you be buying your old clothes if there were no landlords? Many's the fine jacket you've got from them; maybe you'd like to have a look into my wardrobe.'

The man looked at him for a moment.

'I guess you've left most of it over yonder,' said he, for Ned's accent had betrayed him. 'We don't deal in American cloth!'

A shout of laughter went up, and feeling he had been outmatched Ned did not stop again till he came upon some pig-jobbers, dexterous in lifting the pigs into the creels by their hind-legs and their tails, so that they hadn't time to squeal.

'He do be wanting a sup of water, but I can't leave the sheep,' said a herdsman, speaking of his dog.

'Then I'll be going and getting him one.'

The jobber looked at Ned in surprise.

'You'll be wanting a drink yourself?'

'Yes,' he answered. 'A drink!' he cried; 'anything! Lemon squash, ginger beer, lemonade!'

'We have no call for them drinks.'

'Then porter and quickly! Or spirit John Jameson seven-year old.'

'We have none.'

'Porter.'

'Will you have it here, or shall I bring it into the taproom?'

A seat in the cool taproom appealed to him, for he had been on his legs since early morning; but such a reek met him on the threshold that he could not pass it.

'A fine warm smell, sir,' was the remark of a drover in Ned's ear.

'I can't stand it,' Ned said, and went out, his eye alighting on some forty or fifty calves penned in a corner, with a small patch of hair clipped from the left shoulder of every one of them.

'The mark of the butchers that have bought them, a couple of Frenchmen who have gone back to Dublin to get their notes changed. It's for them that the fellows in the taproom do be waiting, drinking the money they have had in advance for the calves, and it's them that can afford to get drunk this morning should they feel disposed, considering the price they got for their bastes three pounds ten up to four pounds apiece. A few gallons of porter divided up between them won't be felt.'

'Not until the morning,' Ned interjected.

'Them fellows have heads on them as hard as the rocks on the hills, and a fine price them French butchers will make on the calves for finer I've never laid eyes on if they follows my advice, which is not to wather the bastes; even if they do be losing four or five, they'll be gainers in the end.'

'So while the calves are dying of thirst, those that reared them will be drinking!'

'Or retching! For as many as fifteen gallons they've drunk between them, and I doubt if there will be one sober enough among them to count the Frenchmen's money.'

'Do you know who that man is the one that's just gone by he that's wearing the straw hat you don't?'

'Well, that's Mr. Cronin, one of the biggest dairymen in the County of Dublin, milking more than sixty cows, and with the benefit of spring water at his very door to help him through the winter. You can't but know his house if you come from Tallagh, about a mile down the road, straight as you can go from Mrs. Grattan's. And if you don't know the house itself, you've heard tell of his daughter Ellen?'

'I have heard Mrs. Grattan speak of a girl with red hair.'

'That's her,' said the drover. And as their roads were not the same, Ned bade the owner and the flock good-bye, and walked on immersed in thoughts of the affability of the Celt. But he had not gone very far when the sound of wheels awoke him from his reveries.

'If you'd like a lift it's no trouble at all, for don't I be passing Mrs. Grattan's gate?'

'Well, thank you,' he answered, and settled himself by the side of Mr. Cronin, a plump, elderly man, with a long white nose and a small, insignificant chin. As soon as Cronin shifted his hat Ned saw that he was bald, and he began to wonder if the fringe of white hair had ever been red hair. 'Children generally inherit their parents' complexion,' he said to himself; and he piled Cronin with questions, hoping he would turn his head, for a profile presents a very incomplete likeness. But Cronin's head remained fixed; and Ned began to hope that Ellen did not inherit Cronin's gift of silence.

Long, level silences, gapped here and there with a word or two, represent the conversation that was meted out to him during the ten miles' drive. Yet he had left no subject untouched; the cattle were good but pigs were better in America; the American pig, he dared to suggest, fattened quicker than the Irish. Even that pregnant remark did not succeed in drawing many words from Cronin, and he began to wonder why Cronin had pulled the horse up beside him; not for the pleasure of his conversation, for certain, but there must be a reason.

'Mrs. Grattan often speaks of your daughter.'

'Yes; they are very friendly.'

He expected the conversation to drop at this point, but to his surprise Cronin added, 'And my daughter told me if I was to meet you at the fair, not to pass you on the road without offering you a lift.'

'It was very kind of her.'

Half an hour later Cronin said: 'We're about halfway now,' and the gig rolled on, Ned wondering what sort of a daughter this silent man could have begotten. As he was about to pull up his horse at Mrs. Grattan's gate, Mr. Cronin said: 'There she is up the road in front of us.' It seemed to Ned that it was no more than the merest politeness to ask Mr. Cronin to introduce him to his daughter, but Cronin made no reply; and while Ned was wondering if he should repeat his request, thinking perhaps that Cronin had not heard him, the gig rolled past Mrs. Grattan's door, and he said to himself: 'He is going to introduce me after all. But what a queer man!' And he would have bent his mind still more closely to the study of Cronin if Ellen's back had not engaged his attention at the moment.

'A little woman,' he said to himself; and when the gig stopped, before the first words were spoken, he was deep in admiration of the slight, shapely figure, with a pointed face, and the head crowned with rich red hair gathered up in combs behind the pretty ears. But it was her eyes that fascinated Ned at the time and ever afterwards; long after he had bidden her good-bye for ever he saw her turquoise eyes looking at him through a blue veil.

'So you did what I told you, father. That was good of you.' Then turning to Ned, she said: 'I was afraid father would forget. Mrs. Grattan told me you were going to the fair, and I knew that coming back you would find the way long. Father,' she said, 'you can go on. Mr. Carmady will walk a little way with me.'

Ned had already begun to think of her as a delightful little person, and the wheels of the gig had not gone round many times when she burst into talk like a bird into song.

'I heard from Mrs. Grattan that you are an American, and that you have come here to write about Ireland; and that was why I wished to make your acquaintance. It seemed to me a pity that you should put anything into your book that would prejudice the people in America against the people at home.'

'But I don't intend to write anything that isn't true a book of impressions and memories, that—'

'But, Mr. Carmady, from lack of knowledge you may write things that you would regret afterwards.'

'The judgment of a stranger is always superficial,' he answered thoughtfully, and his acquiescence in the wisdom of her words threw her off her guard and she did not bid him good-bye at the turn of the road as she had intended, and he, seemingly forgetful of everything but her, continued by her side till they came to the gate opening on to the long drive leading to Brookfield through wide pastures where cattle wandered or rested under trees. He pushed open the gate for her, and with a courtesy that was so inveigling that she forgot to dismiss him, and they continued up the dusty drive, Ellen explaining hurriedly that the new Ireland was an Ireland that for centuries had sought refuge underground like a river, but was coming up again.

'We believe that we are sufficient in ourselves; our mistake was that instead of cultivating what was in us we looked to the stranger.'

According to Ellen, Ireland contained everything the race would want for many hundreds of years, not only food and wood and stone, but an art and a literature of her own in the Gaelic. Ned listened at once amused and interested. 'One of the ancient Druidesses,' he said to himself, 'born out of due time.'

And to draw her on still further, he ventured to remind her of the disunion that had always existed. 'A quarter is in Rome, a quarter in England, a quarter in America; and it is out of the remnant of the people at home you would build a nation.'

'You have a great deal to learn,' she said, as Ned opened the second gate for her to pass through. She held out her hand, but he

begged to be allowed to detain her, for he wished to admire with her
the avenue of old yews that led from the second gate to the house,
which he discerned, one corner of it, through the intervening trees.

'Our yew avenue is often admired, and it is not at all strange that
it should attract your eyes. You have no old trees in America except
those that grow in the forests?'

Ned answered that he knew only the American cities, and asked
her if she had travelled much in Ireland, and she told him that of
Ireland she knew only County Dublin and the adjacent counties.

'My mother was a Wicklow woman.'

'As you are not like your father, I suppose you are like your
mother?'

'I am supposed to be very like her. Her portrait is in the dining-
room. You'll see it when you come to visit us. But I have not
mentioned that my father will be very glad if you will come to
supper on Sunday evening.... if you are free.'

'I am free from everything except Mrs. Grattan's mutton chop,
and perhaps she will be able to cozen the chop to wait till Monday
for me.'

Ellen did not know if she should laugh, and wished he would not
put her to the end of her wits to understand him. 'Then we may
expect you to supper on Sunday evening.'

II

'A week divides us,' he said, as he picked his way down the dirty
drive, and a week later, as he returned to his lodging after supper at
Brookfield, he added: 'Dirty as a byre. And all these gates what
purpose do they serve?' he asked, as he opened the second and
kicked up a bullock lying in the roadway. He disturbed several more
from their slumbers, but after the third gate he was on the high road
and his thoughts returned naturally to the evening he had spent with
the Cronins. 'Yes, she gets her prettiness from her mother the same
small, pointed face, the high forehead, the red hair, the same intense
eyes.' 'You are very like your mother,' he had said when she
showed him the portrait, 'and now and again, Mr. Cronin, I catch a
flitting likeness of you in your daughter.' And he repeated the
farmer's words as he walked up the road, 'We are very different, she
being all for an heroic Ireland and I for dairy produce.' He had
laughed, but neither Cronin nor Ellen had joined in the laughter, and
he began to wonder if the farmer were quite serious in his
description of himself and his daughter.

'She didn't understand my joke about the mutton chop, but a sense of humour is not as necessary as many people think for, and we shall be better friends without it. An excellent substitute for humour is excellent fare, and there is no fault to be found with the fare at Brookfield.'

The juicy and savoury leg of mutton that he had eaten, with onion sauce and baked potatoes, reminded him of Mrs Grattan's frugal larder, and he remembered that to save herself trouble she cooked on Sundays and on Thursdays, and that for the rest of the week the joints came up in various forms, hash, mince, or shepherd's pie. Brookfield had come to save him at least once a week from Mrs. Grattan's meals. Cronin had asked him to come next Sunday for billiards, which meant dinner; he would have preferred the invitation for a day between Thursday and Sunday, or one between Monday and Thursday, and if an invitation came for one of those off-days he would not refuse it. All the same, he must not wear out his welcome, and he was almost glad he had much writing to do this next week, and when the hoped-for invitation came he wrote of his 'daily chores,' meaning his articles. But after posting his letter he foresaw certain blank spaces ahead of him, and yielded to the temptation to call at Brookfield without however intending to remain for dinner, but Cronin's face showed his sadness at the thought of losing his billiards and Ellen pouted so angrily that he stayed, vowing to himself that he would not yield again to temptation; and this vow he kept fairly well for the next two or three weeks. All the same when he ventured on a count at the end of the month he found that Mrs. Grattan's lodger had dined at Brookfield eight times, and that there was every prospect of his dining still oftener during the month to come.

'Even so,' he said to himself, 'what matter, since there is no chance of my wearing out my welcome? We suit each other; I am helpful to them and they to me. I shall learn all I want to know about dairy produce from the farmer, and Ellen will tell me all I want to know about Cuchulain and Deirdre.'

On these words he fell to thinking of the pleasant evening that awaited him at Brookfield, so much pleasanter than an evening by himself at Mrs. Grattan's. 'A game of billiards is as welcome to me as to Cronin, so once more I will yield to temptation, for if I don't, what excuse can I give for not yielding? Later on there'll be the autumn rains; I shall have to sit at home.' And convinced that nothing is pleasanter than to yield to temptation, he walked with alert step down the stretch of road between Mrs. Grattan's and

Brookfield, wondering if the guest of the evening would be a leg of mutton or a round of beef, or a pair of chickens. Soup was often absent. 'The Cronins do not eat soup,' he said, 'but they are addicted to apple pies, custards, and treacle pudding.' A memory started up of Mr. Cronin, who last week, whilst carving the chickens, had remarked suddenly that there had been no proper housekeeping at Brookfield since the death of his poor wife, a remark that had caused Ellen to flare up like a little bonfire: 'I don't think you have anything to grumble at, father.' And whilst walking, almost lost in admiration of the August evening, Ned strove to discover a reason for Cronin's remark, but could find none, for both chickens had had handsome breasts; and a very unpleasant quarrel might have arisen between father and daughter if he had not kept his eyes fixed upon Ellen. At the second gate he attributed her silence to a desire to please him and to save the pleasure of the evening.

As he passed through the gate he remembered a passage of arms between father and daughter about another helping of treacle pudding. Ellen had refused the small piece that remained on the dish more than once, but Cronin continued to press her, till at last, yielding to pressure, she accepted the pudding, leaving some of it upon her plate with the words, 'I wish I hadn't taken that second helping.' 'I wish you hadn't, too,' her father answered, 'for I could have done very well with it myself.'

And smiling he passed on through the gate, stopping to admire the avenue of yews and the pretty Georgian house, pillars and portico. 'A manor-house in the eighteenth century,' he said, 'fallen into the hands of the middle classes in the nineteenth; and very happily fallen, too,' he added, for the quiet, regular life of Brookfield appealed to him. There's something in tradition and habits that appeals to the wanderer, and Ned Carmady remembered with pleasure that every evening was the same evening at Brookfield. On rising from the table Cronin never failed to say, 'Well, Ned, are you ready for a game of billiards?' Ned always answered, 'Yes, sir,' and before the third game was over Ellen came in from her garden.

One evening towards the second month of their acquaintanceship she came in looking a little tired, complaining that the garden boy had gone home and that she had had to fill the cans and carry them herself. As Cronin did not reply, she added, 'You keep Ned all the evening, father, playing billiards.'

'You'll have a cigar, Ned?'

Ned took one, and then Ellen, feeling that she had not had her share of Ned for many evenings and that she must assert herself this evening and draw him away from her father (she could not bear another evening of talk about butter and eggs, dairy produce, nor did she wish to speak about the Irish language), said, 'You have told us many things about America and about the people you have met there, but never what made you leave Ireland.'

'I went to England with my father and mother when I was nine, and we settled in Manchester. But the memory of your green country—'

'Don't say "your green country"; say "our green country."'

'Well, the memory of our green country never left me, and I think it was the memory of the green plains of Meath that begot in me such a hatred of brick chimneys and their smoke cloud that when I was sixteen I felt I couldn't live another day in Manchester and joined a travelling circus on its way to the Continent, and might never have set foot in America if the lion hadn't died on me, as you say here. My job was to keep the ventilating slides open, but we met with a storm and I couldn't get about, and when we arrived at Dieppe the finest lion was dead.'

'So the lion died from your seasickness, Mr. Carmady?' the only joke Cronin was ever known to make; and it being his only joke it amused him month after month, year after year, as long as Ned knew him. 'Now, I'd like to hear what happened to you after the death of the lion.'

'They gave me the sack, of course.'

'And what did you say to that, Ned?'

'I took up my hat and said, "There's other things to do in life besides looking after lions," and walked out into the streets of Havre to look for a bedroom. On the floor under me was the proprietor of a cafe chantant, and he came up one day to tell me that I kept him awake at night playing the fiddle, that he fell asleep from sheer weariness, and when he awoke I was still playing. He knew a little English, so we got on together, and he said, "You play the fiddle very well. Why not play it for money in my cafe chantant instead of playing it for nothing here and keeping me awake?" I agreed that it would be wiser, and when I had saved enough money the big liners going to New York tempted me, and I played my fiddle all the way across, and so well that a woman said there was no reason why I shouldn't play in the Opera House. She gave me a letter of introduction to the manager, who, after listening to me for a few minutes, shook his head. "No," he said, "I cannot have you in my orchestra." So I walked out, my fiddle under my arm.'

'And what did you do then?' Cronin asked. 'Weren't you afraid of finding yourself stranded in a great city like New York?'

'There wasn't much time to think about being stranded, for as I stood jingling my pence on the steps of the Opera House I saw a man go by who had come over with me. He asked me if I had been engaged to play in the orchestra and I said I hadn't, and after five minutes' talk he asked me if I could draw a map according to scale; and as I didn't know if I could or couldn't, I thought it better to say I could. I had drawn maps at school in Manchester. The map he wanted was of a certain mining district, and having nothing better to do when I had finished the map, it occurred to me to go and see the mine. In the mornings I did some mining, and in the evenings I played the fiddle. I wrote articles for a mining journal and wandered and wrote and wandered again. In New York I signed an agreement to edit a paper, but it was tiresome expressing always the same opinions, and as the newspaper couldn't change its opinions I volunteered to go to Cuba and write about the insurgents. My articles were inflammatory, of course; they couldn't be else, being an Irishman. And as soon as America declared war against the Spaniards I enlisted, and might have become a general if the war had lasted long enough.'

'Now I am beginning to perceive the Irishman in you,' said Ellen.

'But the war ended, and remembering the green plains of Meath I said, "I will go to Ireland!"'

'I am afraid, Ned, you're a rolling stone. One day you rolled into Ireland, and the day will come when you will roll out of it.'

'No, father; he is going to stay in Ireland. Ireland wants a new leader, and the leader must come from the outside.'

Cronin did not answer his daughter, and a little later he tried to draw Ned into telling stories of his adventures in Cuba; and to please the old man Ned told how one night he and his squad of soldiers had crossed a mountain by a bridle-path leading to a ledge at the top of the mountain a ledge four feet high, over which they had to leap their horses one by one. 'And the clatter was so great that we were afraid the insurgents would hear us. If they had, they would have shot us all.'

'And if that had happened, father, you would have missed many games of billiards!'

'I would, faith,' said Cronin, and fearing perhaps that his daughter would turn the talk on to contemporary politics, he rose out of his armchair saying, 'I'd like to shut up the house.'

'Does he wish me to go?' Ned asked Ellen.

'No. You can stay as long as you like. Father,' she cried after him, 'I am going to walk with Ned to the end of the drive.'

Cronin did not answer.

'He is in a bad humour tonight. I wonder what is the matter with him.'

'Perhaps he does not like me to walk—'

'Doesn't like you to walk with me in the garden? Father isn't as foolish as that!'

And they walked out into the grey moonlight and listened to a corncrake in the meadows a doleful bird it seemed to Ned in the dusky night, with a round moon hanging above a line of distant trees. On his way home he could just distinguish the sluggish roll of the Dublin mountains, dim and grey, and he asked himself if he would like to live in this queer, empty country, accepting its destiny as part of his destiny, the last remnant of barbarous Europe petering out, notwithstanding all Ellen might say to the contrary.

He knew that Cronin would never trouble to ask him what his intentions were regarding Ellen, but it was becoming quite clear to him that he would have to do something: he would have to ask Ellen to marry him, or he would have to bend over and kiss her on the neck without saying anything, and if she accepted his kisses it would be with a view to matrimony, no doubt. He imagined himself kissing her, and when she turned astonished, his face would remain grave, hieratic, as the priest's after he kisses the altar and turns to the congregation. He smiled at his own absurdity, but his smile died away quickly, for in his sudden inspiration he had discovered himself to be without enough will to run away from Ellen's red hair and her turquoise eyes. If he went to Brookfield he would kiss her, and if he kissed her she would expect a proposal of marriage.

His mood veered like a gale all the next day, and when the clock struck four he put on his hat and walked down the road and stopped, surprised, on finding himself at her door.

'Miss Ellen isn't in the house, sir. You'll find her fishing in the garden.' It was more agreeable to Ned to find her in the garden than in the drawingroom, for the garden at Brookfield had always interested him. He had never seen so large a garden or such high walls old red brick walls, and a view of the Dublin mountains, whose purple wastes contrasted with Ellen's rosery and carnations just coming into bloom. And he had found her so often in the garden that he had come to associate her with it; and he liked to remember that five years ago it was a turnip field which her father had yielded to her. Her garden was entirely of her own making, the walls excepted. The fruit trees had been planted by her, and she had designed the walks that followed the walls, and the walk down the middle leading to the mound where the walls branched to the right and left. Green painted posts had been set in a circle, and she had trailed roses from one to the other; lying farther back came a large plot of grass on which they sometimes played tennis. The romance of the garden was, however, its stream, which entered at the right-hand corner and followed the wall, flowing away at the opposite corner; but a tributary turned at right angles and flowed halfway down the garden, disappearing mysteriously underground somewhere about the middle. The banks of this stream were overgrown with many kinds of shrubs, wild thorn, ash saplings, willow weed and meadowsweet, and every kind of briar grew there in profusion; and when some five feet of mud were taken out, trout thrived in the ancient piscine, for Brookfield had once been a monastery.

She was dressed in a striped muslin, variegated with pink flowers, and when she leaned forward, pursuing a trout against the bank with her fishing net, he admired the turn of her figure.

'There's a great big trout,' she said, 'but he's very cunning; he dives and gets under the net. Come and help me to catch him.'

'But how am I to help you to catch him?'

'By going to the gardener and asking him to give you a net.'

'How stupid of me not to have thought of it!' And when he came back with a net, she asked him which side of the stream he would take.

'I'll leave you the side next the wall; it's freer from briars,' he answered.

Not only were there briars to avoid on his side, but roots of trees protruding from the bank, and once he very nearly fell, only saving himself at the last moment. His task was very difficult, but he applied himself to the hunting of the fish up and down the stream, but the fish knew how to escape the nets and dived at the right moment again and again; and so many were the hiding-places in which he could rest that Ned said at the end of the first half-hour: 'I'm afraid we shall never get him.'

Ellen was more persevering. 'Let's try once more.' And they drove slowly up against the bank, Ellen fearing every moment he would jump the net.

'We've got him at last!' said Ned. And when he was laid with the others on the bank, Ellen touched him with her parasol. 'Would he live if we were to put him back again?'

'Put him back after all the trouble we've had to get him out?'

And whilst discussing how inferior the flesh of trout come out of a muddy bottom is to that of trout come out of a pebbly brook, they were conscious of the stillness and the loneliness of the garden under a grey, lustreless sky hanging above the walls. True, there was the gardener, but he was too far away for them to hear his spade, and only if they listened intently could they hear the gurgle of the stream. Now and then a swallow shrieked as it flew past.

'Do you know, Ellen, I shall always remember you by your eyes. You wore a blue veil the day your father brought me home from the fair.'

She had hesitated between a blue and a brown veil, but could not remember what had decided her in favour of the blue. The conversation dropped from time to time, and they both waited nervously for a decisive word.

'I shall always remember you by your eyes.'

'Do you think that you'll never forget my eyes?'

'Not if you allow me to kiss them.' He drew her towards him.

'No, you mustn't,' she said, as she turned her face from his; and then suddenly: 'Are you a Catholic? You see, Ned, I am. If I weren't I'm afraid I'd be very wicked.'

'And what would you do if you weren't a Catholic? Pick pockets?'

'No, I didn't mean that.'

And then Ned told her of her sensuousness and how he had observed it in her eyes, in her manner of approaching him. But she denied the truth of this description of herself.

'Why should you resent it? Nothing is more delightful in a woman or in a man.'

'Oh, Ned, don't talk like that! I don't like to hear you say these things. No one has ever kissed me, and I'm glad of it.'

'How is that? Were you never tempted?'

'Aren't you glad, Ned, that I've never kissed anybody? But you have kissed many women, I suppose.'

'A few. But I never wished to kiss anybody as much as I wish to kiss you.'

'We have only known each other a month. Perhaps you think me very foolish.'

'I am thinking of the great good fortune that brought me to Ireland, to the beautiful green country that I could never forget.'

'I don't think I should have cared for you, Ned, if you hadn't loved Ireland.'

'It was our love of Ireland that brought us together, interested us in each other, and I have learnt to love you much better than I did though I loved you the first time I saw you since I began to learn Irish....with you.'

'But, Ned, you have made very little progress.'

'Now that I know you like me I'll make more.'

'You promise me?.... But you mustn't put your hand on my knee.'

'But the temptation—'

'Well, then, let us get up.'

'No, let us remain. Why should we leave this green bank?' And he pressed her down and then drew her towards him. It's so pleasant to be sitting near you in this garden.'

'Yes, Ned, it would be pleasant to sit here with you if you didn't make love to me I don't like it.'

'Ellen, if we were going to be married would you let me kiss you? But I cannot kiss you here. The gardener is moving about those Jerusalem artichokes. Let us go into the arbour.'

Ellen did not answer, and all the way down the path she wondered if she would follow him into the arbour or refuse to do so at the last moment.

'Ned, are you sure that you love me?' she asked, stopping at the entrance, overcome by a sense of sudden delight.

'Yes, I am quite sure.'

'Then I'll let you kiss me.'

And the moment he put his arm about her waist she fell back upon his shoulder, and when their lips met she closed her eyes.

'Ned, you mustn't kiss me like that,' she cried, struggling from him. 'Let me go!' And then catching sight of Ned's disappointed face, she added, 'It will be different when we are married.'

'But it's so pleasant in this arbour—'

'No, Ned, not again!'

Awed by her determination, he refrained, feeling that if he were going to marry her he would gain more by obedience to her wishes than he would by contravening them.

'Ned, do you love me well enough to marry me?'

'Should I want to kiss you, Ellen, if I didn't?'

'Ned, I am not a fool, and I love you. You will not make me regret?'

'I have never done anybody any harm in my life, and shall not begin by doing you harm.'

'Not willingly, Ned no, not willingly. But we are so different. A month ago we didn't know each other, and now you mean so much to me. Isn't it strange?'

'But what will your father say?'

'Father will say nothing. You know he won't, Ned. He likes you as much as I do.'

'And he likes trout for his supper! We have forgotten the fish, Ellen. I'll run back for them.'

III

'Mrs Grattan, I have got some news. I am going to marry Miss Cronin.... But you don't look surprised.'

'Well, no, sir. You see, you and she have been about a great deal together, and there was no reason only there'll be many a sore heart for many a day, for all the young men in these parts were looking after Miss Ellen, her fine fortune, and her pretty red hair.'

'Yes, it's of her red hair I am thinking.'

And then they talked of Mr. Cronin, who would not withhold his consent, but would give Ellen as many thousand pounds as she asked of him, for she had always led him by the nose.

'But, Mrs. Grattan, do you think she will lead me by the nose?'

'Well, I wouldn't be saying that, sir but there is no knowing. She has always had her way with everybody she met. But you'll be wanting your tea.... There's somebody at the door. You'll excuse me; I must go to it.'

And she came back saying it was Miss Ellen; and for friendliness they all had tea in the kitchen.

'So you have heard the news, Mrs. Grattan? Ned has told you and aren't you surprised?'

'Well, no, then, I'm not. It always seemed to me from the first that you two were suited to each other.'

'You'll never tell me again, Ellen, that we're very different, will you?' Ned interrupted.

'If Mrs. Grattan can't tell me the truth about you, she can tell you the truth about me, for she knew me when I was a little girl.... Father says you are to come back to supper. You must come back, Ned, for we shall have one of the trout for supper.'

'And it would be unlucky if I didn't share with you the trout we caught together.'

As they walked down the road Ellen said, 'As our love began in Ireland we might go for a tour round Ireland when we're married and see the places that Ireland loves best.'

He had seen Tara, but there was no reason why he shouldn't see it again; and he would like to see it in company with Ellen, and point out to her the Rath of the Hostages and the Rath of Grania, and from Tara they would go to the Druid altars.

'And we'll creep into them together through the Druid stones.'

The Abbey of Clonmacnoise was not very far away, and from Clonmacnoise they would go to Cashel to see Cormac's Chapel. There was St. Kevin's bed at Glendalough to be seen, but Killarney they would avoid on account of the views. The Aran islands tempted them, for there was Gaelic Ireland. Along the shores of the Irish lakes there were ruins of chieftains' castles and of monasteries, and on the lake islands ruins of hermits' cells and beehive huts; and after their marriage they went forth to spend the autumn dreaming amid crumbling stones of a past that would never be again, nor anything like it, unless, as Ellen said, the ancient language of the Gael should revive and bring back to Ireland other tales of heroism and chivalry.

'It is all vision and dream,' Ned said, 'but none the worse for that. The world has a course to pursue and we have to follow the world, but not too closely.' And henceforth he yielded himself more and more to Ellen's enthusiasm, for she was his world, and it amused him to think that his father-in-law had liked him better before he began to learn the Irish language and joined the new political movement which, in Ellen's opinion, was going to regenerate Ireland.

'But I remember, father, when you used to sit up till twelve o'clock talking of Parnell.'

Cronin growled a little and lay still farther back in his armchair, crossing his legs and shaking his foot from time to time, but speaking no more till Ellen went upstairs. As soon as she was gone he grew more communicative, venturing to remark that it was difficult to understand what her idea was in wishing to furnish another house on the other side of Dublin when she had this one to live in. Ned was of the same opinion as Cronin, and admitted to the old fellow that he would much rather stop at Brookfield than live in a small house on the other side of Dublin.

'Where there won't be a billiard room.'

Ned kept his countenance, though he was tempted to smile, for he knew that Cronin was thinking he would have to fall back upon the parson for his evening billiards, and the parson's playing had never been to his liking; he always moved his ball. As soon as the conversation turned on the new politics, in his brief, silent way Cronin tried to dissuade Ned against them. But Ned was taken with the desire of political leadership, and whilst the old man talked he remembered that Ellen had told him the people were weary of the older school of politics, and that what was wanted was a young man the people knew nothing about, one who was not hampered with a past. And convinced that he was the very man Ireland needed, he leaned forward and listened deferentially, answering, 'Quite true, sir; I had not thought of that.' All the same, he did not succeed in deceiving the old man. 'I have invested,' he said, 'five thousand pounds in foreign securities in Ellen's name; you are free to advocate whatever policy you may judge best for old Ireland.' And Ned, taken aback by the old man's prescience, asked Cronin if he thought that Ellen would lead him by the nose. Cronin did not answer, and Ned's thoughts returning to Ellen's wish to live on the other side of Dublin in a modern villa, he confessed his preference for Tallagh and the old seventeenth-century stead, and, of all, for the four-poster that Cronin had slept in for the last thirty years without troubling to consider the beauty of the carved cornice.

'My father slept in the bed before me, and I have always found it a good, comfortable bed.'

'We have no tradition in America, and we come over here tempted by the charm of tradition. Your wife, sir, wore a nightcap?'

Cronin continued to pull at his pipe, and Ned continued, 'Ellen is like her mother, and would look very dainty in one of those frilled caps of the 'sixties. But did men wear nightcaps?'

'I never did,' Cronin answered.

'Peg-tops are more comfortable than the tight trousers we wear nowadays.'

'For going about a farm I have found there is nothing to beat a pair of breeches.'

Ned began to wonder what Cronin would look like in a pair of trousers, and whilst he whistled very softly a waltz played in the 'sixties, the door opened. 'There is Ellen come back, and with something on her mind,' he said.

'I have been thinking it over, father, and quite understand that you would like us to remain with you at Tallagh, and we would remain if it weren't that your politics have always been Unionist. All the same, we don't mean to desert you.'

'But the last train is at ten, so there will be no time for a game of billiards after dinner.'

'Father, you are thinking only of your billiards, but I'm thinking of Ned's political career.'

'You would do well, Ellen, to allow Ned to think for himself.'

'But Ned has often said that I am in touch with contemporary politics.'

Mr. Cronin did not answer, and it amused Ned to watch father and daughter. 'Heads for Kingstown, tails for Tallagh,' he said, taking a coin from his pocket. 'Kingstown has it,' and in accordance with the coin's prediction Ned and Ellen went to live in a villa between Kingstown and Dublin, determined to discover happiness in contemporary politics.

All went well with them, but six months later, as he was hurrying away to catch a train, she stopped him at the door.

'Ned, you won't say anything against religion I know you won't. But I beg of you not to say anything against the priests you promise me?'

'I promise you, Ellen. But Ireland will remain the same old lady she has always been until—'

'Until religion is done away with?'

'No, not religion, Ellen, but the priests.'

'If you knew, Ned, how such remarks distress me, I'm sure you wouldn't make them, for I believe that you love me.'

'Of course I love you, Ellen, and shall love you till your hair turns grey.'

'Only till then, Ned?'

'Well, we won't discuss that question now, Ellen; if I don't start at once I shall miss my train; and I shall have to walk quickly to catch it. Do you feel well enough for so long a walk?'

'No good will come of attacking the priests. And then, dear, think of the grief it would bring to me!'

'I shall never speak again of the priests as magicians, but nobody can help having opinions, Ellen. All we can do is to refrain from expressing opinions that give pain to others.'

'But I should like you to be yourself, Ned. I hate the thought that you are surrendering any of your opinions for my sake.'

'You are worth more than an opinion. Good-bye, darling.'

On his return from the meeting he found her waiting for him at the station, a smile in her eyes, her parasol aslant, and they walked down the fine stretch of road shaded with trees talking of their mutual life, amid calm pasturages decorated with cows lying in golden lights amid the long shadows.

'It is a pity to go indoors. The evening is so fine. Won't you come round the garden?' She knew that he cared very little for flowers, but she always hoped to win his love for her garden. 'If you would only work in the garden a little, Ned, you'd soon begin to distinguish between honesty and rocket.'

'Well, Ellen, I can tell the difference if you give me time to think;

you always have to think whether a sonata is by Beethoven or Mozart I don't. Now, which prelude is this?' And he began to whistle.

'I'll tell you when we get into the house. I can tell better if I hear it on the instrument. Now, look at these flowers and tell me what they are.'

'Give me time, give me time, and I'll work it out.... Monkshood.'

'No, delphinium.'

'Now, Ellen, I wish you wouldn't call larkspur delphinium. All the beauty of the flowers goes once you change their lovely English names to Latin ones.'

Ned was in doubt whether the flowers he was looking at were columbines or Canterbury bells both names were beautiful, but Canterbury bells by far the more beautiful. 'Canterbury is the beautifullest of names, and it is delightful to hear bells choiring over an English landscape on Sunday morning.'

'Why not over an Irish?'

Ned admired the instinct which drew her from flower to flower, for she seemed to divine the wants of every flower and to know where she would find the caterpillars and the snails. She carried a basket on her arm into which she put these gnawing insects. It was not a basket of 'Indian woof,' and she did not tell Ned to carry the insects into distant woods 'far aloof.' Her sensibilities were not so fine as Shelley's, and she was content to let Ned trample upon the caterpillars that had eaten up the hollyhocks.

'In another month the poppies will be over everything,' she said, 'and my pansies are beautiful. See these beautiful yellow pansies. But you're not looking at my garden.'

'Yes, I'm taking it all in, but I was thinking just then of that apple-tree; for there is no finer one in Ireland it is as large as a house! The branches shoot straight out, making, as it were, a little roof; and when there is the moon, yellow as a nectarine among the boughs—'

'Only by comparing one thing with another do you seem to be able to appreciate Nature. If you think the blue of the lobelia reminds you of my eyes, try to remember its name.'

'Tonight the moon is much farther away than when it lay—'

'Like a nectarine among the boughs of an apple-tree.'

'Now the moon is quite different, sailing away up there in icy scorn.'

'Much purer.'

'All the same, I didn't kiss you that night.'

'But you'll kiss me tonight,' and she raised her face to his.

'And which moon do you like the better? The cold, spiritual moon or the nectarine moon?'

'My dear Ned, the moon is never like a nectarine the moon is just the moon.'

'And nothing but the moon, whereas you have a soul.'

He put his arm about her waist; they passed from the garden through the wicket, moved by a desire to see the long fields and the woods sloping down to the shore.

'Only the grey sky,' he said, 'with the fleeting moon in it, and a great stream of white light striking across the sea past the last rocks of that lonely little headland. How small the world is compared with the sky tonight!'

'But the earth is always small compared with the sky.'

'Not always, Ellen.'

And they turned their faces up the grey hillside, going up a little path which led them past a ruined church and over a stream which was difficult to cross, the stepping-stones being placed crookedly. A little farther on they stopped to admire a group of three lonely ash-trees, and he wondered if Ellen was as sensible as he to the mystery of the cattle moving through the furze.

'They seem,' he said, 'nearer the earth than human beings are.'

And he asked Ellen to sympathise with him in the idea that there are not many things in the universe, but one thing divided indefinitely. And when they had seated themselves on a Druid stone their talk drifted from themselves to Ireland, to the time when the primitive races assembled for some rite round the very stone on which they were sitting.

'We shall always think the same; do you not feel that?'

'You're thinking,' she said, 'of America, thinking that if you go there you'll come back with different ideas about Ireland and about me. Isn't that what you are thinking?'

'In a way; one doesn't like to break the spell, and I feel that a spell is upon me.'

'Ned, you mustn't give way to superstition. You must do what you think right.'

'But I don't know that I think any one thing more right than another.'

'Yes you do, Ned.'

'What I am considering is the hardship it imposes upon me to leave you at such a time. We have been married hardly more than a year, and I am asked to leave you; for if I go to America it will be for at least three months four, perhaps.'

'Of course, if you thought that any other woman would tempt you and that you would be unfaithful to me and to Ireland, dear—'

'My dear Ellen, there is no question of that. I am thinking of myself and yourself.'

'If you succeed in America you will come back the first man in Ireland.'

'Even so what is that to me or you? It would be more natural for you to be sorry I am going.'

'I am sorry you are going, of course, Ned; but if you come back a great success I shall be very glad.'

'You will be very lonely.'

'Very likely.... but, Ned, I shall not be looking very well for the next two months.'

'You mean on account of the baby? The next few months will be a trying time for you, and I should like to be with you. Would you like to go into the house now?'

'No, dear: the night is very beautiful.'

And passing through the wicket, they sat down to rest on the seat under the apple-tree.

'But you don't look as if you wished me to stay.'

'Yes, Ned, I do I shall miss you. Of course, it will be very lonely here without you, but perhaps it will be better. When you come back I shall have got back my figure, and perhaps you will like me better than ever.'

'You have so little confidence in my love, Ellen, that you only wish me to see you when you are looking.... charming.'

'It seems to me, Ned, that if a woman wishes to retain a man's love when she marries such a man as you, he must only see her when—'

'But that isn't like you at all. My dear Ellen, you're crying? What is the meaning of these tears?'

'I don't know, Ned. It is foolish of me, and under this apple-tree, too, where we have spent so many pleasant hours.'

'In about six years there will be one who will appreciate the tree as we have never appreciated it. I can see the little chap running after the apples.'

'But, Ned, it may be a girl.'

'Then it will be like you, dear.'

Ned shook the boughs, and their apple-gathering seemed portentous.

'The sound of apples falling in the dusk and a new life coming into the world.'

'But you're sorry to leave me?' she answered, conscious of some estrangement, for she guessed that he was glad he had obtained her consent to go to America.

'Of course I am sorry to leave you, but you say it is my duty to go and I suppose it is, though for the moment I am not conscious of any duty but you.'

IV

A knock came to the door.

'A telegram from home,' he said.... 'A new life has come into the world, and though it does cost a shilling a word, they might have let me know how she is! There is no answer,' he said to the boy, and fell to thinking of her gemlike eyes, her pretty oval face, and her red hair scattered about the pillow. At first he was not certain whether the baby was lying by the side of the mother, but now he saw his child, and thrilled with a sense of wonder for birth and death never cease to be wonderful. 'Never,' he said; and he marvelled at his vision, so clear was it. He could see his wife and child in the room he knew so well, the curtains with the fruit pattern upon them, the pale wallpaper with roses climbing up a trellis, and pretty blue ribbons intervening between each line of roses. He could see the twilight and the bulky nurse passing to and fro, and began to wonder if the child was like him or like Ellen. He had often thought of Ellen as a beautiful marble very rarely as a mother. But he was due at the meeting in about twenty minutes; the notes of his speech lay on the table. He gathered them up and put them in his pocket, and drawing a sheet of paper towards him he began a letter to his wife. He wished to tell her.... he sought for turns of phrase that would veil his thought becomingly from himself and from Ellen. But he must tell her that she would find no difficulty in getting goat's milk at the foot of the Dublin mountains, or a peasant woman. 'The curve of your breast is worth all the world to me,' he was about to write, but decided that it would be better to omit all bodily appreciations, and went to the meeting wondering what Ellen would think of his letter, afraid it would shock and trouble her; she would remember his admiration of her with pleasure, but she would consider the rights of the child; and when the tenth day came the day his letter would probably be handed to her, he was thinking how he might remedy his mistake by telegram.

He refrained, and it was lucky he did; for she had been suckling her baby several days before Ned's letter arrived from Chicago, and when she told the nurse her husband's wishes, the nurse was sorry that Mrs. Carmady had been troubled, for she was still very weak. At that moment the child began to cry; Ellen put him to her little cuplike breast, and as he drew his milk from it her tears fell again. She wept, for she felt her baby might be robbing her of her husband's love, more precious to her than anything else in the world. It was all she had, all she cared to have, and before long she began a letter to Father Brennan, asking him to come to see her as soon as he conveniently could. He did not, however, side with her against the doctor; he even refused to express any opinion on the subject whether a mother was justified in suckling her child herself or in passing it over to a foster-mother. It was entirely a question for the doctor, and if the doctor advised such a course, she would be wrong not to follow it. To get the priest over on her side she tried to tell him that Ned's letter had been inspired by his admiration of her breasts, but the priest either would not or could not understand, and he was glad when the nurse came in with the news that the doctor was in the parlour.

'It is a question for the doctor, Mrs. Carmady,' he said, bidding her good-bye, glad to escape from embarrassing questions.

A moment after the doctor entered; there was some whispering, and Ellen guessed he had brought a foster-mother with him. She wept again, and turned her head aside so that she might not see her baby fix his lips on the countrywoman's breast. But very soon the wet-nurse was accepted for Ned's sake.

'What do you think, nurse? Do you think I shall ever have a waist again?'

The nurse assured her that she could perceive no difference in her figure, but when they put on her stays it was quite clear that she had grown stouter.

'I'm quite a little mother!'

She did not expect him for two months, and in two months her figure would have lost all traces of motherhood; and the day she went to meet him at the station she said, as she strolled, waiting for the train to come up, 'I never wore so becoming a hat.'

Ned was in one of the end carriages, and she would have liked him to jump out of the carriage into her arms. The first kiss, however, was none the worse for the little delay, and they walked on in silence, unable to speak, so intense was their happiness; and when Ned stopped at the corner of the road to admire the gown, the hat, and her pretty red hair, he remembered the letter he had written in answer to the telegram.

'I've had many qualms about the letter I wrote to you from Chicago. After all, a child's right upon the mother is the first right of all. I wrote the letter in a hurry, and hardly knew what I was saying.'

'We got an excellent nurse, Ned, and the boy is doing very well.'

'So you said in your letters. But after posting my letter I said to myself, "If it causes me trouble, how much more will it cause her!"'

'Your letter did trouble me, Ned. I was feeling very weak that morning and the baby was crying for me, and I didn't know what to do; so I sent up a note to Father Brennan asking him to come and see me, and he came down and told me that I was quite free to give my baby to a foster-mother.'

They walked on in silence, and Ned tried to forget that his wife was a Catholic.

'Shall I go upstairs and see the baby, or will you bring him down?'

'I'll bring him down.'

And it was a great lump of white flesh, with blue eyes and a little red down on its head, that she carried in her arms.

'He seems a beautiful boy, and healthy and sleepy.'

'I took him out of his bed, but he never cries. Nurse said she never heard of a baby that didn't cry. Do you know, I'm sometimes tempted to pinch him to see if he can cry! I called him after you, Ned. It was Father Stafford who baptised him.'

'So he has been baptised!'

'He wasn't three days old when he was baptised.'

'Of course, he could not have gone to heaven if he hadn't been baptised.'

'Ned, I don't think it kind of you to say these things to me. You never used to say them.'

'I am sorry, Ellen. Come, sit upon my knee and forget your priests and all that concerns them.'

As she came to Ned the faint cloud of resentment which still lingered in her face provoked his laughter, for he guessed what was passing in her mind.

'You wouldn't have me different, but you would prefer me not to speak about priests?'

'No, darling; you shouldn't use the word "priest," but "religion" you confuse the two. But this is not the moment for theological discussion.'

She did not know whether she hated him or loved him. The thought crossed his mind that there was something of the religious prig in her, but this depreciation was swept away when he began to find in her the same enticing, winning sensuality that he had left.

'How pleased you look!' he said when she came to his bed.

'Would you have me look sullen?' she asked, making him feel vexed at his words, and to redeem them he said:

'You were cross with me whilst walking from the station.'

'No, I was not cross, Ned. But kick off those pyjamas; I would be nearer to you.'

And in the morning, knowing it would please her, he said as she stepped out of her bath: 'Baby has robbed you of no line of your beauty.'

V

Whilst waiting for him at the station she often prayed that God would save Ned's political career, which certainly would be ruined if he continued to attack the priests; and when the train rolled into the station and they walked home under showery skies, sheltered by the same umbrella, she tried to get him to speak of the meeting.

'What did you say, dear? Were the people stirred? And who were the other speakers?'

And that he should answer in general terms, almost refusing to take her into his confidence, left no doubt that he had spoken of the priests' exactions. It would have pleased her if he had expressed regret at leaving her next morning, but he went away quite cheerfully, and she returned to the house remembering his complaints of the long drives on outside cars and the tedium of his evenings in inn parlours. 'He no longer objects to inn parlours!' And on his return she asked him to tell her of the beds he had slept in, and was surprised to hear him describe them all as excellent.

'And the food?' she ventured to ask.

'The food was all right the Irish inn is improving.'

She kept herself from saying, though the words came to her lips, 'Improved within the last three months!'

'But I am glad to get home,' he said, putting his arm about her as if he had guessed her thoughts. 'Where is baby?'

She liked him to be fond of his baby, but....'Baby is asleep.'

'Let us go into the garden, and you can show me your flowers.'

'You recognise a fuchsia when you see it, and that's about all!'

He did not answer this very rude remark, but watched her sewing, wondering at the slenderness of her fingers and their agility. The silence lengthened out, and feeling at last that he must not wait for her to break it, and that it was for him to set a good example, he said: 'Put that tiresome sewing away, and come and sit upon my knee.'

'You see, Ned, I am hardly more to you now than any other woman. You come here occasionally to spend a day or two with me. Our married life has dwindled down to that. You play with the baby and when it's time for him to go to bed, you go to the piano, or you write letters, or you read. You are writing a book, and I don't know what's in it.'

'I haven't spoken about politics lately, Ellen, for I thought you had lost interest in them.'

'You are absorbed in your own ideas, Ned, and you sleep now in the spare room.'

'But I come to see you in your room.'

'Sometimes,' she said sadly. 'But that isn't my idea of marriage, nor is it the custom of the country, nor is it what the Church wishes.'

'I think, Ellen, you are very unreasonable, and you are generally so reasonable.'

'Well, don't let's argue any more.' She stuck her needle in her work, folded it up, and put it into the work-basket. 'I am going to bed....'

'He has gone to the piano and will play Bach till midnight, keeping me awake, without caring whether I live or die! I hate him!' she said, 'I hate him!' and then stopped, for the confession of her feelings had alarmed her. A moment after she knew that she did not hate Ned, but she found him different from what she expected. She undressed, listening to Bach's interminable twiddles, and wept through many preludes and fugues. Later she must have heard them in a dream, for when the door opened (it passed over the carpet softly), she started out of a doze and heard Ned saying he hoped the piano had not kept her awake. She heard him lay the candle on the table and come over to her bedside, and leaning over her, he begged her to turn round and speak to him.

'My poor little woman, I hope I've not been cross with you this evening.'

She turned away petulantly, but he picked up the red hair lying on the pillow. He wooed her, and in spite of herself she could not keep back her happiness.

'You do love me a little, Ned,' she cried, 'and all is not over between us?'

And when he came into her bed the immediate past faded like a bad dream and they were back again in the first months of their married life.

'Don't you feel, Ned, that we never loved each other more than we do now in this bed, where we have spent so many happy hours? And promise me that whatever happens you will never be angry with me again.'

'Never is a big word, Ellen.'

All the same he promised, and after breakfast he said: 'Are you going to walk with me to the station?'

'Of course I am, Ned. To walk with you to the station is part of the unity of our life what we met for, what brought you over from Cuba—'

'My dear Ellen! We are very dear to each other, but let us not exaggerate, for every exaggeration is followed by a reaction'; and the words were no sooner out of his mouth than he was sorry for them. Why should he have chided her? Why should he not have allowed her to enjoy her happiness while it was with her? But as if she had not heard his words she went on chattering. 'She only hears the voice of her own happiness singing within her,' he said as he waved his hand to her from the carriage window. 'A good little woman!'

'God is good to have kept the weather fine, for the best part of the day is walking to the station with him, for it reminds me that in a few hours I shall go to the station again to bring him back to our house to dinner.' And so intent was she on her own happiness that she did not delay in her garden but passed into the house, going into the breakfast room to see if the maid had taken the breakfast things away, but in truth moved to go into the room for it was there that she had last seen Ned; and the same motive led her into Ned's study.

'He has the pleasantest room in the house, and I chose it for him!'

She had bought the bookcase in which he kept all his books, a beautiful piece of mahogany with a pretty top to it. She had bought the writing-table, too, and the inkstand and blotter. Ned had chosen the carpet. She wished for a brighter colour, but he said he liked an old Turkey. And thinking that he had chosen wisely, she dropped herself into his armchair and looked round for something to read. The bookcase was free to her, but she thought she would like to read what Ned was writing staying her hand for a moment to ask herself if it were as indiscreet to look into his manuscripts as it would be to read his letters. His manuscripts seemed to her like newspaper articles.

'But Ned does not write any more for American papers!' And her curiosity stirred, she continued her search for knowledge, discovering very soon that the articles she had glanced through were written for a newspaper which Ned was to edit called The Heretic. Her father was dead; they were now rich; and from the article introducing The Heretic to the public she learnt that the agrarian movement, redolent of landlords, was to be followed by an anticlerical movement.

'To rid Ireland of her priests,' she said. 'And it is my money that will finance a newspaper advocating the suppression of monasteries and convents! Why did I go into that room, and what led me into it?' she asked herself, and the answer came, 'Maybe it was the hand of God.' But no; only the devil could have prompted her to break the implicit covenant with her husband that each should be free to think independently of the other. It was understood that Ned's study was his own room. Why had he left out the manuscripts? And why had she looked into them? His papers were his own as much as his letters, and the consequences of her act affrighted her, so far did they extend, embracing her entire life so it seemed to her, for she would have to tell Ned that she had read his manuscripts and knew all about the newspaper. He would forgive her, but even for the sake of his forgiveness she could not allow him to spend her money on a paper that would advise men and women to leave their money to their relations rather than to priests who would say masses for the repose of their souls. Surely it was not right but there was no need for her to go into that question; it could not be right for her to allow her money to be spent in publishing an anticlerical paper of that she was certain. And the thought sprang suddenly into her mind: Why not consult Father Brennan? 'He will be hearing confessions on Saturday,' she said. But she could not wait till then and hurried forth right to his house.

'Father Brennan, I could not wait till Saturday. I had to come to you at once. I am not certain that what I have come to tell you is a sin, but I wish you to consider it as part of my confession.'

He put on his stole, and she fell on her knees and told him as well as her agitated mind permitted her to tell the differences that had arisen between her and her husband.

'Only religious differences,' she said.

'No differences are worse than religious differences,' the priest answered. And then she related how after walking to the station with Ned she had returned home.

'And not wishing to be separated from him all day, I wandered into his study, for all his intimate life is there the books he reads; he prepares his speeches in that room, and his fiddle hangs on the wall. I felt that I'd like to sit there. We had quarrelled the night before, and I was sitting happy in the remembrance of the promise he had given me never to be angry with me again, no matter what happened, when looking round for a book to read my eyes were caught by the sight of a pile of papers....'

'And you discovered from his papers that his politics are anticlerical?'

'I always knew that. But among his papers I discovered a project for the founding of a newspaper to be called The Heretic. All my money is in Ned's hands.'

'But you can withdraw it from his control; and if you have come here to ask me how you may save your money, my advice to you is to refuse to supply him with funds to publish The Heretic. No paper with such a title could succeed in Ireland.'

'Oh, it isn't the money. A thousand pounds or two thousand pounds we can afford to lose that. But the thought that my money may cause the loss of many thousand souls that is what I am thinking of.'

'I cannot think of anything more unfortunate,' said Father Brennan, a little fat man with small eyes and a punctilious, deferential manner. He spoke in a high voice, almost falsetto.

'I cannot understand how your husband can be so unwise. I know very little of him, but I did not think he was capable of so grave a mistake. The country is striving after unity, and now, when we have almost laid aside our differences for a great national policy, Mr. Carmady comes from America to divide us again. If he tells the clergy that the moment Home Rule is granted an anti-religious party will rise up and drive them out of the country, he will set them against Home Rule, and if the clergy are not in favour of Home Rule who, I would ask Mr. Carmady, will be in favour of it? And I will ask you, my dear child, to ask him I suggest that you should ask him to what quarter he looks for support.'

'Ned and I never talk politics. We used to, but that is a long time ago.'

'He will ruin himself. But I think you said you had come to consult me about something outside of politics.'

'Yes. You see, a very large part of my money is spent in politics, and I am not certain that I shouldn't withdraw my money now that I know for certain what are my husband's politics.'

'You must use your influence to dissuade him.'

'I am afraid that when I tell him you have told me to withdraw my money—'

'You need not say that I told you to do so.'

'I cannot keep anything back from my husband. I must tell him the whole truth,' she said. 'And when I tell him everything, I shall not only lose any influence that may remain, but I doubt very much if my husband will continue to live with me.'

'Your marriage was a love-marriage.'

'Yes, but that is four years ago.'

'I don't think your husband will separate himself from you, but even so I think—'

'You will give me absolution?'

She said this a little defiantly, and the priest wondered. But despite the formula, she felt discouraged, and all the way home the words 'betrayal' and 'treachery' bayed at her heels. She would have to tell him everything, and then he would not go on living with her. She was sure of that, but she knew no more, and her heart seemed to stand still when she entered the house and saw the study door open and Ned looking through his papers.

'I have come back to look for something,' he said. 'It is very annoying. I have lost half the day. Do you know when the next train is?'

She looked out the train for him, and after he had found the papers he wanted they went into the garden.

'Ned, why are you going to Dublin? You're only going to see people who are anti-Catholic, who hate our religion, and are determined to rob us of it if they can.'

'But,' he said, 'why do you talk of these things? We have got on very much better since we ceased to discuss politics together. We've agreed in everything else.'

She did not answer for a long while, and then she said: 'But I don't see how we are to avoid discussing them, for it is my money that supports the agitation.'

'I never thought of that. So it is. Do you wish to withdraw it?'

'I would be wrecking your political career—'

'Don't give it another thought, dear. I shall be able to get on without it.'

'May I go to the station with you?'

'I shall have to hurry to catch the train, and have much to consider.'

The intonation of his voice laid her heart waste; she felt she was done for, and she walked through her garden unable for the first time to attend to her flowers. 'They are thirsty and dying,' she said, and sat down under the apple-tree. Her best days were her school-days. Life was beginning then and now life seemed to her nearly over. She was only five-and-twenty, but she never could take the same interest in politics as she had once taken, nor in books. She felt her intelligence had declined. She was cleverer as a girl than as a woman.... Ned was coming home for dinner, and some time that evening she would have to tell him that she had read his manuscript. He would expect her to come to meet him at the station. But perhaps not. Be that as it may she did not dare.

'After the meeting he will sit in the railway carriage thinking of me, of my treachery, of my betrayal.' Her surmises were not fulfilled; Ned returned home blithe and debonair, and his lightness of heart was the worst blow of all.

'He doesn't care,' she said, and thinking to rouse him out of his indifference, she spoke of Father Brennan.

'I like Brennan,' he said, throwing himself back in his chair. 'He is a clever man. Brennan knows as well as I do there's too much money spent upon religion in Ireland. But did he tell you explicitly that you should give me no more money?'

'Yes. But, Ned—'

'No, no! I am not in the least angry,' he said. 'I shall always get money to carry on my politics.... So you have been looking into my papers?'

'I went into your room to see the time that wasn't the reason, but the pretext. The real reason was that I was so much in love with you that I could sit only in your room; and it was whilst looking round the bookcase, reading the titles of the books, for they were your books, and admiring the pictures on the walls because you had chosen them—Ned, my heart breaks.... I saw the manuscripts and said: "There is the nearest thing to himself."'

'You read the title, then some passages here and there, and walked off to Father Brennan to tell him all about it!'

'I have told you everything, and now I am going to bed.'

He knew she did not expect him to come to her room that night. The sensual coil that had bound them was broken; once more he was a free man. He was glad, and fell to thinking how mysteriously life works out her ends, for they had come to the second period without knowledge of the course or destination of their lives.

'For there are three periods,' he said—'a year of mystery and passion, then some years of passion without mystery, and a period of resignation, when the lives of the parents pass into the children and the mated journey on, carrying their packs. Seldom, indeed, do the man and woman weary of the life of passion at the same time and turn instinctively into the way of resignation, like animals. Sometimes it is the man who turns first, sometimes it is the woman.

In our case it is the man. Each has his and her work to do; each has a different task. She has thrown, or tried to throw, my pack from my shoulders, thwarted me, or tried to thwart me, for to do so is her mission, part of the general mission of woman. But life is interested in the man, too; yet Ellen was sent into my study to read my papers so that she might betray me to the priest.'

He lay awake wondering how she could have brought herself to betray the man she loved to a priest till his thoughts drifted, and he began to examine the question of religious submission in all its bearings, rousing suddenly from his meditations ready to admit that the betrayal was not altogether unexpected. But he had laid no trap; she had walked into one and must pay for her indiscretion. He was sorry that she was the one to suffer, of course, but he could not disguise from himself that he looked forward to the enjoyment of a bed to himself, and when she asked him if his resolution never to come into her room again was irrevocable, he answered: 'I cannot tell you. I am engaged upon my work and have no thought for anything but it.'

She raised her eyes from her sewing and sat looking at him, and then, getting up suddenly, she put her hands to her forehead, saying to herself, 'I will conquer this,' and went out of the room.

'She is at one with herself always,' he said; 'she is one of those whose course through life is straight and not zigzag, as mine is.'

One evening, whilst walking in the garden Ned's talk turned on the thread of destiny we can trace in our lives, and she said: 'But, Ned, you could not live with anyone, at least not always. I think you would sooner not live with anyone.'

He did not care to contradict her, for she had spoken the truth, and he was sorry he was giving pain. 'But I am not the husband that would have suited her,' he said. And then, after a moment's reflection, he added these words spoken like the first in his thoughts 'Another would not have satisfied her instinct; constancy is not everything; and it's a pity I cannot love her always, for none is more worthy of being loved.'

VI

The beautiful outlines of Howth beguiled him from afar, and he approached the secluded clough in the great headland where the Druids had worshipped in reverential spirit. And one day, as he moved about the great stone altars, he was filled with an awe and an ecstasy that lasted whilst climbing up the rocks through the ferns till he reached a high spot whence the sea was visible all round him, with ships, each with a course and a destination. Himself, too, had a course and a destination till his friends, who had promised money for the founding of the new paper, The Heretic, withdrew because Ellen had withdrawn her money; and Ireland, too, had a course and a destination till Ellen, beguiled by Brennan, felt that she could not put her money into a paper whose influence might lose many souls to God her very words.

'She would have given me all her money for any other purpose except the one useful purpose. Anything except the needful! is the cry all the world over. When I told her that the needful in Ireland is a new religion, she asked "Which one?" and I answered, "No matter which, but let her get a new one, for the old is overworn." Then we began to talk of the Church, and to lead her away from the Church I said, "Heretics are interested in religion, the others are content with religious formula, liking it much better, for it is more comfortable."' Seating himself on a rock, he began:

'Jesus himself was a heretic, St. Paul was another, and so was St. Patrick. Other countries have had many heresies and profited accordingly, but Ireland has had only one. When St. Patrick persuaded the Druids to put off their oak-leaves and don the biretta, for two hundred years Ireland gave herself over to the love of Christ continually and intensely. Her prayers prove it. Is not St Patrick's prayer famous all the world over? And there are many hundreds written in the old Irish tongue that tell us how utterly Ireland gave herself over to the worship of Christ. For two centuries little else existed but Christ in Ireland; Ireland breathed Christ, saw and heard Christ during the fifth and sixth centuries. Christ was everywhere above, beneath, within, and without Patrick's own words. The trees and flowers seemed to have had some mysterious and instinctive knowledge of Christ in that happy period when the whole island was collected into monasteries, monks adorning psalters with harmonious interweavings of lines and flowers interspersed with animals and birds, strange devices, all testimony of their love and worship of Christ, and beyond the monasteries were the beehive huts, into which the monks, when they wearied of the too much company of Clonmacnoise, retired with a few followers, to live in the fastness of the forests, where the hazel produced abundant harvest, and there was watercress to be gathered from the rill. Ireland dozed long centuries in the happy aspiration of Christ, the living God, till suddenly God, remembering that happiness could not be allowed to last for ever, sent the Danes up the estuaries and rivers to burn and to pillage. And then, as if God's heart had softened, Brian Boru came and defeated the Danes. God, indeed, seemed to have wished to do something with Ireland in the tenth century, for the Cross of Cong, the Tara brooch, and Cormac's Chapel are works of art; but he changed his mind, and ever since Ireland sinks deeper, struggling all the while to free herself, but held back by the parish priest; were another St Patrick to appear she would not listen.'

And Ned began to regret the numbers of the newspapers that he had already projected mentally. The articles that were to appear in the first number, in the second, in the third, in the fourth he knew them all. He knew even the paragraphs of the first and second numbers, certainly of the first; articles and paragraphs that were on paper in the study that Ellen had violated, articles and paragraphs that would never see the light that the printer sheds. And so he wandered on, admiring the large, windless evening and the bright bay, till suddenly there came a whirring sound, and high overhead he saw three geese flying through the still air. War had broken out in South Africa; Irishmen were going out to fight once again the stranger abroad.

The birds vanished into the air, and the sea lay before him bright and beautiful, and among the hills a little mist rose, clothing the lovely outlines of Howth, reminding him of pagan Ireland, till he began to think of Usheen and his harp. 'Will Usheen ever come again?' he asked.

The mist thickened he could see Howth no longer. 'A dolorous land of nuns and rosaries!' and as if in answer to his words the most dolorous melody he had ever heard came out of the mist. 'The wailing,' he said, 'of an abandoned race.' And he wandered on calling to the shepherd, but the mist was so thick in the hollows that neither could find the other.

After a little while the shepherd began to blow his flute again, and Ned repeated the melody over and over to himself as he walked home: 'Don't speak to me,' he said to Ellen, 'I am going to write something down.' And this is what he wrote:

'A mist came on suddenly, and I heard a shepherd playing this folk-tune. Listen to it.... Isn't it like the people? Isn't it like Ireland? Isn't it like everything that has happened? It is melancholy enough in this room, but no words can describe its melancholy on a flute played by a shepherd in the mist. It is the song of the exile, the cry of one driven out into a night of wind and rain, a prophetic echo. A mere folk-tune, mere nature, raw and unintellectual; and these folk-tunes are all that we shall have done, and by these, and these alone, shall we be remembered.'

'Ned,' she said at last, 'I think you had better go; you're wearing your heart out here.'

'Why do you think I should go?'

'I can see you are not happy, nor even contented.'

'Do you remember, Ellen, the night you told me that after the siege of Limerick "the wild geese" went to fight the stranger abroad when they could not fight him at home any longer?'

'Yes, I remember.'

'And I was thinking of Ireland and her ruin on the hill of Howth, when I heard a whirring sound, and the wild geese flew through the stillness, going south.'

'And you want to follow them, Ned? And the desire to go is as strong in you as in the wild geese?'

'Maybe; but I shall come back, Ellen.'

'Do you think you will, Ned? How can you, if you go to fight for the Boers?'

'There's nothing for me to do here.'

'For five years you have been devoted to Ireland, and now you and Ireland are separated like two ships.'

'Yes, like two ships. Ireland is still going Romewards, and Rome is not my way.'

'And you and I are like two ships that have lain side by side in the harbour, and now—'

'And now what, Ellen? Go on.'

'There is our child. You love the little boy, don't you, Ned?'

'Yes, he said, 'I love the little boy.... But you'll bring him up a Catholic. You'll bring him up to love the things that I hate.'

'Let there be no bitterness between us tonight, Ned, dear. Let there be only love. If not love, affection at least. This is our last night.'

'How is that?'

'Because, Ned, when one is so bent upon going as you are, it is better he should go at once. I give you your freedom. You can go in the morning, or when you please. But remember, Ned, that you can come back when you please. I shall always welcome your return if you return. But before you go you must bid good-bye to your son, though it be for the last time.'

'How do you know it is for the last time?' he said.

'Though it be for the last time, you need not be afraid to come into my room.' She took her child out of his bed, keeping the little quilt about him so that he might not catch cold. He put his hands into his eyes and looked at his father, and then hid his face in his mother's neck, for the light blinded him, and cried to be put back in his cot.

'Let me put him back,' said Ned; and looking down on the sleeping child he wondered how it was that he could feel so much affection for his son, and at the same time leave him for ever.

'Now, Ned, you must kiss me too; and do not think I am angry with you for going. I know you have lost interest in Ireland, but it will be different when you come back. I am sorry you are going, Ned very sorry; but I should be more sorry to see you stay here and learn to hate me.'

'I shall always love you, Ellen, and to Ireland I shall always be grateful for the revelation of a noble woman; and you must never think that our marriage was waste, nor yet my departure; distance will bring us into a closer and more intimate appreciation of each other.'

'There may be some truth in what you say.'

'Each follows his and her truth, Ellen;' and unable to bear any longer the strain of separation, they turned abruptly into their different rooms.

He left early next morning before she was awake in order to save her the pain of farewells, and all that day in Dublin he walked about possessed by the great yearning of the wild goose when it rises from the warm marshes, scenting the harsh north through leagues of air, and goes away on steady wing-beats. But he did not feel he was a free soul until the outlines of Howth began to melt into the grey drift of evening. There was a little mist on the water, and he stood watching the waves tossing in the mist, thinking it were well that he had left home. If he had stayed he would have come to accept all the base moral coinage in circulation; and he stood watching the green waves tossing in the mist, at one moment ashamed of what he had done, at the next overjoyed that he had done it.

FUGITIVES

ONE of Rodney's patrons was Father McCabe, who had long looked upon the restoration of an Abbey built by the last King of Connaught as his special care. He had been to America and returned with enough money to put a watertight roof over the heads of his parishioners; hitherto they had heard Mass in rain and snow. But the roof robbed the ancient Abbey of much of its picturesqueness, a fact that McCabe was aware of; wherefore he had begun to dream of stained-glass windows, carved lecterns, benches for the poor people and chairs for the gentry, and his thoughts continuing their flight after beauty, he had given orders to the painters practising in Dublin to paint a series of pictures showing the various incidents of Christ's last day on earth. A harmonium was, in the priest's own words, unthinkable in an ancient Abbey, and he had deplored the prices of organs in his meditations, till at last he hardened his heart and wrote to London. An organ, however, needs an organist, and the engagement of a musician who could play sufficiently to satisfy the Bishop, and teach the children to sing, started the story going in the parish that the evil day was not far distant when Father McCabe's creditors would threaten him with bankruptcy.

A clear case this was for the Bishop's intervention, and the Bishop, whilst recognising all that Father McCabe had done for the honour and glory of religion, had tried to persuade him to spend no more money on a relic of the Middle Ages. 'But what is better than a relic of the Middle Ages?' McCabe replied, and he pleaded that the work he had come into the world to do must be continued; and for the continuation of his work and the avoidance of clamorous creditors, he asked the Bishop for leave to proceed once more to America. He was away for two years, and in these years he proved himself an ingenious wheedler, returning with so much money that the Bishop gave him his blessing at the dedication of a church that some French nuns had built in the parish. McCabe had triumphed, and satisfied with his success he built no more. He had impoverished two parishes, but things would right themselves, so he said, and the Bishop, whose faith in Father McCabe was restored,

179

lived in peace and when he died was given a funeral at which all the priests in the diocese sang the Mass. The Archbishop of Tuam preached a moving sermon, not forgetting to praise the taste that Father McCabe had displayed in the roofing of the Abbey, saying 'If it were not for his roof we should be standing today in the rain.'

McCabe was that day the happiest man in a ruined parish, and as likely as not it was the Archbishop's praise which had set him thinking that he could continue in his middle age in the path he had trodden so well in his youth; and three months later he began to be heard of in the newspapers as the propounder of a scheme for the revival of Irish Romanesque. The printer's ink was hardly dry, as the phrase runs, when other paragraphs had appeared saying that Father McCabe was considering still another journey to America, this time in the hope of collecting enough money to build a replica of Cormac's Chapel; and again the priest went forth and again he returned with money, enough for him to give commissions for statues, pictures, and a high altar in keeping with the primal architecture of Ireland. But his thoughts did not stop at the high altar, and becoming involved in a newspaper correspondence, he had asked in a brilliant letter how a church could be dedicated to Our Lady if it did not contain a statue of herself; and there being nobody to gainsay him, he asked if there was anybody in Ireland except John Rodney to whom he could confidently confide his church for decoration.

The altar that Rodney designed was approved of, likewise his sketch for the Virgin and Child, and McCabe returned to Galway elated with his success and filled with hope that Rodney would be able to deliver the statue within three months. But Rodney demurred, saying that the marble he needed was not in Dublin; he was not certain that any marble in Ireland was equal to the Carrara marble, he added, and the Carrara quarries were for the future the priest's chief concern. He wrote many letters to Italy inquiring for prices, and whenever he came to Dublin he proceeded to Rodney's studio to solicit Irish marble for the Virgin and Child; and to commit the sculptor to a definite promise he declared that if Phidias were raised from the grave and shown Rodney's handiwork, he would turn away, saying 'Alas, I had not the advantage of being born in a Christian century!'

Rodney tried to keep a straight face whilst listening to the priest's commendations, saying he hoped to show him a more complete sketch when he came up again from Galway. He did not dare to tell McCabe the truth that he could not carry his sketch any further

without a model, and he pitied the priest, whose dilemma was no
less than his own, for if the Galway replica of Cormac's Chapel was
finished before the Virgin was cut out of marble, the dedication
would have to be postponed. McCabe suggested night work; he
tempted Rodney with money; but Rodney could not bring himself to
accept money in advance of work done, though he sorely needed it
to get to Italy, where beautiful girls and boys knocked at studio
doors every morning. The statue could be sent over to Ireland
safely; there were excellent packers in Italy; and he fell to thinking
how much money he would need to go away on the sly. And then he
was inveigled by hopes that he might after all find his model in
Dublin, saying to himself: 'Everything happens in a world where
nothing happens. The very model I have had in my mind's eye this
long while I may meet round the corner, anywhere.' And it was so.
He came upon the girl where he least expected to find her: in his
solicitor's office, whither he had gone to sign an agreement for one
of McCabe's altars.

As he entered the office he saw a girl rise from her typewriting
machine, and stood watching her, divining long, tapering legs and a
sinuous back. 'Now, what is her face like?' he was asking himself
when Mr Lawrence called him into his room, and all the time the
solicitor was reading the contract to him Rodney was thinking: 'If
her face is in keeping with her figure, she is the very model; and if
her face lacks character I can use another model for the head.... I
think the agreement is a very fair one, Mr Lawrence. I will sign it
when you have had it copied.... I shall see her as I pass out,' he said
to himself. But Mr Lawrence let him out by a different door, and he
wandered back to his studio convinced that if he were to ask the
solicitor's typist to sit to him for the nude she would run to her
confessor, and the clergy would be up in arms. 'All the same, the
discovery of the necessary girl makes my stay in Dublin more
difficult than it is already. I shall think of her, and the altar I have
promised McCabe to deliver before Christmas will be delayed. I
shall lose my patron.' But Luck, that had followed him this long
while, was still concerned with his fortunes, and a few days
afterwards he met the pretty typist in a tearoom; and as they stood at
the desk waiting to present their checks to the accountant, he asked
her if Mr Lawrence was in town.

'He is returning to Dublin tomorrow,' she answered, 'and will
be—'

The accountant interrupted her in the middle of her sentence, and
Rodney was a little annoyed; but he was heartened by the thought

that he would be able to overtake her in the street if he ran a thing he had no need to do, for she had lingered by the door to tell him that Mr Lawrence would be glad to see him with a view to discussing one or two points in the agreement.

'Which agreement?' Rodney asked.

'The agreement for the Virgin and Child that you are carving for Father McCabe.' And on the way to the office she discovered herself to him as a forthcoming girl, telling that Father McCabe was her cousin.

'He was at our house last night and complained to father that you had not yet begun to carve the marble. He wondered what you did in the evenings. A painter, he said, needs the daylight, but sculpture can be done by gaslight. He said your thoughts were always on Italy and that he was afraid you would run away home before you had finished the Virgin.'

'Run away home,' Rodney repeated, laughing. 'He has often told me that I am more Italian than Irish, that he had seen my narrow eyes in an Italian bust, and that if I had lived three hundred years ago I should have been one of Cellini's apprentices.'

Then it was Lucy Delaney's turn to laugh, and before she had finished laughing they were at the door of the office.

'I can't imagine how Father McCabe came to think that I spent my evenings in public houses—'

'Oh, he didn't say that, Mr Rodney!'

'Well, idled my evenings playing patience or billiards.'

'I told him he was mistaken, and that you were at work in your studio until eleven o'clock at night.'

'And how did you know that?'

'The back windows of our house overlook the mews in which you have your studio, and I often sit waiting for your light to go out.'

'And your father?' Rodney asked, now anxious for information.

'Father is the biggest man in Dublin, so it's said, almost as wide as his counter. You have often passed our shop and must have seen him sitting above it, like a Buddha, a paper cap on his head, a knife in his hand, ready to cut butter and cheese for the customers. Now I must go in. I am late as it is.'

And Rodney returned to his studio in the midst of wonder, for it was one of God's miracles certainly that the enormous cheese-mongers should have been able to beget the pattern needed for McCabe's Virgin and Child. 'Why, then, does the Church withhold the gift that comes by right to me the only man in Dublin whose business it is to appreciate her sinuous back and loins?' he asked as he sat hewing a font destined for Cormac's Chapel. 'It would have been better for me if I'd not gone that day to Lawrence's office. If I keep away I shall not meet her. But I cannot keep away; the day will seem so lonely if I do not see her.'

He could not keep his feet from the tearoom the next morning, and on their way to the office the talk turned upon Italy and she said: 'I hope that it is for your health you are going to Italy?'

'I am not going for my health, though I like a warm climate, but in search of a model.'

'But do you need a model to do a statue of the Virgin and Child?'

'Yes,' he answered, without daring to tell her that he needed a nude model, and the next day, when they had eaten the inevitable egg, she told him she had asked her father if she might sit to him for the head of the Virgin. '"It will not be like me in any noticeable way, only the line of the neck and head," were my words.'

Rodney praised her discretion.

'But I can only give you an hour before I go to Mr. Lawrence's office. Will that be enough?'

'You will come on more days than one?'

'Of course. Whenever you ask me.'

And feeling that he was drifting towards the long desired model, Rodney replied: 'Tomorrow.'

It was amusing to do her bust, but the bust was only a pretext. He needed her for the nude, and he took her to the museum and called her attention to all the nudes, ancient and modern, telling her the while that great ladies, princesses and the like, had sat for painters and sculptors. She listened to him complacent, not seeming to care what the grand women of past times had done, but when Rodney stepped back one morning and turned the bust from side to side, saying: 'I don't think I shall do much more to this,' she said:

'You won't need me tomorrow morning, then?'

'As long as I can stand before the modelling stool I shall need you.'

'As long as you are in Ireland, perhaps. But you're going to Italy—'

'In search of a model.'

'Now that you have found one in me I thought you might stay in Ireland.'

'My dear Lucy, I want a nude model.'

'Not for Our Blessed Lady, do you?'

From her look of mixed hesitation and pleasure he guessed that she would sit to him, and breaking an irritating silence he mentioned the fire that he would order to be lighted at seven o'clock. 'There is no danger of your catching cold,' he added, afraid that she might disappoint him.

'I shan't disappoint you.'

And next day he watched her undress herself, surprised and delighted by the clean, shapely little girl, almost a blonde, who stood before him. 'It will be my fault if she does not inspire me!' he said to himself, admiring her whilst he sought the pose; and failing to find it, he asked her to look at the sketch. A look was sufficient for her to understand what he needed, and she held the pose without fatigue as long as a professional model, enjoying the sitting even as he enjoyed the modelling. A perfect communion of work it was, with one quarter of an hour for Lucy to rest and warm herself.

'Do you think you'll be able to find the pose again?' he asked.

'I think so,' she answered, and in her walk to the stove, and her retreat into a corner to save her skin from browning, every attitude was admirable, compelling him to say: 'You couldn't take an ugly pose, Lucy, even if you were to try!' And when the inevitable break came in the morning's work, he said as he bade her good-bye: 'Tomorrow.'

The word 'tomorrow' chilled his ardour, so far away did it seem from Lucy, like centuries, and he wished that he could sleep all day, for how the time would pass without her he did not know. He could not concentrate on McCabe's altar or on any other work. He called upon his friends and went to the museum. But he did not care to see other sculpture, and dared even to breathe to himself: 'All seem dry and insipid compared with what I am doing from Lucy!' It seemed that the day would never pass, but it did, and he went to bed hoping he would sleep the time away. But his desire to be at work again on his statue of the Virgin and Child was so great that he slept hardly at all. Lucy was a little late, a few minutes, but he forgot his loss when she had taken the pose, and many days passed in the same excitement, the same exaltation, till one morning she arrived wheeling a perambulator.

'What is this?' he asked, looking at the smiling child in amazement.

'My baby brother. If you want a model for the Virgin you want a model for the Child.'

'Dear Lucy, how wonderful you are! You think of everything. But won't he tell?'

'Tell? He is only a year old!'

They laughed a good deal over this, and the child in Lucy's arms adding to her beauty, Rodney believed himself to be more than ever successful. The child put out his hand for something, and Rodney cried: 'He puts out his hand to the world!' and when Lucy left the studio he felt himself to be inspired. The only fault was that many hours separated him from Lucy and the child.

The day passed slowly, and rising at six he took his dog for a walk, and as he watched the animal hunting rats in the long grass along the berm of the canal, he said: 'He is as anxious after a rat as I am after my statue. It is nearly time to return. I must not keep her waiting in the mews.' And hastening from the canal to his studio, he saw the woman whom he employed to light his fire waiting in the middle of the roadway. 'She should have left the studio at half-past seven. What is her purpose? Has Lucy arrived? She may arrive at any moment, for it's eight o'clock.' He hastened his steps, and would have run if he had not been ashamed to betray his fear to the charwoman.

'Somebody must have broken into the studio last night, sir, and wrecked it.'

Three or four casts were smashed; the floor was covered with broken plaster and the lay figure was overthrown. His Virgin and Child was no longer on the modelling stool but on the floor, with the modelling stand beside it.

'I can't think who has done this. It's a wicked thing to do, sir. And the statue you had in the Exhibition last year—'

'That doesn't matter,' said Rodney. 'My group has gone.'

'But that was only in the clay. May I be helping you to pick it up? It's not broken altogether, perhaps.'

Rodney waved her aside. He had not strength to do or to think, and as the charwoman closed the door he heard her speak to somebody it didn't matter to whom; nothing mattered now. It was Lucy.

'I have come to tell you,' she said, 'that I cannot sit again but your casts are all broken! What has happened? Tell me. And the statue of the Virgin has anything happened to her?'

'Don't look at it. I am out of my mind.'

She took two or three steps forward. 'Here it is. Would you like me to undo the cloths?'

'A lump of clay is all you'll find underneath. Don't look at me in that way. I tell you, nothing is left but a lump of clay, and I feel as if I shall never do any more sculpture. You said just now that you could not sit to me again. I can see that you suspect somebody. What has happened? Tell me, and be quick about it.'

'They have found out at home that I sat for the Virgin.'

'But they don't know that.'

'Yes, they do. Father McCabe came in last night just after we had closed the shop, and when I brought him upstairs he began to talk to father and mother about his church, and the altars; and then he said you were doing a statue for him. Mother said that you sometimes came to spend an evening with us, and that I sat to you. It was then I saw him give a start. Unfortunately I was sitting under a lamp, and the light being full on my face he had a good view of it, and I could see that he recognised me at once. You must have shown him the statue. It was only yesterday you changed the head.'

'You weren't gone an hour when he called. Now I am beginning to see light. He came here anxious to discuss every sort of thing with me, the Irish Romanesque, the Celtic Renaissance, stained glass, and of course Cormac's Chapel. I thought he would go on for ever arguing about the possibility of returning to origins of art. I had to stop him; he was wasting all my day; and I brought over that table to show him my design for the altar. He said it was not large enough, and he took hours to explain how much room the priest would require for his book and his chalice. I thought I would never get rid of him. He wanted to know about the statue of the Virgin, and he was not satisfied when I told him that it wasn't finished. He prowled about the studio, looking into everything. I had sent him a sketch for the Virgin and Child, and he recognised the pose as the same and began to argue. I told him that sculptors always used models, that even a draped figure had to be done from the nude first and that the drapery went on afterwards. It was foolish to tell him these things. He sent some religion besotted slave to break my statue.'

'I don't think Father McCabe would do that. He has got me into a great deal of trouble, but you are wronging him. He wouldn't get a ruffian to break into your studio.'

Rodney and Lucy stood looking at each other. She had spoken with such conviction that he felt she might be right, but recovering himself he said:

'Who else could have done it except the priest? I know them better than you do. But you didn't finish your story. Tell me what happened when he began to suspect that you had sat for the statue.'

'He asked me if I had seen the statue of the Virgin in your studio. I grew red all over. I could not answer him, and mother said: "Why don't you answer Father Tom?" I could see from his manner that he knew I had sat for the statue, and then he said he wanted to speak to father and mother. Mother said that I had better go to bed.'

'And you went out of the room knowing what the priest was going to say?' Rodney asked, melting into sympathy for the first time. 'And then?'

'I waited on the stairs for a little while, long enough to make sure that he was telling them I had sat for the statue. Then father came out and I ran into my room and locked the door, and just as I locked it I heard father say: "My daughter you're insulting my daughter!" You know father is suffering from stone, and mother said "If you don't stop I shall be up with you all night," and so she was. All night I heard father moaning, and today he is so ill that he has been taken to hospital. Mother says that when he leaves the hospital he will turn me out of the house.'

'Well,' said Rodney, 'great misfortunes have happened to us both. It was a cruel thing for the priest to tell your father that you sat for me. And now he has done this!'

Lucy begged of him not to believe too easily that Father McCabe had wrecked his studio. He must wait a little while, she said, and then he had better communicate with the police. They would be able to find out who had done it. 'Now I must go home.'

And letting her leave the studio without bidding her good-bye, without even turning his head, so great was his misery, Rodney fell back into his chair to consider the misfortune that had befallen him. One bright spot amid much gloom there was certainly. The wrecking of his studio had broken the last link that bound him to Ireland. 'There is no place in Ireland for an artist,' he said, 'nor yet for a poor man who would live his life in his own way. The rich leave Ireland for pleasure, and the young fellow who would escape from the priest puts it differently. "Off with me coat," he says, "to earn five pounds that'll take me out of Ireland."' Thank God he was going! There was some satisfaction in taking the irrevocable step that he had not dared to take, and was now compelled to take. 'Paris or Rome which?' he was asking himself, judging them by the only standards he knew, when the opening of the door roused him. It was Lucy. 'Now, whatever has she come back for? Is she, too, a fugitive?'

'It wasn't Father Tom,' she said, 'I knew it wasn't.'

'Do you know who it was, then?'

'Yes, my little brothers, Pat and Taigdh.'

'Pat and Taigdh broke my statue! But what did they do that for?'

'I saw them whispering together. I could see they had a secret. Something inspired me, and when Taigdh went out I got Pat by himself, and I coaxed him and I frightened him. I told him that things had been broken in your studio and that the police were making inquiries. I saw at once that he knew all about it. He got frightened and told me that last night when I went to my room he and Taigdh came out of their room and listened on the stairs. They didn't understand everything that was said; they only understood I had sat for a statue and that the priest did not want to put it up in his church, and that perhaps he would have to pay for it, and if he didn't the Bishop would suspend him you know there has always been talk about Father Tom's debts. Well, they got talking, and Taigdh said he would like to see the statue. They climbed along the wall and got the hasp off the door with the kitchen poker.'

'But why did they break the statue?'

'I don't think they know why themselves. I tried to get Pat to tell me, but all he could say was that he had bumped against a woman with a cloak on.'

'My lay figure!'

'In trying to get out of the studio they knocked down a bust, and after they had done that Taigdh said: "We had better have this one down. The priest doesn't like it, and if we have it down he won't have to pay for it."'

'Oh, it's a great muddle,' said Rodney. 'But there it is my statue is broken. Two little boys have broken it, two little boys who overheard a priest talking nonsense and did not quite understand. I am going away tonight'

'Then I shall not see you again? You said I was a good model.'

'You'd like to go away with me, but what should I do with you? I'm thirty-five and you're sixteen.' He could see that the difference of age did not strike her she was not looking into the remote future. 'I don't think, Lucy, that your destiny is to watch me making statues. Your destiny is a gayer one than that. You want to play the piano, don't you?'

'I should have to go to Germany to study, and I have no money.... Well, I must go back now. Good-bye.'

'A beautiful model,' Rodney said to himself as he watched her going up the mews. 'But there are other girls just as good in Paris and in Rome. So it was two little boys who wrecked my studio, two stupid little boys who have been taught their Catechism and will one day aspire to the priesthood.'

II

A month later Rodney and Carmady met by chance in Piccadilly, not far from the Criterion restaurant and bar.

'Still in London, Rodney?'

'For a few days only, on my way to Italy. And you?'

'I am sailing for America at the end of the week.'

'And the wife?' Rodney asked.

'She is remaining in Ireland.'

'Come into the bar, and we'll drink to the health of our exile.'

Carmady acquiesced, and they made their way to the end of the bar, where there seemed to be more room. But some afternoon boozers encroached upon their privacy, and they were driven for talk into one of the upholstered recesses.

'Nobody is likely to interrupt us here,' said Rodney, and he charged Carmady to put a name upon it.

'Six Jameson out of the bottle.'

'The same for me,' said Rodney, and he ordered the waiter to hasten.

'I heard from Edward Martyn of the wrecking of your studio. A prejudiced account his was, no doubt, there being a priest in it but I think I catch sight of a friend of yours in the crowd.'

And looking up, Rodney called to Harding, who came over to them and after some hesitation sat down, seduced by Rodney's cry: 'Three exiles meet in the Criterion bar, and all three from Ireland!'

'I am not breaking in upon a private talk?' Harding asked.

'Not at all,' replied Rodney. 'We adjourned from the bar so that we might talk more intimately of our exile. You have just come in time to hear how two little boys broke into my studio, and after smashing some casts overthrew the Virgin and Child my masterpiece, if the word does not seem presumptuous.'

'Be not too modest, Rodney. And you are leaving for America, Mr. Carmady, for political and domestic reasons, so I have heard, and as likely as not you will remain there.'

'I have rambled so much in my life,' said Carmady, 'that I may ramble back to Ireland. We have a proverb that no man wanders far from his grave sod, a melancholy saying without much meaning, but very like Ireland and the Irish.'

'Irish atmosphere!' said Rodney.

'My wife refuses to divorce me—'

'How very domestic, Carmady!'

'And we disagree as to how children should be brought up.'

'Religious differences,' Rodney chuckled.

'Edward Martyn tells me,' said Harding, 'that as soon as the old language is revived all differences will disappear. Ireland to him presents the same spectacle as a spring wood: burgeoning trees, nests in the branches—'

'Sculptors carving all day and perhaps all night in their studios,' said Rodney, 'and paintings of sea shores and forests. He reports with some misgivings a saying that when Ireland gets self government the reign of Pericles will be established upon earth again.'

'Martyn is a Catholic,' said Harding, 'and Pericles was a Pagan a subject that we shall be discussing in a few days. I am going to Ireland to spend a long time with him in his Galway castle.'

'It would be wiser for you to go for a cruise in the Mediterranean with Asher,' said Rodney. 'And when you get weary of appreciating his watercolours, ask him to land you at one of the Italian ports, and we'll go to Perugia to see Raphael's first frescoes, and the town itself climbing down into ravines. The streets are hot at midday, but towards evening the people come out to catch the breeze blowing from sea to sea, and from the battlements one sees the lights of Assisi glimmering through the dusk.'

'You tempt me,' replied Harding. 'I had made up my mind to go with Asher, but decided to visit Ireland instead. I should certainly be more at home with you in Perugia than I shall be in Galway with Martyn, wandering from cabin to cabin storing country idiom.'

'How is it that you have never been to Italy?' Rodney asked.

Harding did not answer, and Carmady, taking the responsibility of answering for him, said: 'Because you have always been busy with your own work.'

'Is that a fault?' said Harding.

Carmady shook his head, and rose to his feet. 'I am afraid I must leave you now. Good luck to you, Mr. Harding, in Ireland, and to you, Rodney, in Italy.'

'A strange man, whom I never know whether I like or dislike,' said Harding, his eyes fixed on Carmady as he struggled through the crowd. 'I am sorry for his wife, a pretty little red-haired woman, soused in Catholicism even as Martyn.'

And they talked of Ellen Carmady till Harding wearied of her and asked Rodney to tell him more about Italy.

'You are always at your best when talking of Italy,' he said, 'of Perugia and Assisi.'

'Why not come with me, Harding?'

'It would take a long time to see Italy—'

'It would indeed, for there are more beautiful things in Italy than elsewhere. And there is no country as beautiful. Just fancy a man like you never having seen the Campagna! I remember opening my shutters one morning in August at Frascati. The poisonous mists lay like clouds, but the sun came out and shone through them, and the wind drove them before it. At every moment a hill appeared, and the great aqueducts and the tombs wild grasses at the edge of the tombs waving feverishly, and here and there a pine, or group of pines with tufted heads, like Turner used to draw.... The plain itself is so shapely. Rome lies like a little dot in the middle of it, and it is littered with ruins. The great tomb of Cecilia Metella is there, built out of blocks of stone as big as an ordinary room. He must have loved her very much to raise such a tomb to her memory, and she must have been a wonderful woman.' Rodney paused a moment, and then continued: 'The walls of the tombs are let in with sculpture and there are seats for wayfarers. They will last as long as the world they are everlasting.'

'Three Irishmen meet in London,' said Harding. 'Two are fugitives; one is sailing for America and the other for Italy. Three would have made a better composition.'

'For there to be three fugitives all you have to do is to meet me in Italy.'

'But there are three!' cried Harding, 'though the sex of one is different from the others. I haven't told you that I met your model, Rodney.'

'Lucy Delaney? I didn't know you knew her.'

'A girl stopped me in Piccadilly to ask me the way to the Gaiety Theatre. I told her, adding, however, that the theatre was closed. "What shall I do?" I heard her say, and she walked on. I hesitated, and then walked after her. "I beg your pardon," I said. "Though the Gaiety Theatre is closed there are other theatres equally good. Shall I direct you?" "Oh, I don't know what I shall do," she answered. "I have run away from home. I set fire to my school and came over to London thinking I might go on the stage." I asked her to come down Berkeley Street, for I was curious to know who this girl was who had come over to London to go on the stage, and as we walked she told me that she had set fire to her school so that she could get away in the confusion. I hoped I would not meet anybody I knew, and let her babble on till we came to the square. The square shone like a ballroom, with a great plume of green branches in the middle and every corner a niche of gaudy window boxes. Past us came the season's stream of carriages, the women resting against the cushions looking like finely cultivated flowers, and as soon as there was a block in the stream of carriages I took Lucy across. We could talk unobserved under the trees. "I am nearly seventeen," she said, "and

I was sent back to school because I sat for a sculpture." "What did you sit for?" I asked, and she answered: "For a statue of the Blessed Virgin, and a priest told on me." "Then you're Lucy Delaney," I said, "and the sculptor you sat for is John Rodney, one of my intimate friends."'

'What an extraordinary coincidence,' said Rodney. 'I never thought that Lucy would stay in Ireland. Go on with your story.'

'Well, when I found out who she was there seemed no great harm in asking her home to have some tea. She had arrived that morning in London with threepence in her pocket, so I told the footman to boil a couple of eggs. I would have liked to offer her a substantial meal, but that would have set the servants talking. When she had finished a second plateful of buttered toast she began to walk round the room, noticing the pictures as she went. It is extraordinary how quick a girl is to acquire the ideas of a man she likes, and when I asked her if you had made love to her, she said you had not, that you were always too busy with your sculpture.'

'One can't think of two things at the same time. If I had met her in Paris it would have been different.'

'Unfortunately I was dining out that evening,' Harding continued. 'It was hard to know what to do. At last I thought of a lodging-house kept by a praiseworthy person, and took her round there, and, cursing my dinner party, I left her in charge of the landlady. When I got home I looked out a photograph of some women bathing. I expected her about twelve the next day, and she found me hard at work. "Oh, I didn't know that you were a painter," she said. "No more I am now," I answered, "but I used to be. And thinking of Rodney's statue, and what I can see of you through that dress, I thought I'd try and do something like you." "I'm thinner than that," she said. "You've been very good to me. I should have had to sleep in the park last night if it hadn't been for you. Do continue to be good to me and get me on the stage, for if you don't I shall have to go back to Dublin, or to America." "America!" I said. "Do you want to go to America?" She didn't answer, and when I pressed her, she said: "Well, all the Irish go to America. I didn't mean anything more; I'm too worried to know what I am saying." And then, seeing me turn round to look at my picture, she added: "I will sit to you one of these days, but I'm too unhappy and frightened now. I don't like saying no; it is always disagreeable to say no." And seeing it would give her no pleasure to sit, I did not ask her again.'

'I'm sorry,' said Rodney. 'You missed seeing something very beautiful.'

'I daresay she would have sat if I'd pressed her, but chance had put her under my protection and it seemed cowardly to press her, for she could not refuse. Suddenly we seemed to have nothing more to say to each other, and I asked her if she'd like to see a manager; and as it seemed a pity she should waste herself on the Gaiety Theatre, I took her to see Sir Edward Higgins. But the mummer was going out to lunch with a lord, and could think only of the people he was going to meet, so we went to Dorking's Theatre and found Dorking with his acting manager. The acting manager had been listening for a long while and wasn't sorry for the interruption; but we hadn't been talking for more than two or three minutes when the callboy brought in a bundle of newspaper cuttings, and the mummer had not the patience to wait until he was alone one reads one's cuttings alone. He stuck his knees together and opened the bundle; columns of print flowed over his knees; and after telling us what the critics were saying about him, mention was made of Ibsen, and we wondered if there was any chance of getting the public to come to see a good play. You know how the conversation drifts.'

'So you couldn't get her an engagement,' said Rodney. 'I should have thought she was suited to the stage.'

'If there had been time I could have done something for her; she's a pretty girl. But, you see, all these things take a long time, and she wanted an engagement at once. When we left the theatre I began to realise the absurdity of the adventure and its danger, but the law that is over us compelled me to take her to lunch. "What a number of butlers!" she said, and after lunch I tried to come to terms with myself. "She is a pretty girl," I said, "but she looks odd in her country clothes. Shall I take her to some countryside where neither of us is known? But landladies are inquisitive, and if I am asked if Lucy is my wife I shall be puzzled to give a discreet answer."'

'Perhaps no discreet answer was possible!' said Rodney. 'What happened after that?'

'A fellow came up to me at the club and asked me if I had seen the detectives. Fear is a terrible thing, Rodney; there is nothing so demoralising. You know my staid old club of low ceilings and black mahogany, where half a dozen men sit dining and talking of hunting and two-year-olds. There is a man in that club who has asked me for the last ten years what I am going to do with my two-year-olds. He cannot remember that I never owned a two-year-old. But that night he wasn't tipsy, and his sobriety impressed me. He sat down at my table and after a while leaned across and asked me if I knew that two detectives had been asking after me. "You had better look to this," he said. "These things often turn out devilish unpleasantly. Of course, there is nothing wrong, but you don't want to appear in the police court."'

'Had she told, Harding?'

'She was more frightened than I was when I explained to her what had happened, but the mischief was done. She had written to her people saying she had met a friend of Mr. Rodney, and that he was looking after her. She was quite simple and truthful, and notwithstanding my fear I was sorry for her, for we might have gone away together somewhere. But of course that was impossible now; her folly left no course open to me except to go to Dublin and explain everything to her parents.'

'I don't see,' said Rodney, 'that there was anything against you.'

'No; but I was judging myself according to inward motives, and for some time I did not see how admirable my conduct would seem to an unintelligent jury. And there being nothing to do between London and Holyhead, I composed the case for the prosecution, the case for the defence, and the judge's summing-up, and I think it was at Rugby Junction that I began to hear the judge saying I had acted with great discretion and kindness. All the same, I should have appeared in a police court on a charge of abducting a girl, a seventeen-year-old maiden, and not everybody would be duped by outward appearances; many would have guessed the truth, and though we are all alike, every one of us tries to hide the secret of our common humanity.... I had forgotten to ask Lucy for the address of her parents. I knew only the name and that they were cheese-mongers, so I had to visit every cheese-monger called Delaney. My peregrinations were too absurd. "Have you got a daughter? Has she left you and gone to London?" And it was not until the evening that I found the Delaneys I was seeking. The shop was closed, but there was a light in the passage. One of the boys let me in, and I went up the narrow stairs.'

'I know them,' said Rodney.

'And the room—'

'I know it!'

'The horsehair chairs full of holes—'

'And the rails they catch you about here, across the thighs.'

'The table in the middle of the room, the smell of the petroleum lamp, and in the great chair—'

'I know,' said Rodney, 'the Buddha seated! An enormous head, with a smoking cap and a tassel hanging from it.'

'The great cheeks hanging, and the little eyes (intelligent eyes, too) under the eyebrows, the only animation in the face. He must be sixteen stone.'

'He is eighteen!'

'The long clay pipe, and the fat hands with the nails bitten.'

'I see you have been observing him, Harding!'

'The brown waistcoat with the white bone buttons, curving over the belly, the belly shelving down into the short fat thighs, and the great feet wrapped in woollen slippers.'

'He suffers terribly, and hardly dares to stir out of that chair on account of the stone in the bladder, which he won't have removed.'

'How characteristic the room is,' said Harding—'the piano against the wall near the window.'

'I know. Lucy used to sit there playing. She plays beautifully.'

'Yes, she plays very well.'

'Go on,' said Rodney. 'What happened?'

'You remember the mother, a thin woman with a pretty figure and faded hair, and features like Lucy's?'

'Yes.'

'Well, I had just begun my explanation of how a girl came up to me and asked me the way to the Gaiety Theatre, when this little woman rushed forward and taking hold of both my hands, said: "We are so much obliged to you! We do not know how to thank you!" A chair was pushed forward—'

'Which chair?' asked Rodney. 'I know them all. Was it the one with the hole in the middle? or was the hole in the side?'

'"If it hadn't been for you," said Mrs. Delaney, "I don't know what would have happened." "We've much to thank you for," said the big man, and he begged to be excused for not getting up. His wife interrupted him in an explanation regarding his illness, and gradually I began to see that from their point of view I was Lucy's saviour, a white knight, a modern Sir Galahad. They hoped I had suffered no inconvenience when the detectives called at the club; they had communicated with Scotland Yard only because it was important that Lucy should be recovered at once, for she was engaged to be married to a mathematical-instrument maker, who was on his way from Chicago. He was at that moment on the Atlantic, and if it hadn't been for my admirable conduct Mrs. Delaney did not know what story she could have told to Mr. Wainscott.'

'So Lucy is going to marry a mathematical-instrument maker from Chicago?'

'Yes,' replied Harding, 'and she is probably married to him by

now. It went to my heart to tell her that her mother was coming over
to London to fetch her, and that the mathematical-instrument maker
would arrive early next week. But I had to tell her these unpleasant
things, for I could not take her away in Owen Asher's yacht; her age
and the circumstances forbade an agreeable episode amid the Greek
islands. Poor little Lucy! She slipped down on the floor very
prettily, and her hair fell on my knees. "It isn't fair," she said.
"You're going away on a yacht and I'm going to Chicago." And
when I lifted her up she sat upon my knees and wept. "Why don't
you take me away?" she said. "My dear Lucy," I answered, "I'm
forty and you're seventeen." Her eyes grew enigmatic. "I shall
never live with him," she said.'

'Did you kiss her?' Rodney asked.

'We spent the evening together, and I was sorry for her.'

'Then you don't know for certain that she married Wainscott?'

'Yes, I do. Wainscott wrote me a letter.' And after some searching
in his pockets Harding found the letter.

"'DEAR SIR, Mr. and Mrs. Delaney have told me of your
kindness to Lucy, and Lucy has told me of the trouble you took
trying to get her an engagement, and I write to thank you. Lucy did
not know at the time that I had become a partner in the firm of
Sheldon and Flint, and she thought she might go on the stage and
make money by singing, for she has a pretty voice, to help me to
buy a partnership in the business of Sheldon and Flint. It was a kind
thought. Lucy's heart is in the right place, and it was kind of you,
sir, to take her to different managers. She has given me an exact
account of all you did for her. We are going to be married tomorrow,
and next week we sail for the States. I live, sir, in Chicago City, and
if you are ever in America Lucy and myself will esteem it an honour
if you will come to see us. Lucy would write to you herself if she
were not tired, having had to look after many things.
I am, dear sir,
Very sincerely yours,
JAMES WAINSCOTT.'"

'Lucy wanted life,' said Rodney, 'and she will find her adventure
sooner or later. Poor Lucy!'

'She is of the stuff that great women are made, and will make a
noise in the world yet.'

'It is well she has gone, for it's many years since there was
honour in Ireland for a Grania.'

'Maybe you'll meet her in Rome,' said Harding, 'and will do another statue from her.'

'It wouldn't be the same thing. Ah, my poor statue, now but a lump of clay! Strange stories are told in Dublin about that statue. It appears that after seeing it Father McCabe went straight to Father Brennan, and the priests sat till midnight, sipping their punch and considering this fine point of theology: if a man may ask a woman to sit naked to him, and then if it would be justifiable to employ a naked woman for a statue of the Virgin. Father Brennan said: "Nakedness may not be in itself a sin, but it leads to sin and is therefore unjustifiable." At their third tumbler of punch they had reached Raphael, and at the fourth Father McCabe held that bad statues were more likely to excite devotional feelings than good ones, bad statues being further removed from perilous nature.'

APPENDICES

IN THE CLAY

THE keen morning air excited the dog's instinct; he hunted the rats through the long grass that grew about the canal with more than usual eagerness, and Rodney watched with more than usual admiration the summer trees reflected in the still water and the white clouds showing through the branches. He thought of his work, his memory of his work was as pleasant as the morning, and he lingered until the first boat passed through the lock, and with a mind happy as the clouds he walked to his studio, thinking of Lucy's beautiful face that he had succeeded in modelling. But when he turned into the mews in which his studio was situated, he saw the woman whom he employed to light his fire standing in the middle of the roadway; he could not see her face, but she seemed like one alarmed and the doors of his studio were wide open.

He hastened his steps, and he would have run if he had not been ashamed to betray his fears to the charwoman.

'I'm afraid someone has been into the studio last night. The hasp was off the door when I came this morning. Some of the things are broken.'

Rodney heard no more. He stood on the threshold looking round the wrecked studio. Three or four casts had been smashed, the floor was covered with broken plaster, and the lay figure was overthrown. Rodney saw none of these things, he only saw that his Virgin and Child was not on the modelling stool, and he hoped that the group had been stolen, anything were better than that it should have been destroyed. But the group, now a mere lump of clay, lay on the floor, and the modelling stand lay beside it.

'I cannot think,' said the charwoman, 'who has done this. It was a wicked thing to do. Oh, sir, they have broken this beautiful statue that you had in the Exhibition last year,' and she picked up the broken fragments of a sleeping girl.

'That doesn't matter,' said Rodney. 'My group is gone.'

'But that, sir, was only in the clay. May I be helping you to pick it up, sir? It is not broken altogether, perhaps.'

Rodney waved her aside. He was pale; he could not speak, and he was trembling. He had not the courage to untie the cloths, for he knew there was nothing underneath but clay, and his manner was so strange that the charwoman was frightened. He stood like one dazed by a dream. He could not believe in reality, it was too mad, too discordant, too much like a nightmare. He had only finished the group yesterday!

He still called it his Virgin and Child, but it had never been a Virgin and Child in the sense suggested by the capital letters, for he had not yet put on the drapery that would convert a naked girl and her baby into the Virgin and Child. He had of course modelled his group in the nude first, and Harding, who had been with him the night before last, had liked it much better than anything he had done, Harding had said that he must not cover it with draperies, that he must keep it for himself, a naked girl playing with a baby, a piece of paganism. The girl's head was not modelled when Harding had seen it. It was the conventional Virgin's head, but Harding had said that he must send for his model and put his model's head upon it. He had taken Harding's advice and had sent for Lucy, and had put her pretty, quaint little head upon it. He had done a portrait of Lucy. If this terrible accident had not happened last night, the caster would have come to cast it tomorrow, and then, following Harding's advice, he would have taken a 'squeeze,' and when he got it back to the clay again he would have put on a conventional head, and add the conventional draperies, and make the group into the conventional Virgin and Child, suitable to Father McCabe's cathedral.

This was the last statue he would do in Ireland. He was leaving Ireland. On this point his mind was made up, and the money he was going to receive for this statue was the money that was going to take him away. He had had enough of a country where there had never been any sculpture nor any painting, nor any architecture to signify. They were talking about reviving the Gothic, but Rodney did not believe in their resurrections or in their renaissance, or in their anything. 'The Gael has had his day. The Gael is passing.' So he had said the night before last to Harding: they had a long talk about the Gael, and he had told Harding that he had given up the School of Art, that he was leaving Ireland, and Harding had thought that this was an extreme step, but he had said that he did not want to die, that no one wanted to die less than he did, but he thought he would sooner die than go on teaching. He had made some reputation, and had orders that would carry him on for some years, and he was going where he could execute them, to where there were models, to where there was art, to where there was the joy of life, out of a damp, religious atmosphere in which nothing flourished but the religious vocation.

'Good Heavens! How happy I was yesterday, full of hope and happiness, my statue finished, and I going to meet Harding in Rome. The blow has fallen in the night. Who had done this? Who has destroyed my statue?'

He fell into a chair, and sat helpless, like his own lay figure, like one on whom some stupor had fallen, and he was as white as one of the casts; the charwoman had never seen anyone give way like that before, and she left the studio quietly.

In a little while he got up and mechanically kicked the broken pieces of plaster aside. The charwoman was right, they had broken his sleeping girl: that did not matter much; but the beautiful slenderness, the grace he had caught from Lucy's figure those slendernesses, those flowing rhythms, all these were gone; the lovely knees were ugly clay. Yes, there was the ruin, the ignoble ruin, and he could not believe in it; he still hoped he would wake and find he had been dreaming, so difficult is it to believe that the living have turned to clay.

In front of him there was the cheval glass, and overcome though he was by misfortune he noticed that he was a small, pale, wiry and very dark little man, with a large bony forehead. He had seen, strangely enough, such a bumpy forehead, and such narrow eyes in a Florentine bust, and it was some satisfaction to him to see that he was the typical Italian.

'If I had lived three hundred years ago,' he said, 'I should have been one of Cellini's apprentices.'

And yet he was the son of a Dublin builder! His father had never himself thought to draw, but he had always taken an interest in sculpture and painting, and he had said before Rodney was born that he would like to have a son a sculptor. And he waited for the little boy to show some signs of artistic aptitude. He pondered every scribble the boy made, and scribbles that any child at the same age could have done filled him with admiration. But when Rodney was fourteen he remodelled some leaves that had failed to please an important customer; and his father was overcome with joy, and felt that his hopes were about to be realised. For the customer, who professed a certain artistic knowledge, praised the leaves that Rodney had designed, and soon after Rodney gave a still further proof of his desire for art by telling his mother he did not care to go to Mass, that Mass depressed him and made him feel unhappy, and he had begged to be allowed to stay at home and do some modelling. His father excused his son's want of religious feeling on the ground that no one can think of two things at once, and John was now bent on doing sculpture. He had converted a little loft into a studio, and was at work there from dusk to dusk, and his father used to steal up the ladder from time to time to watch his son's progress. He used to say there was no doubt that he had been forewarned, and his wife had to admit that it did seem as if he had had some prevision of his son's genius: how else explain the fact that he had said he would like to have a son a sculptor three months before the child was born?

Rodney said he would like to go to the school of art, and his father kept him there for two years, though he sorely wanted him to help in the business. There was no sacrifice that the elder Rodney would not have made for his son. But Rodney knew that he could not always count upon his father's help, and one day he realized quite clearly that the only way for him to become a sculptor was by winning scholarships. There were two waiting to be won by him, and he felt that he would have no difficulty in winning them. That year there was a scholarship for twenty-five pounds, and there was another scholarship that he might win in the following year, and he thought of nothing else but these scholarships until he had won them; and he started for Paris with fifty pounds in his pocket, and a resolve in his heart that he would live for a year and pay his fees out of this sum of money. Those were hard days, but they were likewise great days. He had been talking to Harding about those days in Paris the night before last, and he had told him of the room at the top of the house for which he paid thirty francs a month. There was a policeman on one side and there was a footman on the other. It was a bare little room, and he used to live principally on bread. In those days his only regret was that he had not the necessary threepence to go to the café. 'One can't go to the café without threepence to pay for the harmless bock, and if one has threepence one can sit in the café discussing Carpeaux, Rodin, and the mysteries until two in the morning, when one is at last ejected by an exhausted proprietor at the head of numerous waiters.'

Rodney's resolutions were not broken; he had managed to live for nearly a year in Paris upon fifty pounds, and when he came to the end of his money he went to London in search of work. He found himself in London with two pounds, but he had got work from a sculptor, a pupil of Dalous: 'a clever man,' Rodney said, 'a good sculptor; it is a pity he died.' At this time Garvier was in fairly good health and had plenty of orders, and besides Rodney he employed three Italian carvers, and from these Italians Rodney learned Italian, and he spent two years in London earning three pounds a week. But the time came when the sculptor had no more work for Rodney, and one day he told him that he would not require him that week, there was no work for him, nor was there the next week or the next, and Rodney kicked his heels and pondered Elgin marbles for a month. Then he got a letter from the sculptor saying he had some work for him to do; and it was a good job of work, and Rodney remained with Garvier for two months, knowing very well that his three pounds a week was precarious fortune. Some time after, the sculptor's health began to fail him and he had to leave London. Rodney received news of his death two years afterwards. He was then teaching sculpture in the art schools of Northampton, and he wondered whether, if Garvier had lived, he would have succeeded in doing better work than he had done.

From Northampton he went to Edinburgh, he wandered even as far as Inverness. From Inverness he had been called back to Dublin, and for seven years he had taught in the school of art, saving money every year, putting by a small sum of money out of the two hundred pounds that he received from Government, and all the money he got for commissions. He accepted any commission, he had executed bas-reliefs from photographs. He was determined to purchase his freedom, and a sculptor requires money more than any other artist.

Rodney had always looked upon Dublin as a place to escape from. He had always desired a country where there was sculpture. The day his father took him to the school of art he had left his father talking to the head master, and had wandered away to look at a Florentine bust, and this first glimpse of Italy had convinced him that he must go to Italy and study Michael Angelo and Donatello. Only twice had he relaxed the severity of his rule of life and spent his holidays in Italy. He had gone there with forty pounds in his pocket, and had studied art where art had grown up naturally, independent of Government grants and mechanical instruction, in a mountain town like Perugia; and his natural home had seemed to him those narrow, white streets streaked with blue shadows. 'Oh, how blue the shadows are there in the morning,' he had said the other night to Harding, 'and the magnificent sculpture and painting! In the afternoon the sun is too hot, but at evening one stands at the walls of the town and sees sunsets folding and unfolding over Italy. I am at home amid those Southern people, and a splendid pagan life is always before one's eyes, ready to one's hand. Beautiful girls and boys,' he said, 'are always knocking at one's doors. Beautiful nakedness abounds. Sculpture is native to the orange zone the embers of the renaissance smoulder under orange trees.'

He had never believed in any Celtic renaissance, and all the talk he had heard about stained glass and the revivals did not deceive him. 'Let the Gael disappear,' he said. 'He is doing it very nicely. Do not interfere with his instinct. His instinct is to disappear in America. Since Cormac's Chapel he has built nothing but mud cabins. Since the Cross of Cong he has imported Virgins from Germany. However, if they want sculpture in this last hour I will do some for them.'

And Rodney had designed several altars and had done some religious sculpture, or, as he put it to himself, he had done some sculpture on religious themes. There was no such thing as religious sculpture, and could not be. The moment art, especially sculpture, passes out of the domain of the folk tale it becomes pagan.

One of Rodney's principal patrons was a certain Father McCabe, who had begun life by making an ancient abbey ridiculous by adding a modern steeple. He had ruined two parishes by putting up churches so large that his parishioners could not afford to keep them in repair. All this was many years ago, and the current story was that a great deal of difficulty had been experienced in settling Father McCabe's debts, and that the Bishop had threatened to suspend him if he built any more. However this may be, nothing was heard of Father McCabe for fifteen years. He retired entirely into private life, but at his Bishop's death he was heard of in the newspapers as the propounder of a scheme for the revival of Irish Romanesque. He had been to America, and had collected a large sum of money, and had got permission from his Bishop to set an example of what Ireland could do 'in the line' of Cormac's Chapel.

Rodney had designed an altar for him, and he had also given Rodney a commission for a statue of the Virgin. There were no models in Dublin. There was no nakedness worth a sculptor's while. One of the two fat unfortunate women that the artists of Dublin had been living upon for the last seven years was in child, the other had gone to England, and the memory of them filled Rodney with loathing and contempt and an extraordinary eagerness for Italy. He had been on the point of telling Father McCabe that he could not undertake to do the Virgin and Child because there were no models. He had just stopped in time. He had suddenly remembered that the priest did not know that sculptors use models: that he did not know, at all events, that a nude model would be required from which to model a Virgin, and he had replied ambiguously, making no promise to do this group before he left Ireland. 'If I can get a model here I will do it,' he had said to himself. 'If not, the ecclesiastic will have to wait until I get to Italy.'

Rodney no more believed in finding a good model in Dublin than he believed in Christianity. But the unexpected had happened. He had discovered in Dublin the most delicious model that had ever enchanted a sculptor's eyes, and this extraordinary good fortune had happened in the simplest way. He had gone to a solicitor's office to sign an agreement for one of Father McCabe's altars, and as he came in he saw a girl rise from her typewriting machine. There was a strange idle rhythm in her walk as she crossed the office, and Rodney, as he stood watching her, divined long tapering legs and a sinuous back. He did not know what her face was like. Before she had time to turn round, Mr. Lawrence had called him into his office, and he had been let out by a private door. Rodney had been dreaming of a good model, of the true proportions and delicate articulations that in Paris and Italy are knocking at your door all day, and this was the very model he wanted for his girl feeding chickens and for his Virgin, and he thought of several other things he might do from her. But he might as well wish for a star out of heaven, for if he were to ask that girl to sit to him she would probably scream with horror; she would run to her confessor, and the clergy would be up in arms. Rodney had put the girl out of his head and had gone on with his design for an altar. But luck had followed him for this long while, and a few days afterwards he had met the pretty clerk in a tearoom. He had not seen her face before, and he did not know who it was until she turned to go, and as she was paying for her tea at the desk he asked her if Mr. Lawrence were in town. He could see that she was pleased at being spoken to. Her eyes were alert, and she told him that she knew he was doing altars for Father McCabe, and Father McCabe was a cousin of hers, and her father had a cheesemonger's shop, and their back windows overlooked the mews in which Rodney had his studio.

'How late you work! Sometimes your light does not go out until twelve o'clock at night.'

Henceforth he met her at tea in the afternoons, and they went to the museum together, and she promised to try to get leave from her father and mother to sit to him for a bust. But she could only sit to him for an hour or two before she went to Mr. Lawrence, and Rodney said that she would be doing him an extraordinary favour if she would get up some hours earlier and sit to him from eight to ten. It was amusing to do the bust, but the bust was only a pretext. What he wanted her to do was to sit for the nude, and he could not help trying to persuade her, though he did not believe for a moment that he would succeed. He took her to the museum and he showed her the nude, and told her how great ladies sat for painters in the old times. He prepared the way very carefully, and when the bust was finished he told her suddenly that he must go to a country where he could get models. He could see she was disappointed at losing him, and he asked her if she would sit.

'You don't want a nude model for Our Blessed Lady. Do you?'

There was a look, half of hesitation, half of pleasure, and he knew that she would sit to him, and he guessed she would have sat for him long ago if he had asked her. No doubt his long delay in asking her to sit had made her fear he did not think her figure a good one.

He had never had such a model before, not in France or in Italy, and this time he had done the best piece of work he had ever done in his life. Harding had seen it, and had said that it was the best piece that he had done. Harding had said that he would buy it from him if he got rid of the conventional head and when Harding had left him he had lain awake all night thinking how he should model Lucy's head, and he was up and ready for her at eight, and had done the best head he had ever done in his life.

Good God! that head was now flattened out, and the child was probably thrown back over the shoulders. Nothing remained of his statue. He had not the strength to do or to think. He was like a lay figure, without strength for anything and if he were to hear that an earthquake was shaking Dublin into ruins he would not care. 'Shake the whole town into the sea,' he would have said.

The charwoman had closed the door, and he did not hear Lucy until she was in the studio.

'I have come to tell you that I cannot sit again. But what has happened?'

Rodney got up, and she could see that his misfortune was greater than her's.

'Who has done this?' she said, 'Your casts are all broken.'

'Who, indeed, has done this?'

'Who broke them? What has happened? Tell me. They have broken the bust you did of me. And the statue of the Virgin has anything happened to that?'

'The statue of the Virgin is a lump of clay. Oh don't look at it. I am out of my mind.'

She took two or three steps forward.

'There it is,' she said.

'Yes, there it is,' he said. 'Don't speak about it, don't touch it.'

'Something may be left.'

'No, nothing is left. Don't look at me that way. I tell you nothing is left. It is a lump of clay, and I cannot do it again. I feel as if I never could do a piece of sculpture again, as if I never wanted to. But what are you thinking of? You said just now that you could not sit to me again. Tell me, Lucy, and tell me quickly. I can see you know something about this. You suspect someone.'

'No, I suspect no one. It is very strange.'

'You were going to tell me something when you came in. You said you could not sit to me again. Why is that?'

'Because they have found out everything at home, that I sat for you, for the Virgin.'

'But they don't know that—'

'Yes, they do. They know everything. Father McCabe came in last night, just after we had closed the shop. It was I who let him in, and mother was sorry. She knew he had come to ask father for a subscription to his church. But I had said that father and mother were at home, and when I brought him upstairs and we got into the light, he stood looking at me. He had not seen me for some years, and I thought at first it was because he saw me grown up. He sat down, and began to talk to father and mother about his church, and the altars he had ordered for it, and the statues, and then he said that you were doing a statue for him, and mother said that she knew you very well, and that you sometimes came to spend an evening with us, and that I sat to you. It was then that I saw him give a start. Unfortunately, I was sitting under a lamp reading a book, and the light was full upon my face, and he had a good view of it. I could see that he recognised me at once. You must have shown him the statue. It was yesterday you changed the head.'

'You had not gone an hour when he called, and I had not covered up the group. Now I am beginning to see light. He came here anxious to discuss every sort of thing with me, the Irish Romanesque, the Celtic renaissance, stained glass, the possibility of rebuilding another Cormac's Chapel. He sat warming his shins before the stove, and I thought he would have gone on for ever arguing about the possibility of returning to origins of art. I had to stop him, he was wasting all my day, and I brought over that table to show him my design for the altar. He said it was not large enough, and he took hours to explain how much room the priest would require for his book and his chalice. I thought I should never have got rid of him. He wanted to know about the statue of the Virgin, and he was not satisfied when I told him it was not finished. He prowled about the studio, looking into everything. I had sent him a sketch for the Virgin and Child, and he recognised the pose as the same, and he began to argue. I told him that sculptors always used models, and that even a draped figure had to be done from the nude first, and that the drapery went on afterwards. It was foolish to tell him these things, but one is tempted to tread on their ignorance, their bigotry; all they say and do is based on hatred of life. Iconoclast and peasant! He sent some religion besotted slave to break my statue.'

'I don't think Father McCabe would have done that; he has got me into a great deal of trouble, but you are wronging him. He would not get a ruffian to break into your studio.'

Rodney and Lucy stood looking at each other, and she had spoken with such conviction that he felt she might be right.

'But who else could do it expect the priest? No one had any interest in having it done except the priest. He as much as told me that he would never get any pleasure from the statue now that he knew it had been done from a naked woman. He went away thinking about it. Ireland is emptying before them. By God, it must have been he. Now it all comes back to me. He has as much as said that something of the temptation of the naked woman would transpire through the draperies. He said that. He said that it would be a very awful thing if the temptations of the flesh were to transpire through the draperies of the Virgin. From the beginning they have looked upon women as unclean things. They have hated women. Women have to cover up their heads before they go into the churches. Everything is impure in their eyes, in their impure eyes, whereas I saw nothing in you but loveliness. He was shocked by those round tapering legs; and would have liked to curse them; and the dainty design of the hips, the beautiful little hips, and the breasts curved like shells, that I modelled so well. It is he who blasphemes. They blaspheme against Life... My God, what a vile thing is the religious mind. And all the love and veneration that went into that statue! There it is: only a lump of clay.'

'I am sure you are wronging Father Tom; he has his faults, but he would not do such a thing as that.'

'Yes,' said Rodney, 'he would. I know them better than you. I know the creed. But you did not finish your story. Tell me what happened when he began to suspect that you sat for the statue.'

'He asked me if I had seen the statue of the Virgin in your studio. I grew red all over. I could not answer him, and mother said, 'Why don't you answer Father Tom?' I could see from his manner that he knew I had sat for the statue. And then he said he wanted to speak to father and mother. Mother said I had read enough, that I had better go to bed.'

'And you went out of the room knowing what the priest was going to say?' said Rodney, melting into sympathy for the first time. 'And then?'

'I waited on the stairs for a little while, long enough to make sure that he was telling them that I had sat for the statue. I heard the door open, father came out, they talked on the landing. I fled into my room and locked the door, and just as I locked the door I heard Father say, 'My daughter! you're insulting my daughter!' You know father is suffering from stone, and mother said, 'If you don't stop I shall be up with you all night,' and so she was. All the night I heard father moaning, and today he is so ill the doctor is with him, and he has been taken to hospital, and mother says when he leaves the hospital he will turn me out of the house.'

'Well,' said Rodney, 'great misfortunes have happened to us both. It was a cruel thing of the priest to tell your father that you sat for me. But to pay someone to wreck my studio!'

Lucy begged of him not to believe too easily that Father McCabe had done this. He must wait a little while, and he had better communicate with the police. They would be able to find out who had done it.

'Now,' she said, 'I must go.'

He glanced at the rags that had once covered his statue, but he had not the courage to undo them. If his statue had been cast the ruin would not be so irreparable. It could be put together in some sort of way.

Who could have done it but the priest? It was difficult to believe that a priest could do such a thing, that anyone could do such a thing; it was an inhuman thing to do. He might go to the police as Lucy had suggested, and the police would inquire the matter out. But would that be of any satisfaction? a wretched fine, a few days' imprisonment. Of one thing he was sure: that nowhere except in Ireland could such a thing happen. Thank God he was going! There was at least satisfaction in knowing that only twelve hours of Ireland remained. Tomorrow evening he would be in Paris. He would leave the studio as it was. Maybe he might take a few busts and sketches, a few books, and a few pictures; he must take some of them with him, and he tried to formulate some plan. But he could not collect his thoughts sufficiently to think out the details. Would there be time to have a case made, or should he leave them to be sold, or should he give orders that they should be sent after him?

At that moment his eyes went towards the lump of clay, and he wished that he had asked the charwoman to take it out of his studio. He thought of it as one thinks of a corpse, and he took down a few books and tied them up with a string, and then forgot what he was doing. He and his country were two thousand years apart, and would always be two thousand years apart, and then growing superstitious, he wondered if his country had punished him for his contempt. There was something extraordinary fateful in the accident that had happened to him. Such an accident had never happened to anyone before. A most singular accident! He stood looking through the studio unable to go on with his packing, thinking of what Harding and he had been saying to each other. The 'Celtic renaissance!' Harding believed, or was inclined to believe, that the Gael was not destined to disappear, that in making the Cross of Cong he had not got as far as he was intended to get. But even Harding had admitted that no race had taken to religion quite so seriously as the Celt. The Druids had put aside the oak leaves and put on the biretta. There had never been a religious revolution in Ireland. In the fifth and sixth centuries all the intelligence of Ireland had gone into religion. 'Ireland is immersed in the religious vocation, and there can be no renaissance without a religious revolt.'

The door of the studio opened. It was Lucy; and he wondered what she had come back for.

'It wasn't Father Tom. I knew it wasn't,' she said.

'Do you know who it was then?'

'Yes, my brothers, Pat and Taigdh.'

'Pat and Taigdh broke my statue! But what did they do that for? What did I ever do to them?'

'I saw them whispering together. I could see they had a secret; something inspired me, and when Taigdh went out I got Pat by himself and I coaxed him and I frightened him. I told him that things had been broken in your studio, and that the police were making inquiries. I saw at once that he knew all about it. He got frightened and he told me that last night when I went to my room he and Taigdh came out of their room and listened on the stairs. They did not understand everything that was said, they only understood that I had sat for a statue, and that the priest did not wish to put it up in his church, and that perhaps he would have to pay for it, and if he did not the Bishop would suspend him you know there has always been talk about Father Tom's debts. They got talking, and Taigdh said he would like to see the statue, and he persuaded Pat to follow him, and they climbed along the wall and dropped into the mews, and got the hasp off the door with the kitchen poker.'

'But why did they break the statue?' said Rodney,

'I don't think they know why themselves. I tried to get Pat to tell me, but all he could tell me was that he had bumped against a woman with a cloak on.'

'My lay figure.'

'And in trying to get out of the studio they had knocked down a bust, and after they had done that Taigdh said:—"We had better have down this one. The priest does not like it, and if we have it down he won't have to pay for it."'

'They must have heard the priest saying that he did not want the statue.'

'Very likely they did, but I am sure the priest never said that he wanted the statue broken.'

'Oh, it is a great muddle,' said Rodney. 'But there it is. My statue is broken. Two little boys have broken it. Two little boys who overheard a priest talking nonsense, and did not quite understand. I am going away tonight'

'Then I shall not see you again.... and you said I was a good model.'

Her meaning was clear to him. He remembered how he had stood in the midst of his sculpture asking himself what a man is to do when a girl, walking with a walk at once idle and rhythmical, stops suddenly and puts her hand on his shoulder and looks up in his face. He had sworn he would not kiss her again and he had broken his oath, but the desire of her as a model had overborne every other desire. Now he was going away for ever, and his heart told him that she was as sweet a thing as he would find all the world over. But if he took her with him he would have to look after her till the end of his life. This was not his vocation. His hesitation endured but a moment, if he hesitated at all.

'You'd like to go away with me, but what should I do with you. I'm thirty-five and you're sixteen.' He could see that the difference of age did not strike her she was not looking into the remote future.

'I don't think, Lucy, your destiny is to watch me making statues. Your destiny is a gayer one than that. You want to play the piano, don't you?'

'I should have to go to Germany to study, and I have no money. Well,' she said, 'I must go back now. I just came to tell you who had wrecked your studio. Good-bye. It has all been an unlucky business for both of us.'

'A beautiful model,' Rodney said to himself, as he watched her going up the mews. 'But there are other girls just as good in Paris and Rome.' And he remembered one who had sat to him in Paris, and this gave him courage. 'So it was two little boys,' he said, 'who wrecked my studio. Two stupid little boys; two little boys who have been taught their Catechism, and will one day aspire to the priesthood.' And that it should be two stupid little boys who had broken his statue seemed significant. 'Oh, the ignorance, the crass, the patent ignorance! I am going. This is no place for a sculptor to live in. It is no country for an educated man. It won't be fit for a man to live in for another hundred years. It is an unwashed country.'

THE WAY BACK

IT was a pleasure to meet, even when they had nothing to say, and the two men stopped to talk.

'Still in London, Rodney.'

'Yes, till the end of the week; and then I go to Italy. And you? You're going to meet Sir Owen Asher at Marseilles.'

'I am going to Ireland,' and, catching sight of a look of astonishment and disapproval on Rodney's face, Harding began to explain why he must return to Ireland.

'The rest of your life is quite clear,' said Rodney. 'You knew from the beginning that Paris was the source of all art, that everyone here who is more distinguished than the others has been to Paris. We go to Paris with baskets on our backs, and sticks in our hands, and bring back what we can pick up. And having lived immersed in art till you're forty, you return to the Catholic Celt! Your biographer will be puzzled to explain this last episode, and, however he may explain it, it will seem a discrepancy.'

'I suppose one should think of one's biographer,' and they laughed and talked of a time when everybody would choose his biographer and live accordingly.

'It will be more like yourself to get Asher to land you at one of the Italian ports. We'll go to Perugia and see Raphael's first frescoes, done when he was sixteen, and the town itself climbing down into ravines. The streets are lonely at Midday, but towards evening a breeze blows up from both seas Italy is very narrow there and the people begin to come out; and from the battlements one sees the lights of Assisi glimmering through the dusk.'

'I may never see Italy. Go on talking. I like to hear you talk about Italy.'

'There are more beautiful things in Italy than in the rest of the world put together, and there is nothing so beautiful as Italy. Just fancy a man like you never having seen the Campagna. I remember opening my shutters one morning in August at Frascati. The poisonous mists lay like clouds, but the sun came out and shone through them, and the wind drove them before it, and every moment a hill appeared, and the great aqueducts, and the tombs, and the wild grasses at the edge of the tombs waving feverishly; and here and there a pine, or group of pines with tufted heads, like Turner used to draw... The plain itself is so shapely. Rome lies like a little dot in the middle of it, and it is littered with ruins. The great tomb of Cecilia Metella is there, built out of blocks of stone as big as an ordinary room. He must have loved her very much to raise such a tomb to her memory, and she must have been a wonderful woman.' Rodney paused a moment and then he said, 'The walls of the tombs are let in with sculpture, and there are seats for wayfarers, and they will last as long as the world they are everlasting.'

'Of one thing I'm sure,' said Harding. 'I must get out of London. I can't bear its ugliness any longer.'

The two men crossed Piccadilly, and Harding told Rodney Asher's reason for leaving London. 'He says he is subject to nightmares, and lately he has been waking up in the middle of the night thinking that London and Liverpool had joined. Asher is right. No town ought to be more than fifty miles long. I like your description of Perugia. Every town should be walled round, now we trail into endless suburbs.'

'But the Green Park is beautiful, and these evening distances!'

'Never mind the Green Park, come and have a cup of tea. Asher has bought a new picture. I'd like to show it to you. But,' said Harding, 'I forgot to tell you that I met your model.'

'Lucy Delaney? Where?'

'Here, I met her here,' said Harding, and he took Rodney's arm so that he might be able to talk to him more easily. 'One evening, a week ago, I was loitering, just as I was loitering today, and it was at the very door of St. James's Hotel that she spoke to me.'

'How did she get to London? and I didn't know that you knew her.'

'A girl came up suddenly and asked me the way to the Gaiety Theatre, and I told her, adding, however, that the Gaiety Theatre was closed. 'What shall I do?' I heard her say, and she walked on; I hesitated and then walked after her. 'I beg your pardon,' I said, 'the Gaiety Theatre is closed but there are other theatres equally good. Shall I direct you?' 'Oh, I don't know what I shall do. I have run away from home.... I have set fire to my school and have come over to London thinking that I might go on the stage.' She had set fire to her school! I never saw more winning eyes. But she's a girl men would look after, and not liking to stand talking to her in Piccadilly, I asked her to come down Berkeley Street. I was very curious to know who was this girl who had set fire to her school and had come over to London to go on the stage; and we walked on, she telling me that she had set fire to her school so that she might be able to get away in the confusion. I hoped I should not meet anyone I knew, and let her prattle on until we got to the Square. The Square shone like a ballroom with a great plume of green branches in the middle and every corner a niche of gaudy window boxes. Past us came the season's stream of carriages, the women resting against the cushions looking like finely cultivated flowers. The beauty of the Square that afternoon astonished me. I wondered how it struck Lucy. Very likely she was only thinking of her Gaiety Theatre!'

'But how did you know her name?'

'She told me in the Square. You remember it was at the corner of Berkeley Square that Evelyn Innes stood when she went to see Owen Asher for the first time. She used to tell me how she stood at the curb watching London passing by her, thinking that one day London would be going to hear her sing. As soon as there was a break in the stream of carriages I took Lucy across. We could talk unobserved under the trees.'

'I'm nearly seventeen,' she said 'and I was sent back to school because I sat for a sculpture.'

'What did you sit for?'

'For a statue of the Blessed Virgin, and a priest told on me.'

'Then you're Lucy Delaney, and the sculptor you sat for is John Rodney, one of my intimate friends.'

'What an extraordinary coincidence,' said Rodney. 'I never thought that Lucy would stay in Ireland. Go on with your story.'

'When I found out who she was there seemed no great harm in asking her in to have some tea. Asher will forgive you anything if there's a woman in it; you may keep him waiting half an hour if you assure him your appointment was with a married woman. Well,

Lucy had arrived that morning in London with threepence in her pocket, so I told the footman to boil a couple of eggs. I should have liked to have offered her a substantial meal, but that would have set the servants talking. Never did a girl eat with a better appetite, and when she had finished a second plateful of buttered toast she began to notice the pictures. I could see that she had been in a studio and had talked about art. It is extraordinary how quick a girl is to acquire the ideas of a man she likes. She admired Manet's picture of Evelyn, and I told her Evelyn's story knowing it would interest her. 'That such a happy fate should be a woman's and that she should reject it,' her eyes seemed to say. 'She is now,' I said, 'singing Ave Marias at Wimbledon for the pecuniary benefit of the nuns and the possible salvation of her own soul.'.... What a model you had in Lucy. Her walk tells the length of the limbs and the balance of the body, and my eyes followed her as she moved about the room, and when I told her I had seen the statue and had admired the legs, she turned and said, with a pretty pleased look, that you always said that she had pretty legs. When I asked her if you had made love to her, she said you had not, that you were always too busy with your sculpture.'

'One can't think of two things at the same time. If I had met her in Paris it would have been different.'

'Unfortunately I was dining out that evening. It was hard to know what to do. At last I thought of a lodging-house kept by a praise-worthy person, and took her round there and, cursing my dinner party, I left her in charge of the landlady.'

'Like a pot of jam left carefully under cover. How well I can see you going away saying: "that will be all right till tomorrow."'

'Very likely. It is humiliating to admit it, but it is so; the substance of our lives is woman; all other things are irrelevancies, hypocrisies, subterfuges. We sit talking of sport and politics, and all the while our hearts are filled with memories of women and plans for the capture of women. Consciously or unconsciously we regard every young woman from the one point of view. 'Will she do?' You know the little look that passes between men and women as their hansoms cross? Do not the eyes say: 'Yes, yes, if we were to meet we might come to an understanding?' And I'm sure that when we don't look round through the side windows the woman is disappointed. She looks in the glass and says, 'I can't be looking my best today' That night at my dinner party, while talking to wise mammas and their more or less guileless daughters, I thought of the disgrace if it were found out that I had picked up a girl in the street and put her in charge of the landlady.'

'But one couldn't leave her to the mercy of the street.'

'Quite so; but I'm speaking now of what was in the back of my mind.'

'The pot of jam carefully covered up,' said Rodney, laughing.

'Yes, the pot of jam; and while talking about the responsibilities of Empire, I was thinking that I might send out for a canvas in the morning and sketch something out on it; and when I got home I looked out a photograph of some women bathing. I expected her about twelve, and she found me hard at work.

'"Oh, I didn't know that you were a painter," she said.

'"No more I am now, but I used to be; and thinking of Rodney's statue and what I can see of you through that dress I thought I'd try and do something like you."

'"I'm thinner than that."

'"You're not thin."

'We argued the point, and I tried to persuade her to give me a sitting. She broke away, saying that it wasn't the same thing, and that she had sat for you because there were no models in Dublin. 'You've been very good to me,' she said, 'I should have had to sleep in the Park last night if it had not been for you. Do continue to be good to me and get me on the stage, for if you don't I shall have to go back to Dublin or to America.' 'America,' I said. 'Do you want to go to America?' She didn't answer, and when she was pressed for an answer, she said: 'Well, all the Irish go to America, I didn't mean anything more; I am too worried to know what I am saying,' and then, seeing me turn round to look at my picture, she said, 'I will sit to you one of these days, but I am too unhappy and frightened now. I don't like saying no; it is always disagreeable to say no.' And seeing it would give her no pleasure to sit, I did not ask her again.'

'I'm sorry; you missed seeing something very beautiful.'

'I dares she'd have sat if I'd have pressed her, but she was under my protection, and it seemed cowardly to press her, for she could not refuse. Suddenly we seemed to have nothing more to say to each other, and I asked her if she'd like to see a manager, and as it seemed a pity she should waste herself on the Gaiety Theatre I took her to see Sir Edward Higgins. The mummer was going out to lunch with a lord and could only think of the people he was going to meet. So we went to Dorking's Theatre, and we found Dorking with his acting manager. The acting manager had been listening for a long while and wasn't sorry for the interruption. But we had not been talking for more than two or three minutes when the callboy brought in a bundle of newspaper cuttings, and the mummer had not the patience to wait until he was alone one reads one's cuttings alone he stuck his knees together and opened the bundle, columns of print flowed over his knees, and after telling us what the critics were saying about him, mention was made of Ibsen, and we wondered if there was any chance of getting the public to come to see a good play. You know the conversation drifts.'

'You couldn't get her an engagement,' said Rodney, 'I should have thought she was suited to the stage.'

'If there had been time I could have done something for her; she's a pretty girl, but you see all these things take a long time, and Lucy wanted an engagement at once. When we left the Theatre I began to realize the absurdity of the adventure, and the danger to which I was exposing myself. I, a man of over forty, seeking the seduction of a girl of seventeen for that is the plain English of it. We walked on side by side, and I asked myself, 'what am I to her, what is she to me?' But one may argue with oneself for ever.'

'One may indeed,' said Rodney, laughing, 'one may argue, but there is that law that is over us.'

'Well, the law that is over us compelled me to take her to lunch, and she enjoyed the lunch and the great restaurant. 'What a number of butlers,' she said. After lunch the same problem confronted me: Was I or was I not going to pursue the adventure? I only knew for certain that I could not walk about the streets with Lucy. She is a pretty girl, but she looked odd enough in her country clothes. Suddenly it struck me that I might take her into the country, to Wimbledon.'

'And you took her there and heard Evelyn Innes sing. And what did Lucy think? A very pretty experiment in experimental psychology.'

'The voice is getting thinner. She sang Stradella's Chanson D'Eglise, and Lucy could hardly speak when we came out of church. 'Oh, what a wonderful voice,' she said, 'do you think she regrets?' 'Whatever we do we regret,' I answered, not because I thought the observation original, but because it seemed suitable to the occasion; 'and we regret still more what we don't do.' And I asked myself if I should write to Lucy's people as we walked about the Common. But Lucy wanted to hear about Owen Asher and Evelyn, and the operas she had sung, and I told the story of Tannhauser and Tristan. She had never heard such stories before, and, as we got up from the warm grass, she said that she could imagine Evelyn standing in the nuns' garden with her eyes fixed on the calm skies, getting courage from them to persevere. Wasn't it clever of her? We dined together in a small restaurant and I spent the evening with her in the lodging-house; the landlady let us her sitting-room. Lucy is charming, and her happiness is volatile and her melancholy too; she's persuasive and insinuating as a perfume; and, when I left the house, it was as if I had come out of a moonlight garden. "Thy green eyes look upon me.... I love the moonlight of thine eyes."'

'Go on,' said Rodney 'what happened after that?'

'The most disagreeable thing that ever happened to me in my life. You don't know what it is to be really afraid. I didn't until a fellow came up to me at the club and asked me if I had seen the detectives. Fear is a terrible thing, Rodney, there is nothing so demoralising as fear. You know my staid old club of black mahogany and low ceilings, where half a dozen men sit dining and talking about hunting and two-year-olds. There is a man in that club who has asked me for the last ten years what I am going to do with my two-year-olds. He cannot remember that I never had a two-year-old. But that night he wasn't tipsy, and his sobriety impressed me; he sat down at my table, and after a while he leaned across and asked me if I knew that two detectives had been asking after me. "You had better look to this. These things turn out devilish unpleasantly. Of course there is nothing wrong, but you don't want to appear in the police court," he said.'

'Had she told?'

'She was more frightened than I was when I told her what had happened, but she had done the mischief nevertheless. She had written to her people saying that she had met a friend of Mr. Rodney, and that he was looking after her, and that he lived in Berkeley Square; she was quite simple and truthful, and notwith-standing my fear I was sorry for her, for we might have gone away together somewhere, but, of course, that was impossible now, her folly left no course open to me except to go to Dublin and explain everything to her parents.'

'I don't see,' said Rodney, 'that there was anything against you.'

'Yes, but I was judging myself according to inward motives, and for some time I did not see how admirable my conduct would seem to an unintelligent jury. There is nothing to do between London and Holyhead, and I composed the case for the prosecution and the case for the defence and the judge's summing up. I wrote the articles in the newspapers next day and the paragraphs in the evening papers:.... I had met her at the corner of Berkeley Street and she had asked me the way to the Gaiety Theatre; and, being anxious for her safety, I had asked her why she wanted the Gaiety Theatre, for of course if the case came to trial I should not have approved of the Gaiety, and my disapproval would have won all the Methodists. The girl had told me that she had set fire to her school, and an excitable girl like that would soon be lost I don't know what expression the newspapers would use 'in the labyrinths of London vice,' she was just the kind of girl that a little good advice might save from ruin. She had told me that she knew you, I was her only friend, etc. What could I do better than to take her to a lodging-house where I had lodged myself and put her in charge of the landlady? The landlady would be an important witness, and I think it was at Rugby Junction that I began to hear the judge saying I had acted with great discretion and kindness, and left the court without a stain upon my character. Nevertheless, I should have appeared in a police court on a charge of abducting a girl, a seventeen year old maiden; and not everyone would be duped by outward appearances, many would have guessed the truth, and, though we're all the same, every one tries to hide the secret of our common humanity. But I had forgotten to ask Lucy for the address. I only knew the name, and that the Delaneys were cheese-mongers, so I had to call on every cheese-monger called Delaney. My peregrinations were too absurd. 'Have you got a daughter? Has she left you and gone to London?' And that all day in one form or another, for it was not until evening that I found the Delaneys I was seeking. The shop was shutting up, but there was a light in the passage, and one of the boys let me in and I went up the narrow stairs.'

'I know them,' said Rodney.

'And the room—'

'I know it,' said Rodney.

'The horsehair chairs full of holes.'

'I know the rails,' said Rodney, 'they catch you about here, across the thighs.'

'The table in the middle of the room; the smell of the petroleum lamp and the great chair—'

'I know,' said Rodney, 'the Buddah seated! An enormous head! The smoking cap and the tassel hanging out of it!'

'The great cheeks hanging and the little eyes, intelligent eyes, too, under the eyebrows, the only animation in his face. He must be sixteen stone!'

'He is eighteen.'

'The long clay pipe and the fat hands with the nails bitten.'

'I see you have been observing him,' said Rodney.

'The brown waistcoat with the white bone buttons, curving over the belly, and the belly shelving down into the short fat thighs, and the great feet wrapped in woollen slippers!'

'He suffers terribly, and hardly dares to stir out of that chair on account of the stone in the bladder, which he won't have removed.'

'How characteristic the room seemed to me,' said Harding. 'The piano against the wall near the window.'

'I know,' said Rodney, 'Lucy used to sit there playing. She plays beautifully.'

'Yes, she plays very well.'

'Go on,' said Rodney, 'what happened?'

'You know the mother, the thin woman with a pretty figure and the faded hair and the features like Lucy's?'

'Yes.'

'I had just begun my little explanation about the top of Berkeley Square, how a girl came up to me and asked me the way to the Gaiety Theatre, when this little woman rushed forward and, taking hold of both my hands, said: "We are so much obliged to you; and we do not know how to thank you." A chair was pushed forward—'

'Which chair,' said Rodney. 'I know them all. Was it the one with the hole in the middle, or was the hole in the side?'

'"If it hadn't been for you," said Mrs. Delaney, "I don't know what would have happened." "We've much to thank you for," said the big man, and he begged to be excused for not getting up. His wife interrupted him in an explanation regarding his illness, and gradually I began to see that, from their point of view, I was Lucy's saviour, a white Knight, a modern Sir Galahad. They hoped I had suffered no inconvenience when the detectives called at the Club. They had communicated with Scotland Yard, not because they suspected me of wishing to abduct their daughter, but because they wished to recover their daughter, and it was important that she should be recovered at once, for she was engaged to be married to a mathematical instrument maker who was on his way from Chicago; he was expected in a few days; he was at that moment on the Atlantic, and if it had not been for my admirable conduct, Mrs. Delaney did not know what story she could have told Mr. Wainscott.'

'So Lucy is going to marry a mathematical instrument maker from Chicago?'

'Yes,' said Harding, 'and she is probably married to him by now. It went to my heart to tell her that her mother was coming over to fetch her, and that the mathematical instrument maker would arrive early next week. But I had to tell her these unpleasant things, for I could not take her away in Owen Asher's yacht, her age and the circumstances forebade an agreeable episode amid the Greek Islands. She is charming.... Poor Lucy! She slipped down on the floor very prettily and her hair fell on my knees. "It isn't fair, you're going away on a yacht, and I am going to Chicago." And when I lifted her up she sat upon my knees and wept. "Why don't you take me away," she said. "My dear Lucy, I'm forty and you're seventeen." Her eyes grew enigmatic. "I shall never live with him," she said.'

'Did you kiss her?'

'We spent the evening together and I was sorry for her.'

'But you don't know for certain that she married Wainscott.'

'Yes. Wainscott wrote me a letter,' and after some searching in his pockets Harding found the letter.

"'DEAR SIR Mr. and Mrs. Delaney have told me of your kindness to Lucy, and Lucy has told me of the trouble you took trying to get her an engagement, and I write to thank you. Lucy did not know at the time that I had become a partner in the firm of Sheldon and Flint, and she thought that she might go on the stage and make money by singing, for she has a pretty voice, to help me to buy a partnership in the business of Sheldon and Flint. It was a kind thought. Lucy's heart is in the right place, and it was kind of you, sir, to take her to different managers. She has given me an exact account of all you did for her.

"'We are going to be married tomorrow, and next week we sail for the States. I live, sir, in Chicago City, and if you are ever in America Lucy and myself will esteem it an honour if you will come to see us.

"'Lucy would write to you herself if she were not tired, having had to look after many things.

"'I am, dear sir,

"'Very sincerely yours,

JAMES WAINSCOTT."'

'Lucy wanted life,' said Rodney, 'and she will find her adventure sooner or later. Poor Lucy!'

'Lucy is the stuff the great women are made of, and will make a noise in the world yet.'

'It is well she has gone; for it is many years since there was honour in Ireland for a Grania.'

'Maybe you'll meet her in Paris and will do another statue from her.'

'It wouldn't be the same thing. Ah! my statue, my poor statue. Nothing but a lump of clay. I nearly went out of my mind. At first I thought it was the priest who ordered it to be broken. But no, two little boys who heard a priest talking. They tell strange stories in Dublin about that statue. It appears that, after seeing it, Father McCabe went straight to Father Brennan, and the priests sat till midnight, sipping their punch and considering this fine point of theology if a man may ask a woman to sit naked to him; and then if it would be justifiable to employ a naked woman for a statue of the Virgin, Father Brennan said: 'Nakedness is not a sin,' and Father McCabe said: 'Nakedness may not be in itself a sin, but it leads to sin, and is therefore unjustifiable.' At their third tumbler of punch they had reached Raphael, and at the fourth Father McCabe held that bad statues were more likely to excite devotional feelings than good ones, bad statues being further removed from perilous Nature.'

'I can see the two priests, I can hear them. If an exception be made in favour of the Virgin would the sculptor be justified in employing a model to do a statue of a saint.'

'No one supposes that Rubens did not employ a model for his descent from the Cross,' said Rodney.

'A man is different, that's what the priests would say.'

'Yet, that slender body, slipping like a cut flower into women's hands, has inspired more love in woman than the Virgin has in men.'

'I can see these two obtuse priests. I can hear them. I should like to write the scene,' said Harding.

The footman brought in the tea, and Harding told him that if Mr. Carmady called he was to show him in, and it was not long after that a knock came at the front door.

'You have come in time for a cup of tea, Carmady. You know Rodney?'

'Yes, indeed.'

'Carmady used to come to my studio. Many's the talk we've had about the possibility of a neo-pagan Celtic renaissance. But I did not know you were in London. When did you arrive?'

'Yesterday. I'm going to South Africa. There's fighting going on there, and it is a brand new country.'

'Three Irishmen meet,' said Rodney; 'one seeking a country with a future, one seeking a country with a past, and one thinking of going back to a country without past or future.'

'Is Harding going back to Ireland?' said Carmady.

'Yes,' said Rodney. 'You tried to snuff out the Catholic candle, but Harding hopes to trim it.'

'I'm tired of talking about Ireland. I've talked enough.'

'This is the last time, Carmady, you'll be called to talk about Ireland. We'd like to hear you.'

'There is no free thought, and where there is not free thought there is no intellectual life. The priests take their ideas from Rome cut and dried like tobacco and the people take their ideas from the priests cut and dried like tobacco. Ireland is a terrifying example of what becomes of a country when it accepts prejudices and convention and ceases to inquire out the truth.'

'You don't believe,' said Harding, 'in the possibility of a Celtic renaissance that with the revival of the languages?'

'I do not believe in Catholics. The Catholic kneels like the camel, that burdens may be laid upon him. You know as well as I do, Harding, that the art and literature of the 15th and 16th centuries were due to a sudden dispersal, a sudden shedding of the prejudices and conventions of the middle ages; the renaissance was a joyous returning to Hellenism, the source of all beauty. There is as little free love in Ireland as there is free thought: men have ceased to care for women and women to care for men. Nothing thrives in Ireland, but the celibate, the priest, the nun and the ox. There is no unfaith and the violence of the priest is against any sensual transgression. A girl marries at once or becomes a nun a free girl is a danger. There is no courtship, there is no walking out, and the passion which is the direct inspiration of all the world's music and art is reduced to the mere act of begetting children.'

'Love books his passage in the emigrant ship,' said Rodney. 'You speak truly. There are no bastards in Ireland; and the bastard is the outward sign of inward grace.'

'That which tends to weaken life is the only evil, that which strengthens life the only good, and the result of this puritanical Catholicism will be an empty Ireland.'

'Ireland has always struck me,' said Rodney, 'as a place that God had intended to do something with; but he changed his mind, and that change of mind happened about a thousand years ago. Since then the Gael has been wasting.'

'The Gael will be remembered,' said Carmady, 'if he is remembered, by his little folk tunes. The day before I left Ireland I heard one. The hills were shrouded in mist and I could not find the flute-player; but the tune he played, melancholy enough in itself, sounded in the mist like the death wail of a race. Never did music affect me more profoundly a little eight-bar tune.'

Carmady whistled the melody and Rodney said:

'Melancholy as bog-water and, like the Gael, melancholy and ineffective.'

'Then you think there is no hope for Ireland,' said Carmady.

'Yes, if you could remove America. But that would be a big undertaking. Why this fuss? The Gael was only intended to do a little, and that little he did in the tenth century. Since then he has produced an incredible number of priests and policemen, some fine prizefighters and some clever lawyers; but nothing more serious. He is really a very unimportant person, and he knows it. Has he not sloughed his language and booked his passage? A race is wise in its instinct. My dear Harding, you sit there brooding and looking very cross. But the Tara brooch and Cormac's chapel are not much; every European race has done more, and you know it. Come to Italy and I'll show you a city no bigger than Rathmines, in which Michael Angelo, Donatello, Del Sarto and Da Vinci lived, and contemporaneously. The poor Catholic Celt! What have these great pagans left him to do. And now, in the last hour! The time has gone by; everything has been done, and gloriously. Ireland is too far north. Sculpture does not get farther north than Paris oranges and sculpture! the orange zone and its long cigars, cigars eight inches long, a penny each, and lasting the whole day. They are lighted from a taper that is passed round in the cafés. The fruit that one can buy for three halfpence, enough for a meal. And the eating of the fruit by the edge of the canal seeing beautiful things all the while. But, Harding, you sit there saying nothing. Before you came in, Carmady, I was telling Harding that he was not acting fairly towards his biographer. The biographer will not be able to explain this Celtic episode satisfactorily. Only a Balzac could make it convincing.'

And Rodney laughed loudly, saying that he could imagine a man refraining from any excess that might disturb and perplex or confuse his biographer.

'How did the Celtic idea come to you, Harding? Do you remember?'

'Yes, I remember very well. One day looking across a park with a view of the mountains in the distance, I perceived a pathetic beauty in the country itself that I had not perceived before; and a year afterwards I was driving about the Dublin mountains, and met two women on the road; there was something pathetic and wistful about them, something dear, something intimate, and I felt drawn towards them. I felt I should like to live among these people again. There is a proverb in Irish which says that no man ever wanders far from his grave sod. We are thrown out, and we circle a while in the air, and return to the feet of the thrower. But what astonished me is the interest that everybody takes in my departure. Everyone seems agreed that nothing could be more foolish, nothing more mad. But if I were to go to meet Asher at Marseilles, and cruise with him in the Greek Islands, and go on to Cairo, and spend the winter talking to wearisome society, everyone would consider my conduct most rational. You, my dear friend, Rodney, you tempt me with Italy and conversations about yellowing marbles; and you won't be angry with me when I tell you that all your interesting utterances about the Italian renaissance would not interest me half so much as what Paddy Durkin and Father Pat will say to me on the roadside.'